ROAD TO THE ROSE BOWL®

50 YEARS OF LAWRY'S BEEF BOWL

BY TODD ERICKSON
FOREWORD BY KEITH JACKSON

SILVERBACK

TABLE OF CONTENTS

Numerous print and electronic sources provide detailed Rose Bowl Game summaries and statistics accessible to the college football fan. This book is not intended to fulfill that purpose. I was interested in exploring what the Rose Bowl experience of the Big Ten / Pac-10 pact era meant to the players and coaches. Not just the game itself but also its most enduring pre-game tradition, the Lawry's Beef Bowl.

The recollections shared by former Rose Bowl players and coaches became far too voluminous to fit into the context of the original book design. In fact, several individuals submitted multiple recollections, and a few proved to be quite lengthy. A new section of the book was designed to accommodate as much of the overflow as possible. Located in the Epilogue, these recollections and the photos accompanying them are equally insightful and, certainly, just as significant to the intent of this book.

Todd Erickson
Danville, CA
August 26, 2005

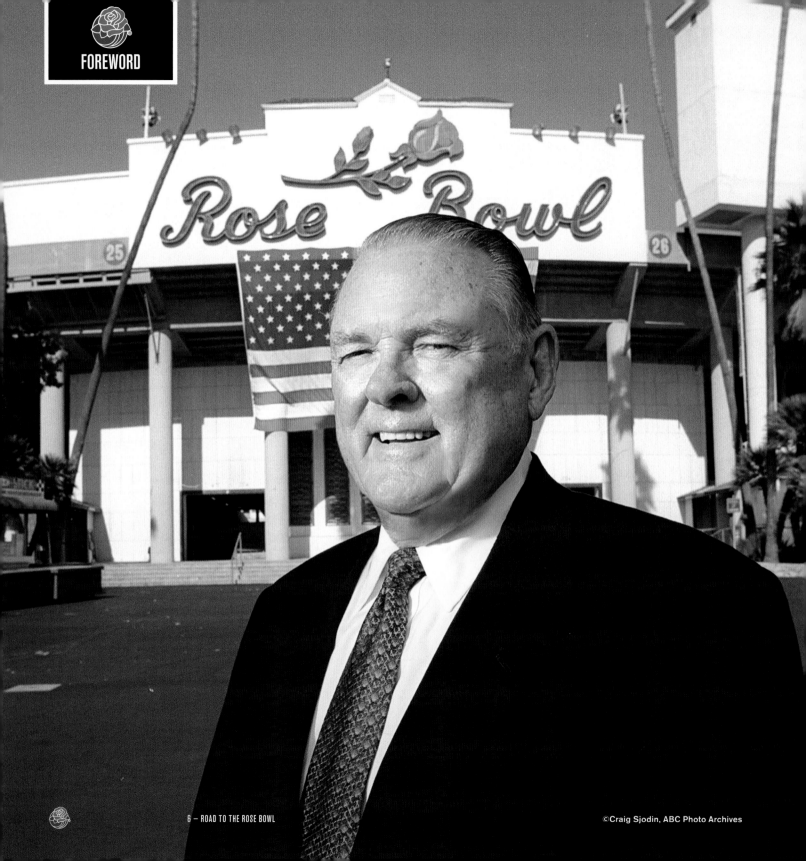

When you have lived three-quarters of a century... it is fun sometimes to shake the old memory and see what falls out. In my case you would guess it would have something to do with Sport since that has been my profession for 53 years, and in particular it would probably involve college football.

I have tried many times to explain WHY college football is my preferred venue in sport but I don't know that I have been successful. Many factors are part of it. Work ethic, the emotions that are available to both player and spectator during the contest. Maybe it is the Festival. If that is so, then the Rose Bowl soars to the fore... for this is one of the great festivals, annually, anywhere.

The final drop of mortar was dropped into the Rose Bowl's historical foundation when the Big Ten Conference and (now) the Pac-10 Conference entered into the agreement to send their champions to the Rose Bowl. It has been in effect for over a half century, interrupted lately, by the BCS, but this transgression has without question aggravated those who are long time Rose Bowl Faithful.

And so it should be because the Rose Bowl match-up of the Big Ten and the Pac-10 is one of those corner-stones that are part of our lives in every hill and hollow... every vale and glen.

This book by Todd Erickson contains a collection of memories from those who have played the game in the past 50 years of the Big Ten / Pac-10 agreement.

Fill 'em with good food from Lawry's and it seems to help their memory.

Enjoy!

Keith Jackson, ABC Sports

A 50-year anniversary, by any standard, is an extraordinary achievement. The Pasadena Tournament of Roses and Lawry's organization commemorate such a milestone in their partnership with the 2006 Rose Bowl Game and the 50th Annual Lawry's Beef Bowl. The Tournament of Roses - Lawry's partnership was the first of its kind in college football, and claims the distinction of being the longest running sponsor partnership in bowl game history.

Imbued by the Rose Bowl's powerful tradition, the Lawry's Beef Bowl has become an essential pre-game rite of passage for those who are privileged to journey the road to the Rose Bowl. My interview with Richard N. Frank, Lawry's chairman and founder of the Beef Bowl event, and a 2005 Rose Bowl Hall of Fame inductee provides fascinating insights into the genesis and development of this celebrated relationship.

The recollections former Rose Bowl players and coaches shared in this book represent a broad range of emotions and compelling or unusual moments both on and off the field. The underlying theme found in the majority of recollections is the special meaning the Rose Bowl tradition holds for these participants and their deep appreciation for being able to contribute to the history of the game.

There is a peculiar bond shared by those who have played the game, even amongst opponents. Many players and coaches shared how friendships had been forged after battling against each other in the Rose Bowl. One quarterback even requested the contact information of his bitter rival from twenty years ago, explaining that he wanted to send belated congratulations for a game well played.

Rose Bowl players are the fiercest of competitors and painful memories of near misses and close losses persist, even decades later. But, there is a healthy respect that prevails within the Rose Bowl fraternity, primarily due to the esteem accorded each Champion team making the journey to Pasadena. One's honor remains intact, even in defeat to a Rose Bowl foe.

Top left: Aerial view of 2004 Rose Bowl Game. Bottom left: 1991 Rose Bowl Game action. Top right: Texas coach Mack Brown with media at Lawry's 49th Annual Beef Bowl. Middle right: Lawry's reprinted coverage from a January 11, 1965 column item in Sports Illustrated magazine for promotional purposes. Bottom right: Texas players at the 2004 Lawry's Beef Bowl.

"You can't pass through life without becoming acquainted with tradition, with legacy, and with a feeling of history, and the Rose Bowl does all that." - Keith Jackson, 1999 Rose Bowl Hall of Fame Induction ceremony

I grew up watching college football on Saturday afternoons with my father and five brothers in Big Ten country. The first college game I attended was Northwestern vs. Wisconsin at Camp Randall Stadium in 1973 with my high school football team. New Year's Day celebrations in our home started in the morning with the Tournament of Rose Parade on the television, a crescendo of familiar aromas wafting out of the kitchen, then culminating with the Rose Bowl Game and lots of tasty holiday food. It was a wonderful tradition; one that I'm sure is replicated with some variation in countless other homes across the nation every year on January 1st.

My children were raised in the midst of some of the Pac-10's storied rivalries and as youngsters they had the opportunity to see USC's Trojans in the Los Angeles Coliseum and the UCLA Bruins on their home playing field in the Rose Bowl Stadium. We later relocated to northern California, and we were able to attend a few Cal and Stanford games together. Of course, like many other college football-loving parents, I was just trying to pass along a semblance of the autumn traditions I had enjoyed as a kid.

College football is steeped in tradition and a rich tapestry of collegiate traditions can be found virtually anywhere throughout the country. Every university relies on fundamental traditions such as school colors, nicknames, mascots, marching bands, fight songs, homecoming festivities, and distinctive game week activities that give meaning and a uniting rally cry to their fan base.

Much of college football's allure can be attributed to the university rivalries that have developed over decades of competition. Usually predicated by conference affiliation and geographic proximity such as the Michigan/Ohio State and Texas/Oklahoma rivalries, there are long distance, non-conference exceptions like the rivalry between USC and Notre Dame. Every rivalry invokes its own unique traditions such as Purdue and Indiana playing for the "Old Oaken Bucket" or Cal and Stanford playing for the "Stanford Axe."

The premiere tradition in college football is the Rose Bowl Game. In addition to being the first New Year's Day game and oldest bowl game in college football history, the Rose Bowl is responsible for several other groundbreaking firsts including being the first sporting event broadcast on national radio, the first bowl game televised to a national audience, and the first college football game televised by satellite in Europe and Japan.

The crowning achievement in the ten-decade history of the Rose Bowl Game is its nearly sixty-year tradition of matching the Big Ten Conference champion against the Pac-10 Conference champion. Constituting the oldest agreement in college football between two major conferences, the power of this Rose Bowl tradition has proven impervious to recent interruptions by BCS computer-generated match-ups.

The Rose Bowl Game is worthy of all the superlatives used to describe it—and more. It isn't just a perennially sold out stadium of devoted fans on New Year's Day and an international television audience of tens of millions informed by golden-voiced play-by-play announcers. It is the sum of all the players who have played in it, and the coaches who have coached in it, the fans who have supported it, and the thousands of Tournament volunteers who have donated their time over the years to make it all possible. It is, first and foremost, a celebration of champions and the Champion spirit.

There have been many historic wins and more than a few startling upsets on New Year's Day in Pasadena. Regardless of the final outcome of any particular game, nothing can take away the fact that both teams had to battle through the proverbial gauntlet of their respective conference foes to even set foot on the Rose Bowl turf as champions.

In 1956, a new event honoring each team was launched by Richard N. Frank of Lawry's, with the approval of the Tournament of Roses. Over time, with careful attention by Frank and the Lawry's organization and the supportive partnership of the Tournament of Roses, the Lawry's Beef Bowl became one of the Rose Bowl's legendary traditions.

In the early years, several Big Ten champions were honored with Lawry's famous prime rib meal near their training facilities or on the Rose Bowl stadium grounds while the Pacific Coast champions were served at Lawry's flagship location in Beverly Hills. There was immediate interest from the sports media, and they were welcomed to attend. The Beef Bowl events provided a perfect setting for reporters to interview the players and coaches away from the practice field, as well as the

opportunity to have some fun comparing the training table appetites of each team.

Eventually, it was noted (and promoted) that the teams consuming the largest amounts of prime rib seemed to be winning on the playing field as well. A tongue-in-cheek item titled "Correct Steer," in the January 11, 1965 issue of Sports Illustrated claimed that "roast beef is better than tea leaves, crystal balls and fortune cookies" for predicting the Rose Bowl victor.

By the mid-Sixties, both teams were attending their own events on separate evenings at Lawry's in Beverly Hills, which were commonly referred to in press kit materials as the "first half" and the "second half" of the Beef Bowl. To this day, only the teams, the Royal Court and Tournament of Roses officials, and select media are invited. The competition is largely mythical, but the exclusivity of each team's private event offers a rare opportunity for sportswriters and television reporters to interact with players and coaches who are momentarily liberated from their typical element of helmets, pads and practice fields.

Over the years, the Lawry's Beef Bowl evolved to become a veritable coronation event—a salute to each team's Champion status—on the "Road to the Rose Bowl." After each team has attended their signature Lawry's event, the game is just a couple days away. There can be little doubt, at this point, that the players and coaches have been inducted into a special fraternity; an elite gridiron brotherhood open only to those who have earned the right to participate in "The Granddaddy of Them All."

CHRYSLER CORPORATION
COURT OF CHAMPIONS

Q&A WITH THE FOUNDER OF LAWRY'S BEEF BOWL RICHARD N. FRANK, CHAIRMAN, LAWRY'S RESTAURANTS, INC. AND 2005 ROSE BOWL HALL OF FAME INDUCTEE

Todd Erickson: What are some of your earliest memories of the Rose Bowl Game?

Richard N. Frank: I was born and raised in Pasadena, so it wasn't surprising that my father took me to the Rose Bowl Game. The first time was to see Alabama vs. Washington State in 1931, when I was eight years old. Apparently, I enjoyed it a lot. Although my dad never seemed to be as interested in athletics and sports as I was, he took me back to the game in 1932 and '33. I missed the 1934 game—we had one of those really wet winters and the game was played in heavy rain. Stanford was playing Columbia, and my dad said I couldn't go. I must have made a fuss about it, because in 1935 and thereafter, he always came up with the tickets. With that one exception, I went to the Rose Bowl Game through grammar school, junior high and high school.

TE: Did the family business have a connection with the Rose Bowl at that time?

My dad's main business was Van de Kamp's Holland Dutch Bakers. From the 1930s into the '60s, it was the largest retail bakery chain in the west, and the second largest in the country. Because it was a local business, Van de Kamp's decided to have a float in the Rose Parade in 1938. They followed with another float in 1939 and in '40.

The 1940 float was a field of tulips in front of a blue Dutch windmill. It was revolutionary for its time because it was the first float that displayed individual flowers in glass tubes. That system is used all the time now, but up until then, flowers had always been glued onto the floats. So you can imagine how much more realistic the

Van de Kamp's float looked. I still remember it vividly, because it was quite beautiful. I forget what the theme of the parade was, but it allowed Van de Kamp's to have the blue windmill, which was their trademark. It wasn't a huge float by today's standards. Floats now are sometimes fifty or more feet long. The 1940 float might have been twenty feet long, but it was spectacular for its era. Nobody had ever seen anything like it in the parade before. It won the grand prize, which in those days was given to the top commercial entry.

TE: Meanwhile, you were still attending all the Rose Bowl Games...

RNF: Yes, my history of going to the Rose Bowl continued. I missed only two other games after 1934. One was the 1942 game between Oregon State and Duke. It was played in Durham, North Carolina, because the attack on Pearl Harbor, which took place just a few weeks before the game, precluded it being played in Pasadena. There was a lot of fear at the time that California might be attacked.

The third Rose Bowl Game I missed was about ten years ago when Stanford played Penn State back in Florida. Being a Stanford fan, I had to see that game, so I went to

Left: The Rose Bowl Stadium's Hall of Fame Pavilion. Top right: Richard N. Frank with Stanford coach Ty Willingham. Bottom right: 1970 Rose Bowl Game spectators.

Florida and watched the Rose Bowl Game afterwards on TV. So, from 1931 to 2005 is what? Seventy-six years?

TE: Seventy-six years! You must be one of the few people who can claim to have attended that many Rose Bowl games. Did you root for any team in particular through those years?
RNF: Sure! I root for Stanford. I went to business school there. Early on, I was a big fan of USC, and still am.

My memories of football when I was young are linked to the radio. Of course, there was no TV back then, and I was fascinated by radio. That's how I think I started getting interested in football, besides going to the Rose Bowl Game. There was a radio sports announcer named Ted Husing, who had a wonderful voice; he was a spellbinder. You'd listen to him and be able to picture the game in your mind.

I'll never forget listening to the play-by-play of a USC-Notre Dame game in which the Trojans kicked a field goal in the last minute to win 16-14. It made a huge

impression on me. So, my fascination with college athletics, particularly football, dates back a long time.

TE: How did the Beef Bowl begin?
RNF: I had a long-time love of the Rose Bowl Game and Rose Parade and thought it would be wonderful if Lawry's could be connected with that great spectacle. In the mid-'50s, I got the idea, "Why not see if the teams would like to dine at Lawry's? It would be something special we could do to add to their pre-game experience. And it would be fun for us. We'd get a kick out of meeting the players."

So I called the Tournament of Roses to see if they would allow the event, and they were amenable. My colleague, Arthur Wynne [former Lawry's executive], also loved football, and he followed up with the conferences to help get it established.

TE: So that was it?
RNF: Yes. I was Lawry's president at the time, and about to become CEO. I was in charge, and I made the decision to

set it in motion. I grew up in Pasadena and the Tournament of Roses was part of my life and important to me. My decision sprang from that. Whatever publicity our company would get from the event was really secondary in my mind. Later on, it became clear that the event had a lot of value not just for Lawry's, but for everybody involved—the players, the coaches and the Tournament.

I don't remember whether we sent letters inviting the teams, or whether the Tournament officials did it in those days, but the Tournament was very supportive. While they didn't come out and endorse it as they do today, they made it available to the two conferences.

TE: Where did the "Beef Bowl" name come from?
RNF: For the first few years, there wasn't a name. Then we hired a public relations firm for both our restaurant and food products companies. They thought that treating the teams to dinners was a great idea and came up with the name "Beef Bowl." We really liked the name; it conveyed the connection between the dinners and the Rose Bowl Game.

TE: A photo of the first year's event shows one of the teams being fed outdoors...
RNF: Yes. Iowa and Oregon State in 1956 [for the 1957 Rose Bowl Game] were the first teams we treated to dinner. Forest Evashevski was the Iowa coach, and he said, "I haven't got time to send the players to the restaurant, but if you want to come out to the practice field, they would enjoy the dinner." But the Pacific Coast Conference was happy to come to Lawry's, and always has. Of course, the PCC became the AAWU for a few years, then the Pac-8, and since 1978 it's been the Pac-10.

TE: Was it just Iowa that wanted to be fed on the practice field? How did you manage to feed a football team away from the restaurant?
RNF: We had a few glitches at first, because coach Woody Hayes brought Ohio State to the Rose Bowl the next year. 1957 [for the 1958 Rose Bowl Game] was the only time he ever let his players participate in our prime rib meal. We fed them near the practice field. We trucked one of our famous serving carts and all the food out to the location, and it was difficult. Those carts weigh a ton! Art Wynne organized everything and

we went out on location to serve the team, meet the players and welcome them to the meal.

For a few years, things were a little bit unsettled, as far as the Big Ten teams were concerned. The West Coast teams were always happy to come to the restaurant. By the mid-'60s, both teams were coming to Lawry's.

But Woody Hayes would never bring his teams to the restaurant, even after we discontinued serving on the playing field. He said, "We don't want our boys distracted; we can't take them away for an afternoon or an evening to be fed. We're out here for one purpose only and that is to win that football game. That's all that counts. To hell with any entertainment! We're not gonna do it."

After Stanford's final touchdown in the 1971 game against Ohio State my wife Mary Alice claims that I shook my fist and yelled "Damn it, Woody, take that!"

But that was Woody. Ohio State coach Earl Bruce, who followed him, was glad to bring his team to the restaurant for the Beef Bowl, and all of the Ohio State coaches since have followed suit.

TE: How did you get the Big Ten teams to come to the restaurant rather than being served at the field?
RNF: It wasn't a matter of getting them to come—it was my decision. In 1964, I decided we were no longer going to take meals to the practice field. If the teams wanted to participate, they would have to eat in the restaurant. Feeding the teams on the practice field wasn't doing us any good. It was too costly and too much trouble, and defeated the whole idea of giving the players the experience and enjoyment of a meal at Lawry's. We'd continue to serve any team that wanted to dine with us, but if a team didn't want to come, so be it.

I don't recall the details, but we did give in one more time. The 1965 Michigan Rose Bowl team really wanted to eat outside at the Rose Bowl, so we accommodated them. But from that point on, the Beef Bowl took place only in the restaurant. Both conferences endorse the event and the teams love it and look forward to it.

Top Left: RNF with USC's 1963 Rose Bowl team. Lower left: RNF with Washington QB Bob Schloredt. Top right: Iowa's 1957 Rose Bowl team eating at the practice field. Lower Right: 1961 Rose Queen Carole Washburn serves Washington players outside the Rose Bowl.

TE: Did the teams ever come to Lawry's on the same night?

RNF: Never. The teams always came on separate nights for two reasons: First, we didn't have the space to accommodate two teams at the same time. That was true even in the early years, when just the teams and their coaches came to the event. As the years went by, Tournament officials began joining us on both nights, and later on, the Rose Queen and Court also began attending. And, of course, after the first few years, we started getting many members of the press. The radio and TV crews with their equipment take up quite a bit of room. Each night of the Beef Bowl has become a big event, with a lot of people thronging the restaurant. The players come at about 4:30 p.m., and the event ends by 6:30, so we don't lose an entire evening's business.

The other and maybe even bigger reason we invite the teams on different nights is that we determined it was more special to honor them separately for their championship accomplishments.

TE: One of the long-time legends of the Beef Bowl is that the team that eats the most beef wins the Rose Bowl Game...

RNF: Well, that was a twist that came from somebody in our P.R. firm. At any rate, it made a good story for the press, and you know, at first, I was kind of intrigued by the concept. But how do you account for one team that brings in more players on its squad than the other? In the early years, we had no restrictions on how much a player could eat.

Eventually, I concluded that it was not in the company's best interest to promote a media image of football players as gluttons. I thought it was in poor taste for the restaurant and damaging to the teams. And the universities felt much the same. We mutually decided not to have a contest anymore. So, we changed the name from the "Beef Bowl" to the "Beef Scrimmage" for a few years. We wanted to get away from "Beef Bowl" because the term "Bowl" suggested a contest.

TE: But, then you changed the name back to "Beef Bowl" a few years later...

RNF: Yes, we felt the name "Beef Scrimmage" was, essentially, meaningless. We liked the name "Beef Bowl" much

better, as I said before, because it suggests the Rose Bowl and I don't think it necessarily suggests a contest. We'd only changed it in an attempt to subdue the idea of the players competing to see who could eat the most beef.

But we've never totally succeeded. The media has never given up on the idea of it being a contest, and they've kept it alive. The legend has grown to the extent that, even at the most recent Beef Bowl, Texas coach Mack Brown came out and told his players, "Boys, don't forget, we have a contest going here!" And, I said, "Now, wait a minute, Mack, you didn't get the message!" But the sports reporters love it, and sometimes the teams love it, too. At one point we had some athletic directors and coaches who didn't want us to push the contest aspect. Now some of those same people look the other way because they no longer feel it's a bad idea.

However, I still think it's a bad idea. We limit the amount of prime rib each player is served to two very generously sized cuts of beef. But the players often find a loophole. What happens when a smaller player gets his second cut and passes it down the table to the big lineman who has already had two? Now he has three. These are things we cannot really control, and they go on behind our backs. All of a sudden, I'll see a group of players and TV cameramen gathering around a table, watching one of their teammates eat his fifth cut, or more, of beef. Now, how the hell did he get that fifth cut?

TE: The players seem to have a lot of fun designating teammates who show the most promise of breaking the legendary all-time record...

RNF: We aren't sure what "the legendary all-time record" is, or if one even exists. And, frankly, we don't want to know. The myth is part of the tradition of the Beef Bowl, and it's the stuff reporters like to pick up on. It just keeps getting bigger and bigger.

TE: What aspect of the events do you enjoy the most?

RNF: It's a pleasure getting to know the coaches, and I often get letters from them thanking me for their event experience. Thanks to Coach Brown, my wife and I will be seeing the Oklahoma-Texas game this year. [Michigan head coach] Lloyd Carr said the same thing: "You want to come to the Ohio State game? We'd

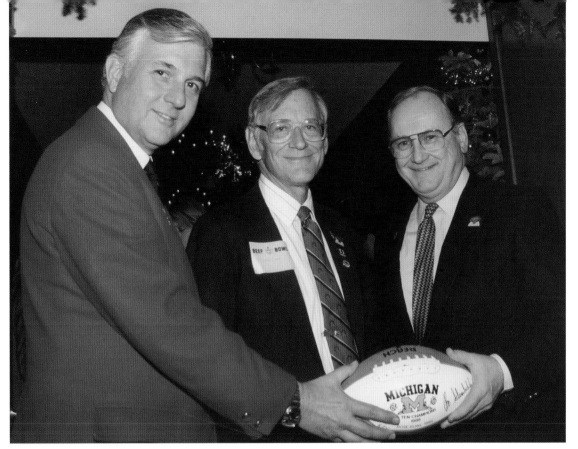

love to have you." And we look forward to that in the next year or two.

So, it has been fun. The coaches have been gracious and hospitable. They're good speakers, quality people. Bo Schembechler is a particularly nice man. I'll never forget the time I mentioned to him that I had tried out for the football team at my alma mater, Pomona College. He replied, "You went out for football with a scrawny neck like yours? You'd last two minutes!" I said, "Well, I didn't last very long, if you want to know the truth. I broke my foot in the first scrimmage!" We had a good laugh over that.

TE: What other unusual situations do you recall?
RNF: Oh sure. Hayden Fry [former head coach of Iowa] brought his team for the 1982 Rose Bowl. I know they had a good time, but four years later, he pulled a "Woody Hayes" and wouldn't bring his team to the restaurant. He thought the 1986 Rose Bowl outcome would be different if he kept his players from being distracted with all of the pre-game events.

After the game, I wrote him a letter that went something like, "Dear Coach Fry, I'm sorry you missed coming to Lawry's for the Beef Bowl because you and your players would have enjoyed it and I doubt it would have made any difference in the outcome of the game. I want to extend a sincere invitation to you: If Iowa ever has the opportunity to play in the Rose Bowl again, we hope you'll bring your team to the restaurant."

He responded promptly, writing, "Mr. Frank, you are absolutely right. The next time we come out there, we'll be in the restaurant." Six years later, Iowa was back at the Rose Bowl and Coach Fry was good to his word and brought his team to Lawry's for the Beef Bowl. That was a great game; Iowa almost won in a shootout with Washington, 46-34!

Joe Tiller, Purdue

"Mr. Frank welcomed our team to Lawry's and introduced me as the head coach of the Washington Huskies who had been there the night before. He quickly corrected himself and apologized, but when I got up to speak, I figured that I couldn't let him off that easily, so I said, 'It's great to be here at the Outback Steak House.' He was good about it and said he deserved it. Of course, we had a wonderful time."

Another time was when I introduced Purdue coach Joe Tiller as the head coach of Washington. The Huskies had been to the restaurant for their event the night before, so I slipped. He got me back pretty good on that one!

I made a similar goof some years ago when Gary Barnett brought Northwestern to the Rose Bowl Game, and he called me on it. You get flustered sometimes!

TE: Do you recall when Joe Paterno and Penn State came out to the Rose Bowl?
RNF: Of course! Richard Riordan, who was mayor of Los Angeles at the time, heard that Paterno and his team would be at Lawry's for the Beef Bowl and he was determined to meet Paterno. Riordan is a restaurant owner, among other things, a very wealthy guy in all kinds of businesses. I don't know if he'd ever been to Lawry's before—at least I'd never seen him there—but, when he heard that Penn State was coming, he made sure he was there. He kind of stole the show because he was the mayor. I just owned the restaurant!

TE: I recall you surprised Coach Paterno with a birthday cake at the Beef Bowl...
RNF: Well, we knew he had celebrated his birthday just five days before, so we wanted to do something special in his honor.

Paterno is a pleasant man. His players were all well-disciplined, dressed in navy blue blazers and matching ties. He said playing in the Rose Bowl was a really big deal to him. And coming to the Rose Bowl is a big deal for most of the teams. The coaches who don't get to come to this game know what the tradition is and what the "Granddaddy" really means. Out of all of the bowl games, it is the one game they would most like to have a chance to play in.

My years of observing the teams at the Beef Bowl have given me a unique perspective on how they express their esteem for the Rose Bowl Game. It's indicated by a lot of seemingly little things—the way they dress, how they act, their attitudes during the pre-game events. In the early years, all of the teams came in blazers and ties, and we could tell they felt that being at Lawry's was something special. Unfortunately, in the last 20 years, there have

been some exceptions where the teams came shabbily dressed, ate and left without so much as a thank you. There's such a difference between that kind of behavior and teams like Penn State and Northwestern, who were all real gentlemen. When Stanford joined us in 1999 [2000 Rose Bowl] the entire team rose when the Queen and Court came into the dining room.

This is a reflection on the coaches. For many of the players, the Beef Bowl is the first time they've ever been to a fine dining establishment like Lawry's, and you can tell whether a coach has prepared his team to dress and act befitting the occasion.

Maybe this makes me sound stuffy and old-fashioned. But it's really a matter of respect—the respect the players have for themselves, their team and the game. When they're at the Beef Bowl, they're in the public eye, and the press and the Tournament notice what they do.

TE: That sure is true. Many consider it the most prestigious pre-game event for each team. It's their coronation as champions on the road to the Rose Bowl.
RNF: Yes, Tournament officials say it's the pre-game event they most look forward to, and I am frequently told it is the players' and coaches' favorite tradition, something they anticipate. The public seems to love it, too. I travel around the country a lot, and everywhere I go, people always ask me, "Are you still feeding those teams?"

The Beef Bowl wouldn't have grown into the success it is without the support of our staff. Our co-workers have a great affection for the Beef Bowl, and take pride in making it the best it can be. We have a meeting every year, about a month after the Beef Bowl, to discuss how we can improve it the next time around. I think that's why it keeps getting better over time.

There are many individuals who contribute, but in particular, Bryan Monfort, Colleen Donatucci, Dick Powell and Todd Johnson have made the Beef Bowl come alive. They have done a lot of things to enhance the experience in just the past decade. For example, Colleen arranged for the Big Ten and Pac-10 university banners that are displayed in the restaurant's main dining room during the holidays leading up to the Rose Bowl Game.

TE: What are some of the other enhancements you've made to the events?

RNF: We've added many special touches over the years to make the experience even more memorable for the teams, and they have become Beef Bowl traditions. We wanted to welcome the players with some fanfare, so we came up with the idea of putting a red carpet from the team buses to the entrance of the restaurant, and having our servers and staff line up alongside to greet the players. Except for the teams that are local, the university bands are rarely in Southern California in time for the Beef Bowl, so we arranged for the official Tournament of Roses band from Pasadena City College to be there each night, playing each team's fight song as they enter the restaurant. We hang the team's banner at the entrance to the restaurant, and our valet parking attendants wear the team's jerseys.

The pièce de résistance, other than the prime rib, is The "Road to the Rose Bowl," a video that is shown both nights of the Beef Bowl. It's another wonderful enhancement. It starts out with the history of the Rose Bowl and the Beef Bowl, and ends with clips of the great plays from the teams' regular season. A separate video is made for each team to spotlight their achievements. Players often ask us if they can get a copy, and we're happy to make it available to them.

Jack French, former CEO of the Tournament, came up with the idea for the video. Tournament officials also suggested we have a printed program, which includes a history of the Beef Bowl, some historic pictures and team highlights. We give the programs to the players, and it's a nice souvenir of their visit to Lawry's.

TE: The early years were rather simple affairs compared to today's events...

RNF: Yes, it's just an evolution, none of these things happened originally. It started very quietly. The team came and enjoyed the meal, but nothing in particular was done besides that. We would walk around and welcome the players and shake their hands. Then, as time went on, the Tournament felt we should add some ceremony to the evening, to make it more of an event, and bit-by-bit, the extras were added, some at the suggestion of the Tournament, others through ideas on our part.

Originally, I didn't receive autographed footballs from each of the teams. That began back in the mid-Sixties. It's become a fun tradition. Each year, my daughter, Susie, designs and develops a special exhibit for the restaurant's lobby with archival photographs and other memorabilia depicting the history of the Beef Bowl and highlighting the teams we're hosting that year. At the conclusion of the last Beef Bowl event, we add the latest autographed balls from that year's teams, and they remain on display until the next year.

Over the years I'd accumulated so many autographed balls, it got to the point where I said to myself, "What am I going to do with all of these footballs? I've had them for years. Heck, I'll give them to the Tournament." And so they have them archived over there now and can be used for displays and whatever. That was another tradition that happened as the event matured. You keep adding little things every year and it just gets bigger and bigger.

TE: Some of the Beef Bowl memorabilia has become pretty popular with the players and collectors, like the annual pin.

RNF: Yes, the pins. We've never changed the design of the pin, only the color and the names of the teams from year to year. We've had those pins for twenty years or more. Our servers proudly wear the pins to show the

Top left: Purdue coach Joe Tiller with RNF at 2000 Lawry's Beef Bowl. Bottom left: Penn State coach Joe Paterno at the 1994 Lawrys' Beef Bowl. Top right: USC band member entertains red carpet crowd before USC team arrival at 2003 Lawry's Beef Bowl. Middle right: KTLA sports anchor Ed Arnold interviews Bryan Monfort of Lawry's. Bottom right: Texas players check out program at 2004 Lawry's Beef Bowl.

Top left: Lawry's Beef Bowl pin for 1996 Rose Bowl Game. Lower left: RNF with USC coach Pete Carroll, athletic director Mike Garrett, and son Richard R. Frank (2003 Lawry's Beef Bowl). Top right: Main lobby display case at Lawry's The Prime Rib in Beverly Hills.

number of Beef Bowls at which they've helped to serve the players. Our guests are always intrigued by the pins and ask the servers about them. And that gives the server a chance to talk about how much she enjoys taking care of the teams.

We had commemorative mugs for the players for a number of years in the '80s, but we felt the pins made better collectibles because everyone involved with the Tournament of Roses Parade and the Rose Bowl has a collectible pin. Over the last few years, we've also given the teams small footballs with their team logos on them, and the players really like those. And the 2005 Rose Bowl trading cards last year became a big hit with everyone, too.

TE: The first-ever Rose Bowl trading cards, as far as I could tell in my research.

RNF: Well, it's all because the Tournament of Roses has been a wonderful partner over the years. I've gotten to know the Tournament presidents over the last twenty years, and many have become good friends. Lawry's has become an appreciated and esteemed member of their program. They think highly of us and the feelings are mutual. We pretty much open up their season with a dinner at our Tam O' Shanter Inn restaurant for the Rose Queen and her Court. It's one of the first opportunities for the Queen and Court to appear in public. Both Lawry's and the Tournament consider it to be an important event, and it's a chance for that year's Tournament officials to meet us. Everything we do in conjunction with the Tournament makes the program stronger.

TE: Do you feel the Beef Bowl in Dallas (in conjunction with the Cotton Bowl) has established its own sort of tradition over the years?

RNF: Yes, the Beef Bowl at Lawry's The Prime Rib, Dallas, first began in 1982. As soon as I knew we were going to be opening the Dallas restaurant, I wrote to the Cotton Bowl committee and offered them the restaurant for the Beef Bowl. They accepted, and it's become a great tradition in Dallas. The players and the coaches enjoy it, and we do, too.

A number of teams have been to both Beef Bowls over the years. UCLA has been to both of them, and now Texas.

We've hosted Oregon, Ohio State, USC, and Oklahoma in Dallas as well as in Beverly Hills.

Take Mack Brown, for instance. He had been to our Dallas restaurant as a guest, but I met him for the first time several years ago, when he brought his team to the Cotton Bowl version of the Beef Bowl. He impressed me as being a genuinely nice man. Then, he brought his team to the 2005 Rose Bowl. When we were having dinner together at the Beef Bowl for the Longhorns, I said, "You know, Mack, next year is the fiftieth anniversary of the Beef Bowl, and the Rose Bowl will also host the national championship game. Here's a chance for you to come back two years in a row." He replied, "Don't think I haven't thought about that! And don't be too surprised if we're there!"

I wrote a letter to USC coach Pete Carroll to remind him of the Beef Bowl's upcoming fiftieth anniversary. The Trojans were national champions the past two years and USC has a long history of coming to both the Rose Bowl and the Beef Bowl.

We never know who we'll be welcoming from year to year, and rooting for the teams and speculating on who'll be at the Beef Bowl is part of the fun of it all.

TE: We've taken a look back over the years, but now with the fiftieth anniversary finally here, what do you envision in the future?

RNF: Well, I certainly would like to see the Rose Bowl Game continue to be the most coveted bowl game in which to play. The BCS has really made an impact on the tradition of the Pac-10 / Big Ten match-up and I think a majority of the fans are disappointed by it. A couple of years ago, USC and Iowa should have been playing each other in the Rose Bowl instead of across the country. And the last time the Rose Bowl hosted the BCS national championship game, we didn't have any schools from either the Big Ten or Pac-10, it was Nebraska and Miami. Last year, I really thought California deserved to come to the Rose Bowl, but Texas won out in the computer polls. I wasn't too unhappy because Texas had a darn good team.

I just hope that the bowl games continue to be relevant. As long as they are, the Rose Bowl will be the most important game. It would be nice to see a Big Ten or

Pac-10 team get into the BCS national championship game during Lawry's fiftieth Beef Bowl year, but we'll be here to welcome any team that does.

If they ever have a national tournament, as they do with NCAA basketball, I would hope that the Rose Bowl would be where they play that game every year. The Rose Bowl would make the most sense as the location because it draws the biggest crowd, pays out the biggest money, and is the oldest and most prestigious tradition of all the bowl games.

Barring some event like a national tournament that might change the importance of the Rose Bowl, I can't see any reason why Lawry's Beef Bowl won't continue to thrive for many years to come. Why shouldn't it? I think players are always going to like a champion's style prime rib meal.

TE: I understand you have just been nominated for induction into the Rose Bowl Hall of Fame with the Class of 2005. In the 17-year history of the Hall of Fame it's been extremely rare for an individual other than a player, coach or Tournament official to be recognized. Can you describe what this honor means to you?

RNF: I am overwhelmed! This is a signal honor. I never dreamed of, or considered it to be a possibility because it is so unusual—in fact, when I was told I had been nominated, it actually took me a few minutes to believe what I had heard. From the start, I have felt tremendously gratified just to be associated with the Tournament and the Rose Bowl Game. That feeling has grown even stronger over the last fifty years, as I've had the privilege of getting to know the Tournament staff and witnessing, first-hand, their skill and dedication. To be recognized in this way, by an organization I hold in such high esteem, and to be given a place in a tradition I love, is one of the crowning honors of my life.

HAIL TO THE CHAMPIONS!

It's late in the afternoon on December 30th at Lawry's The Prime Rib in Beverly Hills. Parking valets wearing the visiting university's football jerseys greet the last of the Tournament of Roses officials to arrive. They join a couple dozen other Tournament officials and their spouses inside the restaurant who have already been mingling with the athletic director of the university, Lawry's executives, and members of the Royal Court.

Moments later, a Tournament of Roses university entertainment committee member receives a call on his cell phone notifying him the team buses are five minutes away. The news spreads rapidly throughout the assemblage. Lawry's managers on walkie-talkies summon their staff to the reception line. In less than a minute, two-dozen employees are lining the red carpet walkway from curbside to the restaurant's entrance. Many of the guests migrate to the front lobby and main entrance to join in greeting the team.

The Pasadena City College band strikes up the rousing school fight song while television news cameramen jockey for the best position. They record an amusing cutaway shot when the Lawry's female staff members playfully mimic a Las Vegas showgirl kick line sequence.

"Here they come!" cries one of the red carpet greeters leaning a bit too far off the curb into the northbound traffic on La Cienega Boulevard. A Beverly Hills police officer nudges her back toward the red carpet just as four team buses pull into view escorted by a police motorcade. Inside the buses, the players are abuzz regarding the enthusiastic reception awaiting them.

With the band playing, the greeters clapping in unison, university banners proudly displayed on the restaurant's columned entrance, and satellite uplink trucks parked in every available space, the excitement is palpable. Each bus edges forward to unload proud coaches and wide-eyed student athletes anxious to make the red carpet walk at Lawry's in Beverly Hills.

On separate evenings both Big Ten and Pac-10 Conference champions travel this brief but significant stretch of glory road known as the Lawry's Beef Bowl. Here, they will enjoy some of the reward for their hard work and sustained effort over the past year. And here they will begin to comprehend the tradition of the "Granddaddy" and the fraternity of champions they have joined.

It's one thing to read or hear about the hoopla surrounding the Rose Bowl and the buildup before the big game, and quite another to experience it. It seems to reach its fever pitch by the time both teams have made their appearance at the Beef Bowl. The strenuous practices and preparation are behind both teams. Their game plans are solid and have shifted into a fine-tuning mode. Game day could be as few as 48 hours away.

Similarly, months of planning and preparation go into honoring the Rose Bowl-bound conference champions at Lawry's each year. Preparatory activities reach a frenetic pace during the month of December when the Tournament of Roses officially announces the two university football teams that will meet in the Rose Bowl Game. On the day of each event all of the elements finally come together. Whether it's game time or show time, the fundamentals are the same: Teamwork, execute the game plan as flawlessly as possible, and adapt as necessary to unforeseen situations.

11:15 a.m.

Banners welcoming the visiting team have just been secured to each of the main entryway columns.

11:47 a.m.

Gregorio Franco readies the aged Midwestern corn fed prime beef roasts for the oven. A really hungry team will put away nearly 20 of these roasts in less than two hours.

12:17 p.m.

Paul from Balloon Bookie proves elusive to the photographer but adds a festive accent to the Beef Bowl atmosphere with team color balloons.

1:20 p.m.

Todd Johnson, general manager of Lawry's The Prime Rib Beverly Hills, tapes an interview with Don Shane of ABC-7 Detroit.

This timeline represents the most recent Lawry's Beef Bowl honoring the University of Michigan's 2005 Rose Bowl team.

2:07 p.m.

Robert Sotomayor makes sure every place setting has a program and mini-football.

2:24 p.m.

Kim Kurek puts the finishing touches on each place setting. In the background is the giant screen where the team-customized presentation of "Road to the Rose Bowl" will be projected.

2:47 p.m.

Staging Technologies run their final checks on the audio and video equipment.

2:54 p.m.

Tino Figueroa prepares containers filled with just-made creamy mashed potatoes for the Lawry's serving carts.

3:01 p.m.

Satellite uplink trucks from local television stations stake claims to the most convenient curbside space on La Cienega Boulevard and prepare their equipment.

3:10 p.m.

Sous Chef Deodato Guzman checks on the prime rib roasts. They are almost done.

3:25 p.m.

Colleen Donatucci of Lawry's discusses the seating chart with Peter Boyle, a member of the Tournament of Roses university entertainment committee.

3:29 p.m.

Todd Johnson, general manager, reviews last minute details of the event game plan with staff members.

3:37 p.m.

The team is scheduled to arrive in less than 30 minutes and Executive Chef Walter Eckstein is pleased to see that the heated serving carts are stocked and ready to roll.

3:40 p.m.

The Tournament of Roses officials have all arrived and the Pasadena City College marching band begins playing energetic fanfares to get everyone pumped up for the team's arrival.

3:55 p.m.

The call comes in that the team buses are only five minutes away. Less than a minute later, Lawry's staffers have lined up along the red carpet and the ladies get playful with their version of a showgirl kick line.

3:59 p.m.

As the police motorcade arrives in the background, Todd Johnson signals there are four team buses to unload.

4:00 p.m.

Like clockwork, the team buses arrive. Valet Captain Pepe Cornejo guides the first bus up to the red carpet.

4:07 p.m.

Head Coach Lloyd Carr leads his team off the bus and onto the red carpet.

4:08 p.m.

The Lawry's red carpet reception from a player's perspective. At the end of the red carpet, players and coaches are greeted by Tournament of Roses officials, the Royal Court, Richard N. Frank and other Lawry's executives.

4:15 p.m.

Offensive lineman Grant DeBenedictis eagerly embraces the Big Ten champions' red carpet reception.

4:20 p.m.

While the team is being seated, Coach Carr and a couple players meet with sports reporters in the media room. Here, cornerback Marlin Jackson responds to a question.

4:28 p.m.

2005 Rose Queen Ashley Moreno and her Court are formally introduced and escorted to their tables by Tournament of Roses chaperones.

4:33 p.m.

Safety Jamar Adams joins in the fun to help Gina Griem prepare the Lawry's spinning salad for his teammates.

4:39 p.m.

Following the official welcomes and introductions Richard N. Frank, and his son Richard R. Frank, president and CEO of Lawry's, pose for a photo with Dave Davis, 2005 president of the Tournament of Roses, and Michigan head coach Lloyd Carr.

4:45 p.m.

Madeline Martin serves the main course of Lawry's prime rib to linebacker Chris Graham.

5:23 p.m.

Detroit ABC-7's Don Shane wants to know if 6'4" 319 lb. offensive lineman David Baas plans to go after the mythical Beef Bowl record held by former Wolverine Ed Muransky while Derek Bell enjoys his meal.

5:35 p.m.

Horsing around in a photo for the Associated Press, freshman QB Chad Henne "passes" a loaf of sourdough bread to All-American receiver Braylon Edwards while Queen Ashley pretends she's going to try to intercept.

5:45 p.m.

Just before the lights go down for the event-ending "Road to the Rose Bowl" video, Michigan players Kevin Dudley, Jerome Jackson, Carl Tabb and Brian Thompson escort Princess Allison Pedro to the podium to award her with an autographed mini-game ball for her awe-inspiring appetite.

ROSE BOWL GAME
1957
OREGON STATE vs. IOWA

Frank Negri, Oregon State

"January 1st, 1957 was a huge day in my life. Not only was I going to play in the Rose Bowl but our first child was due to be born that day. My wife and I were from Los Angeles so returning there to play in front of family and friends was a dream come true. Oregon State flew all the wives down to Pasadena a few days before the game so they could enjoy the Rose Parade. My wife was the only one left behind but the people of Corvallis were wonderful to her, offering all kinds of invitations to share game day with them. A store even sent a TV to the hospital, just in case, so she wouldn't miss the game. The thing I most remember about the game is trying to block the great Alex Karras. Me 5'9, 170 lbs.: Karras 6'3, 260 lbs. He threw me around like a rag doll. The game was still a dream come true, and by the way—the baby girl did not arrive until January 13th."

OREGON STATE BEAVERS
HEAD COACH: TOMMY PROTHRO
1956 RECORD: 7-2-1 (5-1-1) PCC CHAMPIONS

DATE	OPPONENT	RESULT
Sep 22	at Missouri	W 19-13
Sep 29	at USC	L 13-21
Oct 6	at Iowa	L 13-14
Oct 13	California	W 21-13
Oct 20	at Wash. St.	W 21-6
Oct 27	UCLA	W 21-7
Nov 3	Washington	W 28-20
Nov 10	at Stanford	W 20-9
Nov 17	at Idaho	W 14-10
Nov 24	Oregon	T 14-14

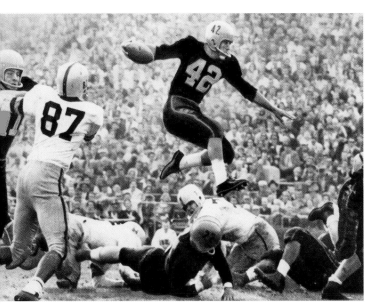

SCORE BY QUARTERS	1 - 2 - 3 - 4	FINAL SCORE
OREGON STATE	0 - 6 - 6 - 7	19
IOWA	14 - 7 - 7 - 7	35

UNIVERSITY OF IOWA HAWKEYES
HEAD COACH: FOREST EVASHEVSKI
1956 RECORD: 9-1 (5-1) BIG TEN CHAMPIONS

DATE	OPPONENT	RESULT
Sep 29	at Indiana	W 27-0
Oct 6	Oregon State	W 14-13
Oct 13	Wisconsin	W 13-7
Oct 20	Hawaii	W 34-0
Oct 27	at Purdue	W 21-20
Nov 3	Michigan	L 14-17
Nov 10	at Minnesota	W 7-0
Nov 17	Ohio State	W 6-0
Nov 24	at Notre Dame	W 48-8

Kenny Ploen, Iowa

"Forest Evashevski, had us travel to the West Coast prior to Christmas so we could become acclimatized to the weather. He also wanted us to experience the flavor of the West Coast. We attended a number of shows including one hosted by Bob Hope. When Bob came on stage his opening comment was, 'When I first heard the name Forest Eveshevski, I thought it was a National Park in Russia.' It brought down the house and put a lot of smiles on all the Iowa players."

The Beavers lost to Iowa by a whisker on the road early in the regular season (14-13) but they surrendered that many points in the opening quarter off touchdown runs by Hawkeyes Kenny Ploen and Collins Hagler. By halftime, the score was 21-6. Hagler ripped off a nifty 66-yard TD scamper that put Iowa up 28-6 in the third quarter. Ploen ended up with 9 of 10 passing for 83 yards and a score, while also contributing 59 more yards on the ground. His counterpart, Joe Francis, provided 203 total yards (73 yards rushing, 10 of 12 passing for 130 yards) including a 35-yard strike to Sterling Hammick. Oregon State made a battle of it in the second half, but it wasn't enough to overcome the cushion Iowa had built up in the first period.

Top left: Iowa defenders Collins Hagler and Don Dobrino break up a pass intended for an Oregon State receiver. Bottom left: 1957 Royal Court at the game. Top right: Beaver QB Joe Francis leaping over Iowa line as Iowa's #87 Frank Gilliam tries to shed a block. Bottom right: Iowa players being treated to a prime rib meal on their Southern California practice field at the inaugural Lawry's Beef Bowl.

ROSE BOWL GAME

1958

OREGON vs. OHIO STATE

SCORE BY QUARTERS	1 - 2 - 3 - 4	FINAL SCORE
OREGON	0 - 7 - 0 - 0	7
OHIO STATE	7 - 0 - 0 - 3	10

Jack Crabtree,
QB, Oregon

"The thing that sticks in my mind the most is the humiliation and bad press we got before the game. I think we were something like 40-point underdogs and the press said we didn't belong there playing the #1 team in the nation, even though we did win the PCC. Then, after the game, when we had proven we could hang with Ohio State, the press said we were the best West Coast Rose Bowl team since 1941. Anyway, if they were #1, then we were #2."

UNIVERSITY OF OREGON DUCKS
HEAD COACH: LEN CASANOVA
1957 RECORD: 7-3 (5-2) PCC CHAMPIONS

DATE	OPPONENT	RESULT
Sep 21	at Idaho	W 9-6
Sep 28	Pittsburgh	L 3-6
Oct 5	UCLA	W 21-0
Oct 12	San Jose State	W 26-0
Oct 19	at Washington St.	W 14-13
Oct 26	California	W 24-6
Nov 2	at Stanford	W 27-26
Nov 9	Washington	L 6-13
Nov 16	at Southern Cal	W 16-7
Nov 23	Oregon State	L 7-10

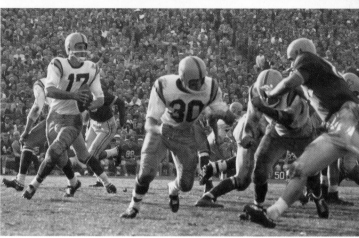

Ohio State came into the game as huge favorites with the UPI national championship already under their belt but the Buckeyes barely squeaked out a victory with the help of two Duck turnovers in the second half. Both teams entered the contest with stingy defensive units and that's the way the game played out. The Buckeyes had given up only 85 total points during the regular season and the Ducks had yielded just 87. Ohio State marched 79 yards and scored on a Frank Kremblas 1-yard run on their first possession, but their offense was held in check the rest of the game. Jim Shanley put the Ducks' only points on the board with a touchdown run in the second quarter to even the score before halftime.

Oregon had a chance to go ahead in the third quarter but their 24-yard field goal attempt just missed its mark. Ohio State managed to drive deep into Duck territory at the beginning of the fourth quarter, but they had to settle for a 24-yard field

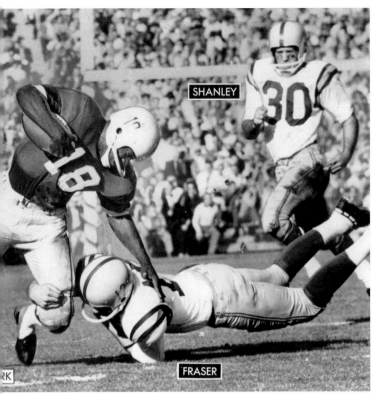

SHANLEY

30

FRASER

goal—from the exact same spot where Oregon had missed minutes earlier. Oregon receiver Ron Stover had 10 receptions for 144 yards, but his costly fumble in Buckeye territory with less than 11 minutes in the game all but dashed the Ducks' comeback hopes. The fumble occurred when Stover hit the ground hard and the ball squirted loose, a ruling that would not have occurred under modernized rules. Oregon had one final drive underway near the end of the game and ran out of time at midfield.

Webfoot QB Jack Crabtree kept the Buckeyes off balance throughout the game with 10 of 17 passing for 135 yards and effective ball control. Oregon never punted in the game and outmatched Ohio State in total yards (351 to 304) and first downs (21 to 19). Don Clark (14 rushes, 82 yards) and Bob White (25 for 93 yards) accounted for the bulk of OSU's offense. Jim Shanley had 59 yards rushing on 11 carries for the Ducks.

OHIO STATE UNIVERSITY BUCKEYES
HEAD COACH: WOODY HAYES
1957 RECORD: 8-1 (7-0) BIG TEN CHAMPIONS

DATE	OPPONENT	RESULT
Sep 28	Texas Christian	L 14-18
Oct 5	at Washington	W 35-7
Oct 12	Illinois	W 21-7
Oct 19	Indiana	W 56-0
Oct 26	at Wisconsin	W 16-13
Nov 2	Northwestern	W 47-6
Nov 9	Purdue	W 20-7
Nov 16	Iowa	W 17-13
Nov 23	at Michigan	W 31-14

PRESS BOX FACTS

Woody Hayes was named the 1957 National Coach of the Year by college football sportswriters.

Top left: Oregon's Charlie Tourville leaps to catch a pass in first half action. Middle left: Duck QB Jack Crabtree rolls out to pass in the fourth quarter while Jim Shanley seals off the outside rush. Bottom left: Oregon's Jim Shanley fields a punt in the third quarter. Top center: Buckeye Don Clark fights off a Duck tackler. Top right: Buckeye players and coaches enjoy the Lawry's Beef Bowl meal outside their practice facility. Bottom right: Oregon players swarm to tackle Ohio State ball carrier.

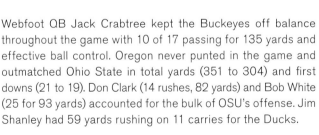

ROSE BOWL GAME

1959

CALIFORNIA vs. IOWA

SCORE BY QUARTERS	1 - 2 - 3 - 4	FINAL SCORE
CALIFORNIA	0 - 0 - 6 - 6	12
IOWA	7 - 13 - 12 - 6	38

Jack Hart, HB, California

"Playing in the Rose Bowl was a great experience, although it was a tough loss to a fine Iowa team. Our team was treated royally during the week, and a highlight was our team dinner at Lawry's. The 1959 Rose Bowl has gotten to be a bigger deal over the years for our team, as Cal has not been back since. I'm often introduced as 'the last player to score a touchdown for Cal in the Rose Bowl.' I like to amend the introduction to 'the most recent, not the last...'"

UNIVERSITY OF CALIFORNIA GOLDEN BEARS
HEAD COACH: PETE ELLIOTT
1958 RECORD: 7-4 (6-1) PCC CHAMPIONS

DATE	OPPONENT	RESULT
Sep 20	Pacific	L 20-24
Sep 27	at Michigan State	L 12-32
Oct 4	Washington State	W 34-14
Oct 11	Utah	W 36-21
Oct 18	at USC	W 14-12
Oct 25	Oregon	W 23-6
Nov 1	at Oregon State	L 8-14
Nov 8	UCLA	W 20-17
Nov 15	at Washington	W 12-7
Nov 22	Stanford	W 16-15

Top left: Jack Hart fights across the goal line for a Cal score. Middle left: Cal defenders pursue #11 Bob Jeter as he scoots around right end. Bottom left: Jack Hart shows his wife how to carve prime rib while fellow Cal players Jack Yerma and Joe Kapp observe at the Lawry's Beef Bowl. Top right: Hawkeye Bob Jeter takes the handoff from Randy Duncan as Willie Fleming seals off the defensive end. Middle right: Iowa mascot "Herky" helps a University of Iowa Scottish Highlander off the train in Los Angeles. Bottom right: Iowa's Jeff Langston clutches the ball for a touchdown in the 2nd quarter.

Iowa continued the Big Ten's dominance over the Pacific Coast Conference in the thirteen-year old Rose Bowl pact with a convincing 38–12 victory. The Hawkeyes led 20–0 at halftime and 32–6 at the end of the third quarter. Many had expected a passing duel between Iowa's Randy Duncan, the runner-up in the Heisman Trophy voting, and Cal's Joe Kapp. In the end, both quarterbacks combined for a total of only 24 pass attempts the entire game. The ground game was a different story with both teams ringing up 643 rushing yards, 429 of those yards gained by Iowa.

©University of Iowa Photo Service

©University of Iowa Photo Service

UNIVERSITY OF IOWA HAWKEYES
HEAD COACH: FOREST EVASHEVSKI
1957 RECORD: 7-1-1 (5-1) BIG TEN CHAMPIONS

DATE	OPPONENT	RESULT
Sep 27	TCU	W 17-0
Oct 4	Air Force	T 13-13
Oct 11	Indiana	W 34-13
Oct 18	at Wisconsin	W 20-9
Oct 25	Northwestern	W 26-20
Nov 1	at Michigan	W 37-14
Nov 8	at Minnesota	W 28-6
Nov 15	Ohio State	L 28-38
Nov 22	Notre Dame	W 31-21

Bob Jeter, RB, Iowa

"We had a great offensive line and I loved running behind them. Laphum, Drake, Lewis, Burroughs, Growinkle and Mertz. They were fast and I didn't have to wait for them. My favorite play was the 134 Counter. I'll never forget when we ran that play against Cal. I took the handoff from Randy Duncan and hit the hole off right guard as usual behind our fullback John Nocera. Instinctively, I cut back to my left against the grain of pursuit. I could see the Cal defenders flying by me in a blur, reaching out for me but missing. Nobody touched me as I hit the sidelines and raced in for the score."

Bob Jeter and Willie Fleming led the powerful Hawkeye rushing attack. Jeter finished with 194 yards on 9 carries including a then-record 81-yard TD scamper. His 21.6 yards per carry average is still a Rose Bowl record. Fleming tallied 85 yards on 9 carries and he ripped off two touchdown runs of 37 and 7 yards in the second half to ice the game. Duncan ended up with one touchdown run and one TD pass on the day. Jack Hart was the only Golden Bear to light up the score board with a 1-yard run in the third quarter and a 17-yard TD pass reception in the final period. Cal failed on two 2-point conversions and Iowa fell short on three 2-pointers and botched one PAT kick.

ROSE BOWL GAME
1960
WISCONSIN vs. WASHINGTON

Bob Schloredt, QB, Washington

"Chesty Walker was one of our coaches, one of the old timers from Texas who had come up to assist Jim Owens. After a kick-off luncheon the day before the game, our team went over to the stadium to see the field for the first time. Chesty took the Backs and led us down to one of the end zones. He told us to take a blade of grass and put it in the heel of our shoe. Then, he led us down to the other end zone, where we did the same thing in the other shoe. Chesty said this would ensure us that we'd visit the end zone a lot during the game. The game ended in our favor 44-8, and it's all because of a couple blades of Rose Bowl end zone grass in the heel of our shoes."

UNIVERSITY OF WASHINGTON HUSKIES
HEAD COACH: JIM OWENS
1959 RECORD: 9-1 (3-1) AAWU CHAMPIONS

DATE	OPPONENT	RESULT
Sep 19	at Colorado	W 21-12
Sep 26	Idaho	W 23-0
Oct 3	Utah	W 51-6
Oct 10	Stanford	W 10-0
Oct 17	Southern Cal	L 15-22
Oct 24	Oregon	W 13-12
Oct 31	at UCLA	W 23-7
Nov 7	Oregon State	W 13-6
Nov 14	at California	W 20-0
Nov 21	Washington State	W 20-0

Top left: Husky QB Bob Schloredt races to turn the corner as #60 Badger LB Jerry Stalcup closes in. Middle left: Wisconsin receiver Ron Steiner hauls in a pass in traffic. Bottom left: Badger All-American Dan Lanphear with Lawry's founder Lawrence L. Frank. Top right: Diagrammed game action. Middle right: Washington players converge on the ball. Bottom right: Husky receiver goes up for the catch.

Wisconsin came in with a defense that had allowed just over 10 points per game during the regular season but Washington's George Fleming accounted for ten points in the first quarter alone with a 26-yard field goal and a 53-yard TD punt return. By halftime Washington held a sizable advantage of 24-8. Unfortunately, the Badger offense proved to be a major handicap with four fumbles in the game and zero red zone points in the second half. The Huskies mounted an impressive scoring drive on their first possession of the second half that put the game out of reach.

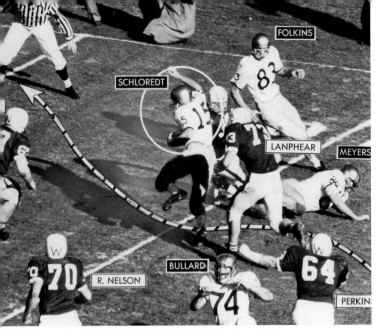

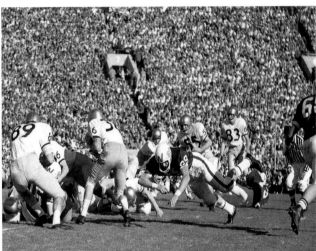

Washington QB Bob Schloredt passed for 102 yards and a score and rushed for 81 of the Huskies 215 total rushing yards. Wisconsin's Dale Hackbart was 11-25 for 153 yards and a 2-point conversion following Tom Weisner's four-yard TD run late in the first half. Washington's win restored a bit of pride to the West Coast after losing 12 of the first 13 Rose Bowl match-ups with Big Ten Conference opponents.

SCORE BY QUARTERS	1 - 2 - 3 - 4	FINAL SCORE
WISCONSIN	0 - 8 - 0 - 0	8
WASHINGTON	17 - 7 - 7 - 13	44

UNIVERSITY OF WISCONSIN BADGERS
HEAD COACH: MILT BRUHN
1959 RECORD: 7-2 (5-2) BIG TEN CHAMPIONS

DATE	OPPONENT	RESULT
Sep 26	Stanford	W 16-14
Oct 3	Marquette	W 44-6
Oct 10	at Purdue	L 0-21
Oct 17	Iowa	W 25-16
Oct 24	Ohio State	W 12-3
Oct 31	at Michigan	W 19-10
Nov 7	at Northwestern	W 24-19
Nov 14	Illinois	L 6-9
Nov 21	at Minnesota	W 11-7

PRESS BOX FACTS

The Pacific Coast Conference dissolved in 1959 and the AAWU (Athletic Association of Western Universities) took its place with 5 schools: USC, UCLA, Cal, Stanford and Washington. Washington State joined in 1962 and Oregon and Oregon State joined in 1964. The conference name changed to Pac-8 in 1968 and then became the Pac-10 in 1978 with the addition of Arizona State and Arizona.

Jerry Stalcup,
LB, Wisconsin

"Playing in the Rose Bowl is the dream of anyone in the Midwest. For years, it was the only bowl game any team in the Big Ten could attend. Now as many as seven teams from the conference play in postseason games each year but there is only one Rose Bowl. When we first visited the Rose Bowl Stadium after arriving in Pasadena we entered halfway up into the stands to a deathly silence. No workers, no fans, no other team. Our next entrance was bedlam! Game Day was unbelievable. We tried to treat it like any other game, but that was impossible. Not everyone can say they played in the Rose Bowl and I am proud and honored that I was able to participate in the Granddaddy of all Bowl games."

ROSE BOWL GAME
1961
MINNESOTA vs. WASHINGTON

Jim Owens, Head Coach, Washington

"I played at Oklahoma for Bud Wilkinson, so it meant a great deal to me when he called a couple days after the game and said, 'That team was the finest prepared team in execution that I've ever seen.'"

Top left: Washington's George Fleming intercepts a pass intended for Dave Mulholland. Middle left: Huskies being served at the Lawry's Beef Bowl. Lower left: Husky field goal attempt. Bottom center: Washington's Charlie Mitchell turns the corner on Minnesota's James Rogers. Top right: Golden Gopher RB Judge Dickson carries the ball in second half action. Middle right: Minnesota defenders wrap up Husky ball carrier. Bottom right: UW defense take down Gopher ball carrier.

UNIVERSITY OF WASHINGTON HUSKIES
HEAD COACH: JIM OWENS
1960 RECORD: 9-1 (4-0) AAWU CHAMPIONS

DATE	OPPONENT	RESULT
Sep 17	Pacific	W 55-6
Sep 24	Idaho	W 41-12
Oct 1	Navy	L 14-15
Oct 8	at Stanford	W 29-10
Oct 15	UCLA	W 10-8
Oct 22	at Oregon State	W 30-29
Oct 29	Oregon	W 7-6
Nov 5	at Southern Cal	W 34-0
Nov 12	California	W 27-7
Nov 19	Washington State	W 8-7

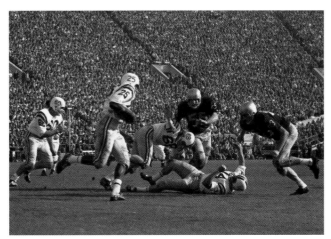

SCORE BY QUARTERS	1 - 2 - 3 - 4	FINAL SCORE
MINNESOTA	0 - 0 - 7 - 0	7
WASHINGTON	3 - 14 - 0 - 0	17

Minnesota entered the game as Big Ten champions and the #1 team in the nation, but they got off to a slow start and faced a 17-point deficit by halftime. Washington's George Fleming kicked a record 44-yard field goal in the first quarter to begin the scoring. Bob Schloredt came off the bench early in the game to engineer several time-consuming drives, one which ended with a TD toss to Brent Wooten early in the second quarter and another that he capped off with a QB sneak for a score with just over 4 minutes left in the half. Schloredt also had a booming punt from inside the Husky end zone during the second quarter that helped prevent the Golden Gophers from securing key field position on the exchange.

Ray Jackson added 60 yards rushing and a key pass reception to Schloredt's 68 yards on the ground. Minnesota's Sandy Stephens rushed for 51 yards but he threw three costly interceptions. Bill Munsey notched the only Gopher score on an 18-yard run in the third quarter.

UNIVERSITY OF MINNESOTA GOLDEN GOPHERS
HEAD COACH: MURRAY WARMATH
1960 RECORD: 8-1 (6-1) BIG TEN CHAMPIONS

DATE	OPPONENT	RESULT
Sep 24	at Nebraska	W 26-14
Oct 1	Indiana	W 42-0
Oct 8	Northwestern	W 7-0
Oct 15	Illinois	W 21-10
Oct 22	at Michigan	W 10-0
Oct 29	Kansas State	W 48-7
Nov 5	Iowa	W 27-10
Nov 12	Purdue	L 14-23
Nov 19	at Wisconsin	W 26-7

Greg Larson,
C/LB, Minnesota

"There was a glitch in the Big Ten's agreement with the AAWU and the Rose Bowl, so we lost valuable training time waiting to hear if we were invited to Pasadena. There was a lot of anxiety. When we were finally invited and could officially practice as a team the coaches worked our tails off. I lost 12 pounds before the game! We left a lot of ourselves on the practice field and played lethargically in the first half. We didn't have the energy we'd displayed all year. I separated my shoulder on the opening kickoff and played the rest of the game with the pain because playing in the Rose Bowl is a once-in-a-lifetime experience."

ROSE BOWL GAME
1962
MINNESOTA vs. UCLA

SCORE BY QUARTERS	1 - 2 - 3 - 4	FINAL SCORE
MINNESOTA	7 - 7 - 0 - 7	21
UCLA	3 - 0 - 0 - 0	3

Marshall Shirk, OT/DT, UCLA

"My most vivid memory of the 1962 Rose Bowl actually occurred the night before the game. To keep a low profile, our coaches moved the team to a hotel outside the immediate area where we had been staying. Everything went well until the clock struck midnight, ushering in the New Year. The bar next to the hotel really started to rock and roll. The partying lasted long past the normal closing time of 2 am and it was insanely loud. My roommate and I took our beds apart and stuffed the mattresses into the windows, but it didn't help much. It was a long, sleepless night followed by a very long afternoon."

UCLA BRUINS
HEAD COACH: BILL BARNES
1961 RECORD: 7-3 (3-1) AAWU CHAMPIONS

DATE	OPPONENT	RESULT
Sep 23	Air Force	W 19-6
Sep 30	at Michigan	L 6-29
Oct 7	at Ohio State	L 3-13
Oct 14	Vanderbilt	W 28-21
Oct 21	Pittsburgh	W 20-6
Oct 28	at Stanford	W 20-0
Nov 4	California	W 35-15
Nov 10	Texas Christian	W 28-7
Nov 18	Washington	L 13-17
Nov 25	Southern Cal	L 10-7

PRESS BOX FACTS

The Big Ten Conference had a "no-repeat" rule in effect from 1946 to 1960. The Pac-10 (then Pacific Coast Conference) had the same rule in effect from 1951 to 1958.

Milt Sunde, T, Minnesota

"As a sophomore behind Bobby Bell and Carl Eller I didn't figure to play much, but Dad was still there for me. At 68, he didn't have much money, having raised three boys by himself after Mom passed away. His bus from Minneapolis to Pasadena arrived just in time to catch the game. The return bus left shortly after the game with several stops along the way. His wallet was stolen in Salt Lake, leaving him with 35 cents. He spent 25 cents on food and saved a dime to make a phone call from the bus station. He insisted missing a couple meals was worth seeing the Gophers win in the Rose Bowl. My dad loved football. When I made it to the NFL, he would go to a high school game Friday night, the Gophers game on Saturday, and the Vikings on Sunday to see me play."

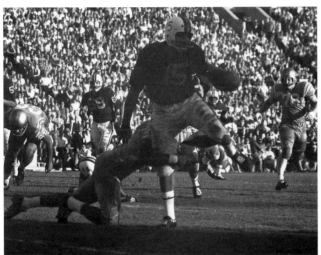

UNIVERSITY OF MINNESOTA GOLDEN GOPHERS
HEAD COACH: MURRAY WARMATH
1961 RECORD: 7-2 (6-1) BIG TEN CHAMPIONS

DATE	OPPONENT	RESULT
Sep 30	Missouri	L 0-6
Oct 7	Oregon	W 14-7
Oct 14	at Northwestern	W 10-3
Oct 21	at Illinois	W 33-0
Oct 28	Michigan	W 23-20
Nov 4	Michigan State	W 13-0
Nov 11	at Iowa	W 16-9
Nov 18	Purdue	W 10-7
Nov 25	Wisconsin	L 21-23

The Golden Gophers returned nearly all their starters from the year before and came back to the Rose Bowl with a vengeance. UCLA put the first points on the board on a Bobby Smith 28-yard field goal, but that was virtually the end of the Bruin offensive output against a Golden Gophers defense anchored by Bobby Bell and Carl Eller. UCLA only managed 107 total yards and 8 first downs in the entire game to Minnesota's 297 total yards and 21 first downs.

Minnesota controlled the clock with two long touchdown drives. QB Sandy Stephens passed for 75 yards and picked up 46 on the ground, including two short yardage scores. Bill Munsey scored the Gophers' other touchdown on a 3-yard run.

Top left: Bruin Bobby Smith knocks down pass intended for Bill Munsey. Bottom left: Rose Queen Martha Sissell, Richard N. Frank, and Tournament of Roses President Arthur Althouse at special luncheon celebrating the Rose Bowl's new press box. Bottom center: Gopher defenders take down UCLA ball carrier. Top right: Bill Munsey carries the ball. Middle right: Minnesota QB Sandy Stephens carries for big yards. Bottom right: Golden Gopher players in line for their Lawry's prime rib meal outside the Rose Bowl.

ROSE BOWL GAME

1963

WISCONSIN vs. USC

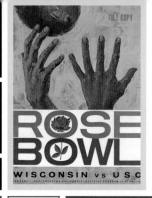

ROSE BOWL

WISCONSIN vs U S C

Hal Bedsole, End, USC

"We'd just gone 11-0 in the regular season, won the Rose Bowl and secured the national championship, but if you would've walked into our locker room before the media was allowed in, you could have heard a pin drop. Everybody's head was hanging because it felt like a loss to us. It was not the feeling of a team that had just won the national championship. John McKay was walking around the locker room trying to convince everyone it was a great win. I know how Wisconsin must have felt because the year before we were losing on the road to #1 Iowa 35-14 at halftime. We almost pulled off the comeback, losing 35-34 on a failed two-point conversion."

USC TROJANS
HEAD COACH: JOHN MCKAY
1962 RECORD: 10-0 (4-0) AAWU CHAMPIONS

DATE	OPPONENT	RESULT
Sep 22	Duke	W 14-7
Sep 29	at SMU	W 33-3
Oct 6	at Iowa	W 7-0
Oct 20	California	W 32-6
Oct 27	at Illinois	W 28-16
Nov 3	Washington	W 14-0
Nov 10	at Stanford	W 39-14
Nov 17	Navy	W 13-6
Nov 24	at UCLA	W 14-3
Dec 1	Notre Dame	W 25-0

Top left: Trojan QB Pete Beathard pursued by Roger Jacobazzi (79) and Ken Bowman (57) in first half action. Bottom left: Tommy Trojan and "Traveler" want to join the Royal Court and USC players at the Lawry's Beef Bowl. Bottom center: USC head coach John McKay beams after his first Rose Bowl victory. USC #40 is Ernie Jones. Top right: Wisconsin goal line defense anchored by #38 James Parnell and #81 Larry Howard. Middle right: Badger QB Ron VanderKelen finds an open receiver behind solid pass protection in the second half. Bottom right: Richard N. Frank welcomes Badgers Ron VanderKelen, Pat Richter, Steve Underwood and Louis Holland to the Lawry's Beef Bowl at Rose Bowl Stadium.

SCORE BY QUARTERS	1 - 2 - 3 - 4	FINAL SCORE
WISCONSIN	0 - 7 - 7 - 23	37
USC	7 - 14 - 14 - 7	42

UNIVERSITY OF WISCONSIN BADGERS
HEAD COACH: MILT BRUHN
1962 RECORD: 8-1 (6-1) BIG TEN CHAMPIONS

DATE	OPPONENT	RESULT
Sep 29	New Mexico St.	W 69-13
Oct 6	Indiana	W 30-6
Oct 13	Notre Dame	W 17-8
Oct 20	Iowa	W 42-14
Oct 27	at Ohio State	L 7-14
Nov 3	at Michigan	W 34-12
Nov 10	Northwestern	W 37-6
Nov 17	at Illinois	W 35-6
Nov 24	Minnesota	W 14-9

Pat Richter, End, Wisconsin

"I was traveling on a red eye flight from LA to Nashville in 1974. I was sitting in an airport chair at 4:30 am and I looked over and saw this gentleman and it was Woody Hayes. I stood up to go say hello and just then his flight must have been called because he jumped up and hustled to the gate. I extended my hand and said 'Coach, Pat Richter' and before I could say another word he said, 'a couple more minutes and you guys would have won that game,' and off he went."

PRESS BOX FACTS

USC's Hal Bedsole and Wisconsin's Pat Richter were both consensus All-Americans for 1962. They combined for 264 yards receiving and 3 touchdowns in the 1963 Rose Bowl.

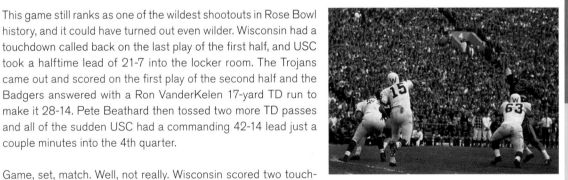

This game still ranks as one of the wildest shootouts in Rose Bowl history, and it could have turned out even wilder. Wisconsin had a touchdown called back on the last play of the first half, and USC took a halftime lead of 21-7 into the locker room. The Trojans came out and scored on the first play of the second half and the Badgers answered with a Ron VanderKelen 17-yard TD run to make it 28-14. Pete Beathard then tossed two more TD passes and all of the sudden USC had a commanding 42-14 lead just a couple minutes into the 4th quarter.

Game, set, match. Well, not really. Wisconsin scored two touchdowns within a 3-minute time frame and then picked up a safety off a bad punt snap. USC free-kicked and Vander Kelen went back to work right away, reeling off three straight completions, the final one a TD pass to Pat Richter before time ran out. Richter ended up with 11 receptions for 163 yards and a score, and Vander Kelen was 33 of 48 for 401 yards and two scores. Beathard was 8 for 12, 190 yards passing and 4 TD's and his favorite target, Hal Bedsole, had 4 receptions for 101 yards and 2 scores. Wisconsin outgained USC 486 to 367 in total yardage and 32-15 in first downs

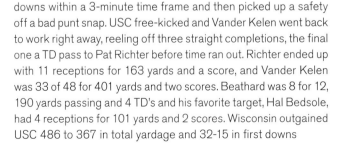

ROSE BOWL GAME

1964

ILLINOIS vs. WASHINGTON

SCORE BY QUARTERS	1 - 2 - 3 - 4	FINAL SCORE
ILLINOIS	0 - 3 - 7 - 7	17
WASHINGTON	0 - 7 - 0 - 0	7

Jim Owens,
Head Coach, Washington

"Our QB Bill Douglas was injured on the first drive of the game and he never returned. Our big RB Junior Coffey was also hurt and couldn't play more than a handful of series in the game. It could have been a much different game, but what a thrill it was to see the match-up of two great All-Americans like Dick Butkus and Rick Redman going at it in the Rose Bowl!"

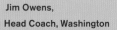

UNIVERSITY OF WASHINGTON HUSKIES
HEAD COACH: JIM OWENS
1963 RECORD: 6-4 (4-1) AAWU CHAMPIONS

DATE	OPPONENT	RESULT
Sep 21	at Air Force	L 7-10
Sep 28	at Pittsburgh	L 6-13
Oct 5	Iowa	L 7-17
Oct 12	Oregon State	W 34-7
Oct 19	Stanford	W 19-11
Oct 26	at Oregon	W 26-19
Nov 2	USC	W 22-7
Nov 9	at California	W 39-26
Nov 16	at UCLA	L 0-14
Nov 30	Washington State	W 16-0

It was a 3-point game near the end of the third quarter and the Huskies were threatening deep in Illini territory when Washington back-up QB Bill Siler tossed his third interception of the game. The Illini began the final quarter with the ball on their 15-yard line. They proceeded to march down the field chewing up valuable clock time along the way. Jim Grabowski banged it in from 10 yards out for the score with only seven minutes remaining.

Top left: Husky receiver Al Libke snags a pass in traffic. Middle left: Washington field goal attempt foiled by Illinois. Bottom left: Illini defender breaks up pass. Top center: Illinois FB Jim Grabowski is tackled after 19-yard gain in the 2nd half. Top right: MVP Jim Grabowski with his dad, Stanley Grabowski, in the post-game locker room. Bottom right: Dick Butkus and his wife at the Lawry's Beef Bowl.

Illinois head coach Pete Elliott previously played in the 1948 Rose Bowl Game for Michigan and was head coach of California's 1959 Rose Bowl squad. His two sons, Bruce and Dave, both played in the Rose Bowl for Michigan. He later went on to become the president of the NFL Hall of Fame from 1979–1998.

UNIVERSITY OF ILLINOIS FIGHTING ILLINI
HEAD COACH: PETE ELLIOTT
1963 RECORD: 7-1-1 (5-1-1) BIG TEN CHAMPIONS

DATE	OPPONENT	RESULT
Sep 28	California	W 10-0
Oct 5	Northwestern	W 10-9
Oct 12	at Ohio State	T 20-20
Oct 19	Minnesota	W 16-6
Oct 25	at UCLA	W 18-12
Nov 2	Purdue	W 41-21
Nov 9	Michigan	L 8-14
Nov 16	at Wisconsin	W 17-7
Nov 28	at Michigan State	W 13-0

Jim Grabowski,
RB, Illinois

"I grew up in a working class neighborhood in Chicago. My father was employed as a butcher and he had to work on most Saturdays so he rarely ever got to see me play football, but when we won the Big Ten Championship he decided to take my mother and sister to the Rose Bowl. I was thrilled that he was finally going to see his first college football game and it wasn't just any college game, it was the Rose Bowl. After the game, the press took many pictures of my dad hugging me as I was presented the Player of the Game trophy. I remember how proud he was and how happy I felt to give something back to a man who sacrificed so much for his family."

The previous three quarters were headbangers with 10 total fumbles—five each by each team. Both of Illinois' other scores came off Washington turnovers and the Huskies also wasted two golden scoring opportunities in the red zone with turnovers. Grabowski was the workhorse on offense for the Illini with 125 yards on 23 carries and Sam Price added 55 yards on 10 rushes. Dave Kopay scored Washington's only points on a 7-yard scamper in the second quarter. Washington played without star QB Bill Douglas who was injured on their first possession of the game. Husky RB Junior Coffey saw limited action due to an ankle injury.

ROSE BOWL GAME
1965
MICHIGAN vs. OREGON STATE

MICHIGAN vs. OREGON STATE 51ST ROSE BOWL GAME

Danny Espalin, Safety, Oregon State

"We were on the field in full uniform with helmets and pads going through our stretching and pre-game drills when Michigan appeared. They were in football pants, no pads, and t-shirts and helmets. They were gigantic. We just looked at them in amazement. We had a pretty good defensive unit so Coach Prothro decided to punt the ball on third down in every series of the first half. It kept us close at halftime. But then those huge Wolverine bodies took their toll on our defense as the game wore on and Michigan kicked the hell out of us in the second half. I wish we could have spent some time touring the Rose Bowl Stadium during game week so I had some memories of that. It seems like you don't see more than five feet in front of you when you are playing the game."

OREGON STATE UNIVERSITY BEAVERS
HEAD COACH: TOMMY PROTHRO
1964 RECORD: 8-2 (3-1) AAWU CHAMPIONS

DATE	OPPONENT	RESULT
Sep 19	at Northwestern	L 3-7
Sep 26	at Colorado	W 14-7
Oct 3	at Baylor	W 13-6
Oct 10	Washington	W 9-7
Oct 17	Idaho	W 10-7
Oct 24	Syracuse	W 31-13
Oct 31	at Washington St.	W 24-7
Nov 7	Indiana	W 24-14
Nov 14	at Stanford	L 7-16
Nov 21	Oregon	W 7-6

Top left: Beaver receiver Doug McDougal scores the game's first TD. Lower left: Michigan's Mel Anthony block OSU's Dick Ruhl to open a hole for Robert Timberlake. Right top center: Mel Anthony eluding Beaver tacklers. Top right: 1965 Royal Court at the game. Bottom right: #77 David Butler and #61 John Marcum block for #19 Carl Ward.

Oregon State broke open a scoreless tie early in the second quarter on a 5-yard pass from Paul Brothers to Doug McDougal. The 11-point favorite Wolverines took a while to adapt to the Beavers' defensive ploys, but when they did, their rushing attack dominated the rest of the game. Mel Anthony raced for 84 yards and a score midway through the second quarter and Carl Ward followed with a 43-yard TD run on the following possession.

Following a blocked Beaver punt, Michigan continued to roll in the second half with Anthony scoring two more times and QB Bob Timberlake adding one more score on a nice 24-yard carry. Anthony ended up with 123 yards on 13 carries, Ward had 88 yards on 10 rushes, and Timberlake picked up 57 yards rushing and 77 in the air. Relying more on the pass, OSU was 19-33 and 179 yards through the air.

SCORE BY QUARTERS	1 - 2 - 3 - 4	FINAL SCORE
MICHIGAN	0 - 12 - 15 - 7	34
OREGON STATE	0 - 7 - 0 - 0	7

 UNIVERSITY OF MICHIGAN WOLVERINES
HEAD COACH: BUMP ELLIOTT
1964 RECORD: 8-1 (6-1) BIG TEN CHAMPIONS

DATE	OPPONENT	RESULT
Sep 26	Air Force	W 24-7
Oct 3	Navy	W 21-0
Oct 10	at Michigan State	W 17-10
Oct 17	Purdue	L 20-21
Oct 24	Minnesota	W 19-12
Oct 31	Northwestern	W 35-0
Nov 7	Illinois	W 21-6
Nov 14	at Iowa	W 34-20
Nov 21	at Ohio State	W 10-0

PRESS BOX FACTS

Michigan head coach "Bump" Elliott played for Michigan in the 1948 Rose Bowl, was an assistant coach at Iowa for the 1957 & 1959 Rose Bowl games, an assistant athletic director at Michigan for the 1970 and 1972 Rose Bowl games, and the Director of Athletics at Iowa during the Hawkeyes' 3 trips to Pasadena in 1982, 1986 and 1991.

Mel Anthony,
FB, Michigan

"My high school coach, Bron Bacevich, taught me that 'What you do in practice, you do in the game.' That is so true. A football team is more than the couple dozen starters you see getting most of the playing time on the field. Our Michigan redshirts and three-deep back-ups were constantly pushing and bringing out the best in our first team. These were guys who had been some of the top players in their high school conferences, so they weren't used to being second or third team players. They took a lot of hard knocks in our scrimmages without getting any of the glory that game day players receive. But they helped our team reach its goals. It was gratifying to me that we played well in the Rose Bowl and these great teammates of ours got the opportunity to play as well."

BIG TEN CONFERENCE

ROSE BOWL GAME
1966
MICHIGAN STATE vs. UCLA

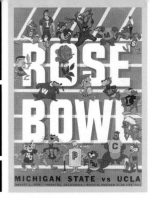

ROSE BOWL

MICHIGAN STATE vs UCLA

SCORE BY QUARTERS	1 - 2 - 3 - 4	FINAL SCORE
MICHIGAN STATE	0 - 0 - 0 - 12	12
UCLA	0 - 14 - 0 - 0	14

Gary Beban, QB, UCLA

"Bob Stiles, laid out on the goal line after stopping Bob Apisa's effort for a two point conversion to tie the game with no time left, to Ducky Drake, UCLA Head Trainer: 'Ducky, do you think SI has finished taking their next cover photo?' Stiles ended up on the cover of the next issue of Sports Illustrated."

PRESS BOX FACTS

Four of the top eight players selected in the 1967 NFL draft were Spartans: Bubba Smith went #1 to the Baltimore Colts, Clint Jones #2 to the Vikings, George Webster #5 to the Oilers, and Gene Washington #8 to the Vikings. UCLA's Mel Farr went to the Lions with the #7 selection.

UCLA BRUINS
HEAD COACH: TOMMY PROTHRO
1965 RECORD: 7-2-1 (4-0) AAWU CHAMPIONS

DATE	OPPONENT	RESULT
Sep18	at Michigan State	L 3-13
Oct 2	at Penn State	W 24-22
Oct 9	Syracuse	W 22-14
Oct 16	at Missouri	T 14-14
Oct 23	California	W 56-3
Oct 30	at Air Force	W 10-0
Nov 6	Washington	W 28-24
Nov 13	at Stanford	W 30-13
Nov 20	at USC	W 20-16
Dec 4	at Tennessee	L 34-37

The undefeated and #2 ranked Spartans were heavy favorites in this rematch of their season opening home game with the #5 Bruins. Led by All-Americans Charles "Bubba" Smith and George Webster, the vaunted Michigan State defense had surrendered just 62 points the entire season. UCLA had given up that many points in their last three regular season games. But the Bruins were battle-toughened from a grueling road schedule that included three trips back East, one to the Midwest and one to the Rockies.

Bruin QB Gary Beban scored the game's first points on a one-yard run following a fumbled punt recovery on the Spartan's 6-yard line. UCLA then surprised Michigan State with an on-side kick, and Beban scored again on another short keeper for a shocking 14-0 lead. Midway through the fourth quarter, the Spartan offense finally started to click with Bob Apisa

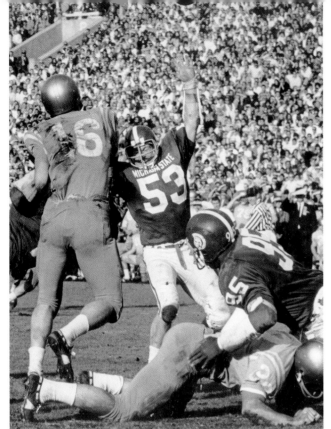

MICHIGAN STATE UNIVERSITY SPARTANS
HEAD COACH: DUFFY DAUGHERTY
1965 RECORD: 10-0 (7-0) BIG TEN CHAMPIONS

DATE	OPPONENT	RESULT
Sep 18	UCLA	W 13-3
Sep 25	at Penn State	W 23-0
Oct 2	Illinois	W 22-12
Oct 9	at Michigan	W 24-7
Oct 16	Ohio State	W 32-7
Oct 23	at Purdue	W 14-10
Oct 30	Northwestern	W 49-7
Nov 6	at Iowa	W 35-0
Nov 13	Indiana	W 27-13
Nov 20	at Notre Dame	W 12-3

Charles "Bubba" Smith, DE, Michigan State

"A couple days before the game, Duffy took the team to a monastery in the mountains to get us away from any distractions. It didn't help one bit. There we were in some creepy, ancient building that reminded me of a funeral home, and they've got crosses lit up on every bedroom door, and clouds drifting in the windows at night. It was freaky! You see, black people aren't exactly used to having clouds floating in our windows at night and coyotes howling. The only thing I can compare it to is those werewolf movies. I tossed and turned all night and didn't get any rest. I could whoop some old werewolf if I'm rested, but not if I'm half asleep. That pretty much sums up how we played the first three quarters of the game. Everybody thought it would be a cakewalk for us, but we were sleepwalking instead. We just weren't prepared, mentally or physically."

scoring on a 38-yard pitchout from QB Jim Raye. The two-point conversion failed. Still trailing by eight points, Bubba Smith partially blocked a punt near midfield. MSU marched down the field and scored with just 31 seconds left on a short run by alternate QB Steve Juday, setting up a do-or-die two-point conversion attempt. Apisa took a quick pitch from Raye and accelerated toward the end zone. He was hit first by Jim Colletto and then defensive back Bob Stiles met him head on to make the final stop just inches short of the goal line. Michigan State had 314 total yards to the Bruins 212, but the Spartans handicapped themselves with five turnovers. It still ranks as one of the most thrilling upsets in Rose Bowl and college football history.

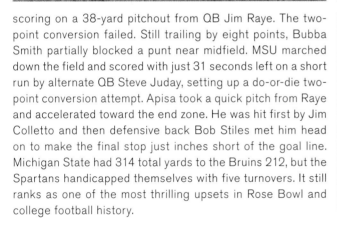

Top left: Officials signal UCLA's second touchdown of the first half by QB Gary Beban. Bottom left: UCLA defenders swarm to the Spartan ball carrier. Top right center: UCLA's Beban throws under heavy pressure from Spartan defense #53 Buddy Owens #95 Bubba Smith. Top right: UCLA QB sweep left. Bottom right: Michigan State head coach Duffy Daugherty (right) with QB Steve Juday and unidentified individual at the Lawry's Beef Bowl.

ROSE BOWL GAME
1967
PURDUE vs. USC

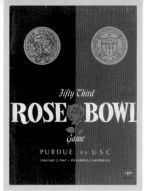

Fifty Third
ROSE BOWL
Game
PURDUE vs USC
JANUARY 2, 1967 · PASADENA, CALIFORNIA

SCORE BY QUARTERS	1 - 2 - 3 - 4	FINAL SCORE
PURDUE	0 - 7 - 7 - 0	14
USC	0 - 7 - 0 - 6	13

Tim Rossovich, DE, USC

"The 1967 Rose Bowl vs. Purdue brings back bitter-sweet memories. I played defensive end and place kicker and I missed two field goals. We lost the game by one point, so just one of them could have been a game winner. We had a chance to win the game in the end and failed the two-point conversion."

USC TROJANS
HEAD COACH: JOHN McKAY
1966 RECORD: 7-3 (4-1) AAWU CHAMPIONS

DATE	OPPONENT	RESULT
Sep 17	at Texas	W 10-6
Sep 24	Wisconsin	W 38-3
Oct 1	at Oregon State	W 21-0
Oct 8	Washington	W 17-14
Oct 15	at Stanford	W 21-7
Oct 22	Clemson	W 30-0
Oct 28	at Miami, FL	L 7-10
Nov 5	California	W 35-9
Nov 19	at UCLA	L 7-14
Nov 26	Notre Dame	L 0-51

Top left: USC's Rod Sherman hauls in one of his 7 catches. Left center: Perry Williams struggles for extra yardage against Trojan Nate Shaw. Bottom left: Don McCall scores for USC. Top right: Purdue QB Bob Griese passes behind good protection. Bottom center: Perry Williams scores his second TD. Lower right: Bob Griese and Purdue coach Jack Mollenkopf autograph ball for Richard N. Frank at the Lawry's Beef Bowl.

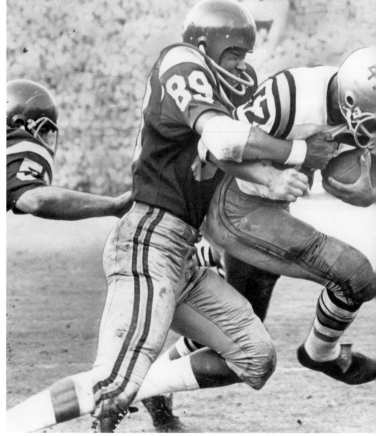

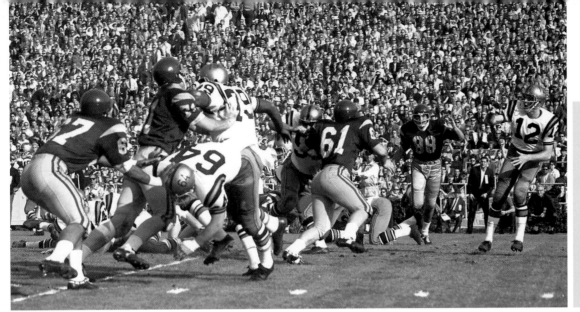

Purdue defensive back George Catavolos intercepted USC's two-point conversion attempt with less than three minutes remaining in the game to secure the Boilermaker victory in their first-ever visit to the Rose Bowl. The Trojans had just pulled within a point on Troy Winslow's 19-yard TD toss to Rod Sherman and momentum was on their side. The game was tied at 7-7 at halftime and remained deadlocked until Perry Williams scored his second touchdown of the game with less than two minutes to go in the third quarter.

Boilermaker Bob Griese was a cool 10 of 18 passing for 139 yards and he picked up 15 more yards on the ground. He also kicked both extra points, which proved to be the difference in the game. Williams had 61 tough yards on 20 carries to go along with his 2 TD's. Rod Sherman had 7 grabs for 102 yards and one TD and Don McCall scored another for USC, but the defenses ruled much of the day. John Charles had 11 tackles for Purdue and Adrian Young had 15 stops for the Trojans.

PURDUE UNIVERSITY BOILERMAKERS
HEAD COACH: JACK MOLLENKOPF
1966 RECORD: 8-2 (6-1) BIG TEN CHAMPIONS

DATE	OPPONENT	RESULT
Sep 17	Ohio	W 42-3
Sep 24	at Notre Dame	L 14-26
Oct 1	SMU	W 35-23
Oct 8	Iowa	W 35-0
Oct 15	at Michigan	W 22-21
Oct 22	at Michigan State	L 20-41
Oct 29	Illinois	W 25-21
Nov 5	at Wisconsin	W 23-0
Nov 12	at Minnesota	W 16-0
Nov 19	Indiana	W 51-6

Bob Griese, QB, Purdue

"Back when I was growing up in Indiana in the Sixties, the Big Ten was all about going to the Rose Bowl. As a kid, you wanted to play for a Big Ten school and have a chance to play in the Rose Bowl. Even today they never talk about the national championship. It's all about winning the Big Ten title and going to the Rose Bowl. Purdue had never been to the Rose Bowl when I arrived there as a student athlete, so to be able to be a part of the team that went there was special. It was even more special because we won."

ROSE BOWL GAME

1968

INDIANA vs. USC

SCORE BY QUARTERS	1 - 2 - 3 - 4	FINAL SCORE
INDIANA	0 - 3 - 0 - 0	3
USC	7 - 0 - 7 - 0	14

Tim Rossovich, DE, USC

"I wasn't the place kicker in the 1968 Rose Bowl game vs. Indiana, just the defensive end, so I didn't have to kick the ball, I only had to kick butt. Hence, we beat Indiana to win the Rose Bowl and the national championship."

Top left: USC's O.J. Simpson breaks through the center of the Hoosier line as #80 Tom Bilunas and #83 Jim Sniadecki converge from the end positions. Left center: The 1968 Royal Court at the game. Lower left: Hoosier DB Nate Cunningham attempts to break up pass intended for USC's Ron Drake. Top right center: USC's Tim Rossovich pursues Hoosier QB Harry Gonso. Top right: Indiana TE Al Gage makes a grab as Trojan #46 Jerry Shaw moves in for the tackle. Bottom right: USC receiver hangs on to ball against Indiana's Cunningham.

USC TROJANS
HEAD COACH: JOHN MCKAY
1967 RECORD: 9-1 (5-1) AAWU CHAMPIONS

DATE	OPPONENT	RESULT
Sep 15	Washington State	W 49-0
Sep 23	Texas	W 17-13
Sep 30	at Michigan State	W 21-17
Oct 7	Stanford	W 30-0
Oct 14	at Notre Dame	W 24-7
Oct 21	at Washington	W 23-6
Oct 28	Oregon	W 28-6
Nov 4	at California	W 31-12
Nov 11	at Oregon State	L 0-3
Nov 18	UCLA	W 21-20

John Pont engineered one of the greatest turnarounds in college football history after Indiana University finished with a 1-8-1 record in 1966. The 1967 version of Indiana pigskin racked up a 9-1 record and the Big Ten title, picked up the nickname of "Cardiac Kids," and tripped to the Rose Bowl for the first time in university history. The Hoosiers were prohibitive underdogs against the top-ranked USC Trojans but their defense kept them in the game until the end. The Trojans scored first on a 2-yard run by O.J. Simpson in the first quarter. Indiana mounted its strongest threat of the game in the second quarter but couldn't capitalize on a first and goal opportunity. Instead they settled for a David Kornowa field goal and very respectable 7-3 score at halftime.

The Trojans manufactured a 45-yard scoring drive midway through the third quarter and held a 14-3 lead heading into the fourth quarter. The Hoosiers responded with a threat, advancing to the USC 37-yard line with just over seven minutes left in the game, but they failed on two attempts at a first down with just inches to go. It was a hard-fought defensive game and the Hoosiers gave USC all they could handle, holding the Trojans to 317 total yards. The Troy defense proved worthy of the national championship by holding Indiana to 189 total yards and their fewest points scored all season.

INDIANA UNIVERSITY HOOSIERS
HEAD COACH: JOHN PONT
1967 RECORD: 9-1 (6-1) BIG TEN CHAMPIONS

DATE	OPPONENT	RESULT
Sep 23	Kentucky	W 12-10
Sep 30	Kansas	W 18-15
Oct 7	at Illinois	W 20-7
Oct 14	Iowa	W 21-17
Oct 21	at Michigan	W 27-20
Oct 28	at Arizona	W 42-7
Nov 4	Wisconsin	W 14-9
Nov 11	at Michigan State	W 14-13
Nov 18	at Minnesota	L 7-33
Nov 25	Purdue	W 19-14

Harold Mauro, C, Indiana

"A record setting crowd of nearly 103,000 and a sea of red cheering for the Hoosiers was a moment never to forget. Losing was very hard to take especially in the Rose Bowl. We lost to the #1 team in the country and Indiana finished 9-2 and ranked # 4 in the nation. Our football squad was proud to represent Indiana University and the Big Ten Conference. As we took off from LA International Airport we all looked back at a sign made compliments of Continental Airlines' ground crew. It spelled out California's feelings about the departing Hoosiers: GOOD SHOW HOOSIERS!"

ROSE BOWL GAME

1969

OHIO STATE vs. USC

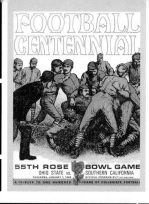

SCORE BY QUARTERS	1 - 2 - 3 - 4	FINAL SCORE
OHIO STATE	0 - 10 - 3 - 14	27
USC	0 - 10 - 0 - 6	16

Sam Cunningham, FB, USC

"The 1969 Rose Bowl game was part of my recruiting experience with USC. To be there and see all the pageantry surrounding the nationally televised game as a recruit with 100,000 people in the stands—all I could think about was getting out there and playing myself."

USC TROJANS
HEAD COACH: JOHN MCKAY
1968 RECORD: 9-0-1 (6-0) PAC-8 CHAMPIONS

DATE	OPPONENT	RESULT
Sep 21	at Minnesota	W 29-20
Sep 28	at Northwestern	W 24-7
Oct 5	Miami, FL	W 28-3
Oct 12	at Stanford	W 27-24
Oct 19	Washington	W 14-7
Nov 2	at Oregon	W 20-13
Nov 9	California	W 35-17
Nov 16	Oregon State	W 17-13
Nov 23	at UCLA	W 28-16
Nov 30	Notre Dame	T 21-21

Undefeated and #1 vs. undefeated #2 in the Rose Bowl Game. You couldn't ask for anything better in college football than that. After a scoreless first quarter, USC jumped out to a 10-0 lead featuring a dazzling 80-yard TD run by O.J. Simpson. But that play seemed to arouse the Buckeyes as they rambled back and put ten points on the board before halftime to knot the score. Jim Otis, who would gain 101 yards on 30 carries for the day, dove over the top for the Buckeyes' first score and Jim Roman added a 26-yard field goal.

The momentum clearly shifted in Ohio State's favor as the game progressed with Rex Kern working the option deftly behind the solid All-American blocking of Dave Foley and Rufus Hayes. Meanwhile, USC coughed up the ball five times, three turnovers by Simpson and two by Trojan QB Steve Sogge. Leading 13-10, the Buckeyes put the game away in the fourth frame when Kern converted two USC fumbles into quick touchdown passes to Leo Hayden and Ray Gillian. That made it 27-10 with just over ten minutes remaining. The Trojans would score once more on a controversial "catch" by Sam Dickerson, but it was too little, too late. The Buckeyes had played 60 minutes of error-free ball against an outstanding Southern Cal team and proved themselves worthy of the title "National Champions."

The 1969 Rose Bowl Game was the first time in Rose Bowl history that the #1 and #2 teams met to determine the National Championship. It was also the first time in the 22-year history of the Big Ten–Pac 8 (formerly PCC and AAWU) Rose Bowl Game pact that both teams entered the game undefeated.

Rex Kern, QB, Ohio State

"Woody said, 'We are not going to the Rose Bowl to eat or talk, but to play football! Be ready to work hard and harder each day so we can be prepared to play the best game of our lives.' We didn't attend the Lawry's Beef Bowl, nor were we allowed to talk to reporters unless Woody approved, which was rare, and if we did, he was right there with us. Woody ended any interview when he wanted—not when the sportswriters wanted, but on his command. Period. After we beat a great USC team with Heisman Trophy winner O.J. Simpson, Jim Murray, the famous Los Angeles Times sportswriter wrote, 'We didn't know if the Ohio State team could use forks, spoons, knives, or if they could even talk, but the nation found out that they sure could play football!'"

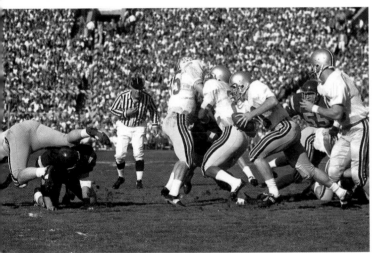

OHIO STATE UNIVERSITY BUCKEYES
HEAD COACH: WOODY HAYES
1968 RECORD: 9-0 (7-0) BIG TEN CHAMPIONS

DATE	OPPONENT	RESULT
Sep 28	SMU	W 35-14
Oct 5	Oregon	W 21-6
Oct 12	Purdue	W 13-0
Oct 19	Northwestern	W 45-21
Oct 26	at Illinois	W 31-24
Nov 2	Michigan State	W 25-20
Nov 9	at Wisconsin	W 43-8
Nov 16	at Iowa	W 33-27
Nov 23	Michigan	W 50-14

Top left: O.J. Simpson tries to wriggle free for more yardage. Lower left: Bob Hope, the 1969 Tournament of Roses Parade Grand Marshal, hams it up with Tournament of Roses president Gleeson L. Payne. Lower inside left: USC coach John McKay instructs QB Steve Sogge. Top right: Jim Otis dives over the goal line for Ohio State's first score. Right center: QB Rex Kern running the Buckeye option behind solid blocking. Bottom right: OSU punter Mike Sensibaugh in action.

1970

1979

ROSE BOWL GAME

1970

MICHIGAN vs. USC

56th Rose Bowl Game

MICHIGAN vs. SOUTHERN CALIFORNIA
JANUARY 1, 1970   PASADENA, CALIFORNIA   OFFICIAL PROGRAM $1.00

PRESS BOX FACTS

The last time Michigan and USC squared off in the Rose Bowl was in 1948. Under the leadership of head coach Fritz Crisler, Michigan won that contest by a score of 49-0 to capture the national championship.

Top left: USC coach John McKay with RB Clarence Davis and QB Jimmy Jones at the Lawry's Beef Bowl. Left top center: Clarence Davis strains for more yardage after a big gain. Top right center: Bo Schembechler leaving the hospital in Pasadena. Top right: Jim Mandich looks for extra yards while USC's Greg Slough closes in. Right middle: Wolverine QB Don Moorhead tries to pass over #72 Al Cowlings in 4th quarter action.

USC TROJANS
HEAD COACH: JOHN MCKAY
1969 RECORD: 9-0-1 (6-0) PAC-8 CHAMPIONS

DATE	OPPONENT	RESULT
Sep 20	at Nebraska	W 31-21
Sep 27	Northwestern	W 48-6
Oct 4	at Oregon State	W 31-7
Oct 11	Stanford	W 26-24
Oct 18	at Notre Dame	T 14-14
Oct 25	Georgia Tech	W 29-18
Nov 1	at California	W 14-9
Nov 8	Washington State	W 28-7
Nov 15	at Washington	W 16-7
Nov 22	UCLA	W 14-12

USC entered the game ranked #4 in the nation, undefeated and once-tied. The Michigan squad was emotionally handicapped, playing without head coach Bo Schembechler and second leading rusher Glenn Doughty. Schembechler had suffered a heart attack the night before the game and Doughty injured his knee earlier in the week. The game turned out to be a hard-nosed defensive battle from the opening kick-off but the final score doesn't reveal the several blown opportunities that Michigan had in the final quarter that might have changed the outcome.

The Trojans picked up the game's first points in the first quarter on a 25-yard field goal by Ron Ayala. Michigan answered with a three-pointer off the foot of Tim Killian from twenty yards out early in the next frame. The score remained deadlocked until late in the third period when Trojan QB Jimmy Jones connected

SCORE BY QUARTERS	1 - 2 - 3 - 4	FINAL SCORE
MICHIGAN	0 - 3 - 0 - 0	3
USC	3 - 0 - 7 - 0	10

with Bob Chandler who then shook off several tacklers for a nifty 33-yard scoring play. And that was the end of the scoring. The Wolverines had the ball deep inside USC's red zone twice in the fourth quarter and came away without any points. They also were driving inside the Trojan 40-yard line when time ran out.

The Wolverines defense held the Pac-8's leading rusher Clarence Davis to just 76 yards on 15 carries and USC's scoring output was 15 points below their regular season average. TE Jim Mandich was Michigan's main offensive threat with 8 receptions for 79 yards.

M

UNIVERSITY OF MICHIGAN WOLVERINES
HEAD COACH: BO SCHEMBECHLER
1969 RECORD: 8-2 (6-1) BIG TEN CHAMPIONS

DATE	OPPONENT	RESULT
Sep 20	Vanderbilt	W 42-14
Sep 27	Washington	W 45-7
Oct 4	Missouri	L 17-40
Oct 11	Purdue	W 31-20
Oct 18	at Michigan State	L 12-23
Oct 25	at Minnesota	W 35-9
Nov 1	Wisconsin	W 35-7
Nov 8	at Illinois	W 57-0
Nov 15	at Iowa	W 51-6
Nov 22	Ohio State	W 24-12

Jim Mandich,
TE, Michigan

"The first thing that struck me being on that field on game day was 'wow—this is every boy's dream come true!' However, that was quickly overshadowed by the spectre that hung over our team that day. We were without Bo. As team captain, I had been called into a meeting late the night before by the assistant coaches to inform me that Coach Schembechler had suffered a heart attack. They didn't know what his condition was, but the game was still going to be played and I was asked to relay this information to the team. Quite frankly, the team was shell-shocked. Our concern for our Coach's life made it difficult to stay focused. And against a very good USC team, we needed to be at the top of our game."

ROSE BOWL GAME

1971

OHIO STATE vs. STANFORD

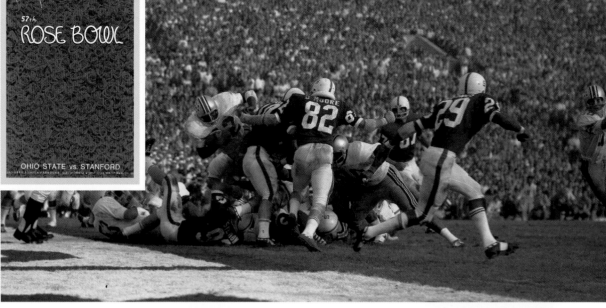

Jim Plunkett, QB, Stanford

"One of the key plays from the game I remember well occurred when we were behind 17-13 in the 4th quarter. Our defense had just stopped Ohio State deep in our territory to regain possession. I called a pass play designed for maximum protection. As we broke the huddle and walked to the line I changed my mind and told tight end Bob Moore that he better release and go out. I ended up getting into trouble as the pocket collapsed. I quickly checked through my first two receivers and saw my third option downfield covered by two defenders. I knew if I threw it high Bob could get up and fight for it. He came down with the ball in what some sportswriters have called 'the Mad Dog Catch' and we went on to score the go-ahead touchdown a few plays later."

STANFORD UNIVERSITY INDIANS
HEAD COACH: JOHN RALSTON
1970 RECORD: 8-3 (6-1) PAC-8 CHAMPIONS

DATE	OPPONENT	RESULT
Sep 12	Arkansas	W 34-28
Sep 19	San Jose State	W 34-3
Sep 26	at Oregon	W 33-10
Oct 3	Purdue	L 14-26
Oct 10	USC	W 24-14
Oct 17	Washington State	W 63-16
Oct 24	at UCLA	W 9-7
Oct 31	Oregon State	W 48-10
Nov 7	Washington	W 29-22
Nov 14	at Air Force	L 14-31
Nov 21	at California	L 14-22

Left top: Stanford's "Thunder Chicken" defense stops Buckeye John Brockington on 4th and goal in the final period. Left center: Stanford's Demea Washington makes the grab early in the fourth quarter. Bottom left: Jim Plunkett with Rose Queen Kathleen Arnett at the Lawry's Beef Bowl. Right top: Ohio State QB Rex Kern runs the option. Right middle: Jim Plunkett is tackled after being forced out of the pocket. Right bottom: Field painting the Rose Bowl gridiron.

Not many college football experts gave John Ralston's Indians much of a chance against the mighty Buckeyes, even with Heisman Trophy-winner Jim Plunkett running the show on offense. Ohio State was led by option whiz Rex Kern, now a savvy senior with one big Rose Bowl win and a national championship under his belt. He had an array of weapons in his option package including John Brockington and Leo Hayden in a backfield that averaged nearly 300 yards on the ground. Ohio State's defense was a force to be reckoned with, too, anchored by All-Universe nose guard Jim Stillwagon.

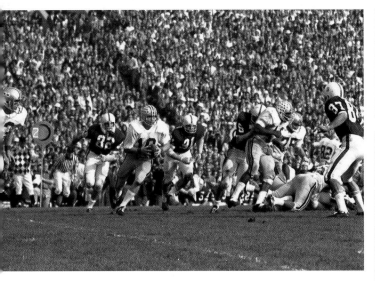

SCORE BY QUARTERS	1 - 2 - 3 - 4	FINAL SCORE
OHIO STATE	7 - 7 - 3 - 0	17
STANFORD	10 - 0 - 3 - 14	27

OHIO STATE UNIVERSITY BUCKEYES
HEAD COACH: WOODY HAYES
1970 RECORD: 9-0 (7-0) BIG TEN CHAMPIONS

DATE	OPPONENT	RESULT
Sep 26	Texas A&M	W 56-13
Oct 3	Duke	W 34-10
Oct 10	at Michigan State	W 29-0
Oct 17	Minnesota	W 28-8
Oct 24	at Illinois	W 48-29
Oct 31	Northwestern	W 24-10
Nov 7	at Wisconsin	W 24-7
Nov 14	at Purdue	W 10-7
Nov 21	Michigan	W 20-9

Surprisingly, Stanford scored the first two times they had the ball to take a 10-0 lead. Ohio State regrouped and answered with a pair of Brockington short smashes across the goal for a 14-10 halftime advantage. The teams traded field goals in the third period to push the score to 17-13. Stanford's bend-but-don't-break defense was giving up huge chunks of rushing yardage to Ohio State but they managed to make the stops when it counted the most. Late in the fourth period, Stanford seemed to suck the life out of the Buckeyes when their "Thunder Chicken" defense stopped Brockington from the one in a tremendous goal line stand. Momentum in their favor, Stanford quickly responded with two scoring drives to put the game away.

Fans were treated to a tremendous quarterback duel between Plunkett (20-30, 265 yards, + 26 yards on the ground) and Ohio State's Rex Kern (20 carries, 129 yards running). Brockington tallied 101 yards on 21 carries and Hayden added 54 yards on 11 tries for the Buckeye attack that churned the field for 380 total rushing yards. Stanford's unsung O-line anchored by John Sande played a vital role in the upset victory, springing Jackie Brown loose and providing Plunkett enough time to find Demea Washington, Randy Vataha, and Bob Moore in the open.

PRESS BOX FACTS

Jim Stillwagon made college football history in 1970 by becoming the first player to win the Outland Trophy and the Lombardi Award in the same year. Stillwagon, a three-year starter at middle guard for the Buckeyes between 1968 and 1970, was a consensus All-American as a junior and senior.

**Jim Stillwagon,
DL, Ohio State**

"Not to take any credit away from Stanford because they played well and beat us, but we had already beat ourselves in the smash-mouth, two-a-day practices Woody ran for two weeks before the Rose Bowl Game. We used to joke that he used those intense scrimmages to get a jump on looking at the younger kids—sort of like a pre-spring practice period. He was wound so tight with a bowl game on the line. We were getting taped up on the flight into Los Angeles so we could hit the practice field the moment we landed, and heaven forbid if he would let us enjoy any of the rewards of the Big Ten title. He said participating in events like Lawry's would only make us soft."
See Epilogue for entire recollection.

BIG TEN CONFERENCE

ROSE BOWL GAME
1972
MICHIGAN vs. STANFORD

John Ralston,
Head Coach, Stanford

"Earlier that season in our second to last game playing San Jose State, our field goal kicker, Rod Garcia, missed 5 field goals. As he prepared for each one, I put my arm around his shoulders trying to relax him, but to no avail. He missed them all. We lost the game 13-12. After the game, the players suggested to me that my confidence-building pep talk wasn't very good. Now, with the game on the line vs. Michigan in front of 100,000 people and millions on TV, the players made sure I didn't get a chance to foul it up. Two huge tackles grabbed me as Rod trotted out on the field. His kick was perfect and we won 13-12 (the exact score we lost by to San Jose State two games earlier)."

STANFORD UNIVERSITY INDIANS
HEAD COACH: JOHN RALSTON
1971 RECORD: 9-2 (6-1) PAC-8 CHAMPIONS

DATE	OPPONENT	RESULT
Sep 11	at Missouri	W 19-0
Sep 18	at Army	W 38-3
Sep 25	Oregon	W 38-17
Oct 2	Duk	L 3-9
Oct 9	at Washington	W 17-6
Oct 16	at USC	W 33-18
Oct 23	Washington State	L 23-24
Oct 30	at Oregon State	W 31-24
Nov 6	UCLA	W 20-9
Nov 13	San Jose State	L 12-13
Nov 20	California	W 14-0

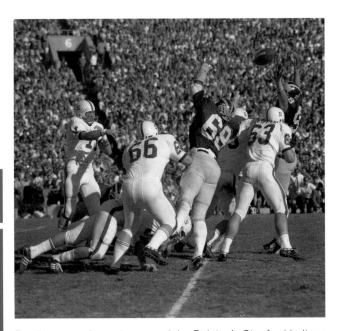

For the second year in a row, John Ralston's Stanford Indians pulled off a huge upset of an undefeated Big Ten powerhouse in the Rose Bowl. Michigan entered the fray with an 11-0 record, averaging 37 points on offense and yielding a mere 6.4 points per game to the opposition. To give you an idea how good this Wolverine bunch was, in a 3-game span vs. Virginia, UCLA and Navy they tossed three shutouts while racking up 140 points. Stanford made it back to the Granddaddy by winning when it counted in Pac-8 action with a 6-1 record. Don Bunce had filled in Jim Plunkett's shoes admirably and Jackie Brown was a dangerous threat to any defense on the run or the fly.

The score was just 3-0 in favor of Michigan in the third quarter when Stanford mounted an amazing goal line stand to halt the Wolverines just inches short of pay dirt. The Indians promptly marched 75 yards and tied the game with a Rod Garcia 42-yard FG. Michigan regained the lead with a Fritz Seyferth 1-yard run and that's when things got really interesting. Stanford faked a punt from their own 33-yard line and Brown bolted for 31-yards and a first down. Several plays later, he broke free again and scored from 24 yards out.

Top left: Stanford QB Don Bunce passes behind solid protection. Bottom left: Richard N. Frank with Stanford head coach John Ralston and QB Don Bunce. Right top: Michigan FB Fritz Seyferth and RB Billy Taylor in action. Right center: Seyferth scores the only Wolverine TD in the 4th quarter. Bottom right: RNF with Coach Bo Schembechler and his wife at the Lawry's Beef Bowl.

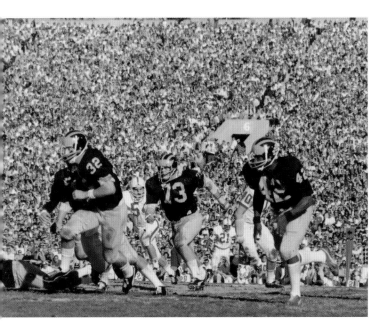

SCORE BY QUARTERS	1 - 2 - 3 - 4	FINAL SCORE
MICHIGAN	0 - 3 - 0 - 9	12
STANFORD	0 - 0 - 3 - 10	13

UNIVERSITY OF MICHIGAN WOLVERINES
HEAD COACH: BO SCHEMBECHLER
1971 RECORD: 11-0 (8-0) BIG TEN CHAMPIONS

DATE	OPPONENT	RESULT
Sep 11	at Northwestern	W 21-6
Sep 18	Virginia	W 56-0
Sep 25	UCLA	W 38-0
Oct 2	Navy	W 46-0
Oct 9	at Michigan State	W 24-13
Oct 16	Illinois	W 35-6
Oct 23	at Minnesota	W 35-7
Oct 30	Indiana	W 61-7
Nov 6	Iowa	W 63-7
Nov 13	at Purdue	W 20-17
Nov 20	Ohio State	W 10-7

Larry Smith,
Asst. Coach, Michigan

"It rained the entire week before the Rose Bowl and there weren't any dry fields in the Los Angeles basin to practice on, so Bo decided to bus the entire team up to Bakersfield where a dry field had been located. Wouldn't you know it ended up snowing in the mountain pass between Los Angeles and Bakersfield after we got there! The buses couldn't make it back through the snow, so United Airlines had to charter an aircraft to fly over and pick the team up the day before the game. The weather turned out fine on game day."

A few minutes later, Michigan's Dana Coin missed a 42-yard field goal attempt but Stanford's Jim Ferguson caught the ball in the end zone and was immediately tackled for a safety by Ed Shuttlesworth. Michigan received the free kick but failed to advance and had to punt the ball back to Stanford. Don Bunce connected on five of six passes to put the Indians within field goal range. With 16 seconds left on the clock, Garcia nailed a 31-yard field goal to secure the upset.

ROSE BOWL GAME
1973
USC vs. OHIO STATE

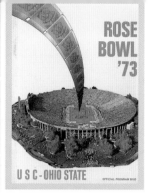

ROSE BOWL '73

U S C - OHIO STATE

OFFICIAL PROGRAM $1.00

SCORE BY QUARTERS	1 - 2 - 3 - 4	FINAL SCORE
USC	7 - 0 - 21 - 14	42
OHIO STATE	0 - 7 - 3 - 7	17

Sam Cunningham,
FB, USC

"One of the most important things about the Rose Bowl is when you get there it's the culmination of a team goal that you set at the beginning of the season. We always felt the Rose Bowl was our house. In our minds, we had that New Year's Day game on our schedule every year and it was a major disappointment to not get there in 1970 and 1971. It was very special to get there my senior year and to achieve our goal of finishing undefeated and #1 in front of family, friends and fans."

USC TROJANS
HEAD COACH: JOHN MCKAY
1972 RECORD: 11-0 (7-0) PAC-8 CHAMPIONS

DATE	OPPONENT	RESULT
Sep 9	at Arkansas	W 31-10
Sep 16	Oregon State	W 51-6
Sep 23	at Illinois	W 55-20
Sep 30	Michigan State	W 51-6
Oct 7	at Stanford	W 30-21
Oct 14	California	W 42-14
Oct 21	Washington	W 34-7
Oct 28	at Oregon	W 18-0
Nov 4	California	W 35-17
Nov 16	at Washington St.	W 44-3
Nov 18	at UCLA	W 24-7
Dec 2	Notre Dame	W 45-23

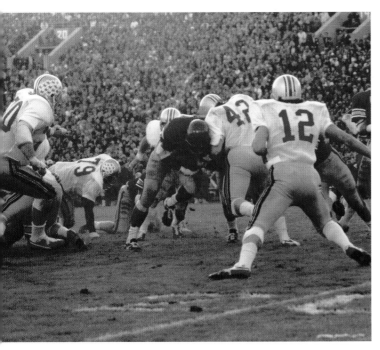

Anthony Davis scored 6 touchdowns vs. Notre Dame during the regular season to help the Trojans defeat the Fighting Irish 45-23. Two of A.D.'s touchdowns were on kickoff returns. He still holds the NCAA record of 218 yards on 3 returns in a single game.

Archie Griffin, RB, Ohio State

"My first Rose Bowl was my freshman year and the experience the night before the game left quite an impression on me. Woody decided to take the team up to a monastery in the mountains the night before the game to get us away from the New Year's Eve celebrations and distractions in the city. He assumed we would be more mentally prepared for the game if we were isolated. But, I couldn't sleep at all that night with the coyotes howling outside and the anxiousness for the game keeping me awake. I was used to the sounds of the city. We lost to a great team; USC could have beaten some pro teams that year. The next year we didn't go to the monastery and we came back and beat the Trojans by nearly the same score."

John McKay's #1 ranked and undefeated Trojans returned to Pasadena after a two-year layoff to face another outstanding Woody Hayes' Buckeye team. The high-scoring Trojan Express was derailed for the first half of the game, which ended in a 7-7 tie. Ohio State's option offense piled up a 2-1 edge in rushing yardage with freshman Archie Griffin accounting for nearly half the output (73 yards on 15 carries).

Part II of this game was a totally different story. USC's offense got back on track and racked up a touchdown on all three of their third quarter possessions. The onslaught continued into the final period with two more scores. Meanwhile the Trojan defense rose to the occasion and held Griffin to 20 yards and forced three turnovers in the second half. Anthony Davis carried 23 times for 157 yards and one TD, and Mike Rae completed 18 of 25 passes for 229 yards to pace the Trojan attack. FB Sam Cunningham set a modern era Rose Bowl record with 4 rushing touchdowns and Charles Young and Lynn Swann both had six receptions. USC was voted the consensus national champion following the game. 23 Trojans from the 1973 squad went on to play in the pros.

	OHIO STATE UNIVERSITY BUCKEYES HEAD COACH: WOODY HAYES 1972 RECORD: 9-1 (7-1) BIG TEN CHAMPIONS		

DATE	OPPONENT	RESULT
Sep 16	Iowa	W 21-0
Sep 30	North Carolina	W 29-14
Oct 7	at California	W 35-18
Oct 14	Illinois	W 26-7
Oct 21	Indiana	W 44-7
Oct 28	at Wisconsin	W 28-20
Nov 4	Minnesota	W 27-19
Nov 11	at Michigan State	L 12-19
Nov 18	at Northwestern	W 27-14
Nov 25	Michigan	W 14-11

Top left: Trojan tailback Anthony Davis scores a TD. Left center: USC FB Sam Cunningham dives over Ohio State defenders for the score. Bottom left: Richard N. Frank with the 1973 Royal Court at the Lawry's Beef Bowl. Right top center: Buckeye defenders swarm to stop Sam Cunningham. Top right: Ohio State coach Woody Hayes.

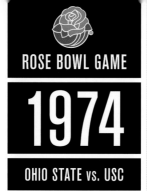

ROSE BOWL GAME
1974
OHIO STATE vs. USC

Pasadena, January 1, 1974 / official souvenir program, $2.00

SCORE BY QUARTERS	1 - 2 - 3 - 4	FINAL SCORE
OHIO STATE	7 - 7 - 13 - 15	42
USC	3 - 11 - 7 - 0	21

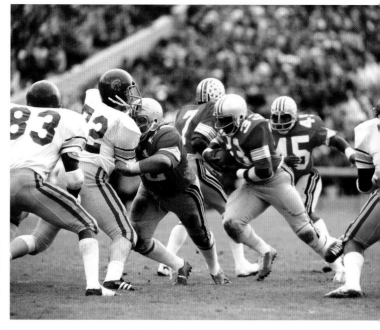

Richard Wood, LB, USC

"Coach McKay would give us some time off after the regular season concluded and then we would come back and practice in sweats. Our practices would be intense—he wanted to make sure we had our timing and execution down and that we were mentally focused on the game, but we didn't do any physical hitting. Coach McKay said, 'You've been hitting all year, if you can't hit by now then something is wrong with you.' I can assure you by game time we were very eager to get physical again."

USC TROJANS
HEAD COACH: JOHN McKAY
1973 RECORD: 9-1-1 (7-0) PAC-8 CHAMPIONS

DATE	OPPONENT	RESULT
Sep 15	Arkansas	W 17-0
Sep 22	at Georgia Tech	W 23-6
Sep 29	Oklahoma	T 7-7
Oct 6	at Oregon State	W 21-7
Oct 13	Washington State	W 46-35
Oct 20	Oregon	W 31-10
Oct 27	at Notre Dame	L 14-23
Nov 3	at California	W 50-14
Nov 10	at Washington	W 42-19
Nov 17	UCLA	W 23-13

In a game some have referred to as "Woody's Revenge," Ohio State and USC offered a cast of characters quite similar to the preceding Rose Bowl Game, but the outcome was completely the reverse. Deadlocked at halftime like the previous year, the Buckeyes spotted USC a go-ahead touchdown by Anthony Davis in the third quarter and then proceeded to light up the scoreboard with the final 28 points of the contest.

The similarities between the two games don't stop there. OSU's Archie Griffin rushed for 149 yards and a score as the primary workhorse out of the backfield and FB Pete Johnson banged in three scores on short yardage situations (compare to Davis' 157 yards and 1 TD, and FB Sam Cunningham's 4 short yardage scores the previous year). Trojan QB Pat Haden logged 229 yards passing, identical to his predecessor in the 1973 Rose Bowl Game.

The difference proved to be Buckeye sophomore signal caller Cornelius Greene and OSU's inspired second half defensive effort. In an MVP performance, Greene ran for 45 yards, a TD and a 2-point conversion on just 7 carries, adding 129 yards on 6 for 8 passing. His skillful timing and execution running the Buckeye option behind two-time All-American offensive lineman John Hicks and Co. was also key in accumulating 288 of the team's 323 total yards on the ground between Griffin, Johnson and himself. Neal Colzie's 56-yard punt return was the catalyst for Ohio State's go-ahead touchdown in the third quarter.

OHIO STATE UNIVERSITY BUCKEYES
HEAD COACH: WOODY HAYES
1973 RECORD: 9-0-1 (7-0-1) BIG TEN CHAMPIONS

DATE	OPPONENT	RESULT
Sep 15	Minnesota	W 56-7
Sep 29	Texas Christian	W 37-3
Oct 6	Washington State	W 27-3
Oct 13	at Wisconsin	W 24-0
Oct 20	Oregon	W 31-10
Oct 27	Northwestern	W 60-0
Nov 3	at Illinois	W 30-0
Nov 10	Michigan State	W 35-0
Nov 17	Iowa	W 55-13
Nov 24	at Michigan	T 10-10

Left top: Ohio State FB Pete Johnson gets the handoff. Left center: Buckeye Neal Colzie returns a punt for big yardage in the 3rd quarter. Bottom left: Richard N. Frank with wife Mary Alice, USC's Anthony Davis and Rose Queen Miranda Barone. Right top center: Pete Johnson breaks free for a big gain. Right top middle: QB Cornelius Greene turns up field with Archie Griffin trailing for the possible pitchout. Top far right: OSU's Woody Hayes is lifted onto his players' shoulders after the Rose Bowl victory.

Cornelius Greene, QB, Ohio State

"Woody was a military historian and he would always sum up the team we were playing and then compare the game to one of the battles Patton had fought. He was brilliant in how he would relate our Buckeye team to Patton's army to get us motivated for battle. His strategy never wavered for the first play of the game against any team. "Run 'em between the tackles. We want a knockout punch on the first play of the game." He wanted us to establish dominance at the line of scrimmage from that first snap and dictate the rest of the game, sort of like Patton's battle strategy..."

ROSE BOWL GAME
1975
OHIO STATE vs. USC

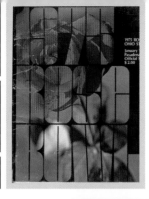

Richard Wood, LB, USC

"Cornelius Greene ran the veer option to near perfection. You didn't know he was keeping the ball until he had turned the corner—and then it was probably too late... When J.K. scored and Coach said we were going for the two-point conversion, we were all a bit taken by surprise for a moment, and then we thought, 'this is for the national championship, this is what we've been playing for all year. Why not put it all on the line right now?' Shelton had an incredible vertical jump. You should see how high up he went to catch the ball. It's really beautiful to watch in slow motion."

PRESS BOX FACTS

Nicknamed "Batman," Richard Wood is USC's only 3-time All-American first teamer.

USC TROJANS
HEAD COACH: JOHN McKAY
1974 RECORD: 9-1-1 (6-0-1) PAC-8 CHAMPIONS

DATE	OPPONENT	RESULT
Sep 14	at Arkansas	L 7-22
Sep 28	at Pittsburgh	W 16-7
Oct 5	Iowa	W 41-3
Oct 12	at Washington St.	W 54-7
Oct 19	at Oregon	W 16-7
Oct 26	Oregon State	W 31-10
Nov 2	California	T 15-15
Nov 9	at Stanford	W 34-10
Nov 16	Washington	W 42-11
Nov 23	at UCLA	W 34-9
Nov 30	Notre Dame	W 55-24

SCORE BY QUARTERS	1	-	2	-	3	-	4	FINAL SCORE
OHIO STATE	0	-	7	-	0	-	10	17
USC	3	-	0	-	0	-	15	18

OHIO STATE UNIVERSITY BUCKEYES
HEAD COACH: WOODY HAYES
1974 RECORD: 10-1 (7-1) BIG TEN CHAMPIONS

DATE	OPPONENT	RESULT
Sep 14	at Minnesota	W 34-19
Sep 21	Oregon State	W 51-10
Sep 28	SMU	W 28-9
Oct 5	at Washington St.	W 42-7
Oct 12	Wisconsin	W 52-7
Oct 19	Indiana	W 49-9
Oct 26	at Northwestern	W 55-7
Nov 2	Illinois	W 49-7
Nov 9	at Michigan State	L 13-16
Nov 16	at Iowa	W 35-10
Nov 23	Michigan	W 12-10

The final score indicates just how well these two foes were getting to know each other after three years of combat in the trenches. The first half developed in what was becoming typical fashion. One team dominated statistically in the first two quarters (in this case it was USC) but the scoreboard reflected a virtual draw.

Ohio State seized the momentum in the third period twice only to lose it both times by failing to score once they penetrated the Trojans' ten-yard line. One field goal out of those two golden opportunity possessions might have changed the outcome of the game. Still, the Buckeyes kept battling and after USC took a 10-7 lead in the final period on a Pat Haden TD toss to Jim Obradovich, Cornelius Greene capped an 82-yard drive with a 3-yard scamper to make it 14-10. Ohio State got a break when they recovered a fumble at the USC 30-yard line, but they had to settle for a 32-yard field goal from Tom Klaban to stretch their lead to seven.

With Anthony Davis sidelined by an injury, Allen Carter became the ground game sparkplug for the Trojans on their final drive into Buckeye territory. With less than three minutes remaining, Haden hit J.K. McKay with a perfect strike covering 38 yards for the score. USC went for the 2-point conversion and Ohio State saw its hopes for a national championship dashed in the arms of Trojan flanker Shelton Diggs who was on the receiving end of another Haden pass. The Buckeyes attempted a 62-yard field goal that fell short as time ran out. In a split title year, USC was named national champion by the UPI coach's poll.

Cornelius Greene, QB, Ohio State

"After three Rose Bowl games in a row, you really know what you like and what you don't like about the entire experience. I can say that we liked everything except one thing. One thing bugged everyone and that was Citrus Junior College. Not that we hated the school, but we hated their practice field. It was a 45-minute bus ride from our hotel to the school, so we were on the road in a bus for nearly two hours every day for two weeks every December for three years."

Left top: Shelton Diggs shows the official the ball he came down with for the game-winning 2-point conversion. Bottom left: Pat Haden looks downfield. Bottom center: Trojan receiver strains for more yardage in the first half. Right top: Ohio State QB Cornelius Greene scampers in for a 4th quarter TD. Bottom right: Greene scrambles away from USC's Art Riley while trying to find an open receiver.

ROSE BOWL GAME
1976
OHIO STATE vs. UCLA

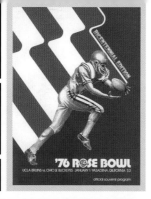

'76 ROSE BOWL
UCLA BRUINS vs OHIO ST. BUCKEYES · JANUARY 1 · PASADENA, CALIFORNIA $2
official souvenir program

SCORE BY QUARTERS	1 - 2 - 3 - 4	FINAL SCORE
OHIO STATE	3 - 0 - 0 - 7	10
UCLA	0 - 0 - 16 - 7	23

Dick Vermeil,
Head Coach, UCLA

"Every career has its highs and lows but that Rose Bowl, that team, that win was as high as you could ever experience in a coaching career. The Super Bowl was equivalent, but I don't know if I have ever experienced anything else that was equivalent to that Rose Bowl win. What those kids did in beating a team that had already soundly beaten them earlier in the season was a great tribute to their athletic ability, their character and their willingness to work hard to win. To represent UCLA in a way that it should always be represented was an honor. It was one of the highlights of my career and one of the highlights of my life."

UCLA BRUINS
HEAD COACH: DICK VERMEIL
1975 RECORD: 8-2-1 (6-1) PAC-8 CHAMPIONS

DATE	OPPONENT	RESULT
Sep 13	Iowa State	W 37-21
Sep 20	Tennessee	W 34-28
Sep 27	at Air Force	T 20-20
Oct 4	Ohio State	L 20-41
Oct 11	at Stanford	W 31-21
Oct 18	at Washington St.	W 37-23
Oct 25	California	W 28-14
Nov 1	Washington	L 13-17
Nov 8	at Oregon	W 50-17
Nov 15	Oregon State	W 31-9
Nov 28	at USC	W 25-22

Top left: Bruin QB John Sciarra under pressure in the pocket #73 is Phil McKinnely. Bottom left: UCLA's Wendell Tyler carries for a big gain. Top right: Buckeye FB Pete Johnson carries in second half action. Right center: Ohio State QB Cornelius Greene heads upfield on the keeper. Bottom right: UCLA head coach Dick Vermeil with Ohio State's Woody Hayes at pre-game event.

OHIO STATE UNIVERSITY BUCKEYES
HEAD COACH: WOODY HAYES
1975 RECORD: 11-0 (8-0) BIG TEN CHAMPIONS

DATE	OPPONENT	RESULT
Sep 13	at Michigan State	W 21-0
Sep 20	Penn State	W 17-9
Sep 27	North Carolina	W 32-7
Oct 4	at UCLA	W 41-20
Oct 11	Iowa	W 49-0
Oct 18	Wisconsin	W 56-0
Oct 25	at Purdue	W 35-6
Nov 1	Indiana	W 24-14
Nov 8	at Illinois	W 40-3
Nov 15	Minnesota	W 38-6
Nov 28	at Michigan	W 21-14

Bo Schembechler was known to have once told his players before their season-ending showdown with archrival Ohio State: "This game is only 30 minutes today, boys. You give me the lead by halftime and I'll beat Woody myself in the second half because he's so damn predictable." When you look back at Woody Hayes' impressive string of four consecutive Rose Bowl appearances in the mid-1970s, one thing is very apparent. Ohio State was either tied or slightly ahead at halftime in each of those games. Something went haywire in the second half of three of those games, and this was one of them.

It was a miracle UCLA was behind by only 3 points at intermission. The Bruins offense managed just 48 total yards in the first half. Conversely, Ohio State penetrated inside the UCLA 33-yard line four times, but they only had three points to show for it. Proving Schembechler correct, Dick Vermeil & Co. made adjustments in the locker room and came out on fire. Behind a revved up defense, the pitch and catch combo of John Sciarra and Wally Henry and Wendell Tyler's rushing, the Bruins opened up a 13-point lead heading into the final frame.

Ohio State closed the gap to six points in the fourth quarter, but two turnovers and a 54-yard touchdown run by Tyler put the game away for the Bruins. Sciarra was an efficient 13-of-19 for 212 yards, Wally Henry had 5 catches for 113 yards and two big scores, and Tyler had 177 yards rushing on 21 carries and a score. Archie Griffin closed out his fourth Rose Bowl with 93 yards on 17 carries. The loss cost the #1 ranked and undefeated Buckeyes the national championship.

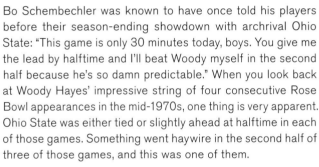

PRESS BOX FACTS

Two-time Heisman Trophy winner Archie Griffin compiled 412 yards rushing on 79 carries (5.2 yards per carry average) in four Rose Bowl Game appearances from 1973–1976.

Brian Baschnagel, WR, Ohio State

"The '76 Rose Bowl was very disappointing since we had blown out UCLA earlier in the year and came into the game ranked #1. I've often thought about how we could have lost that game. During my NFL years, I discussed with many Big Ten and Pac-10 alumni the mindsets of both conferences. In the Big Ten, the Rose Bowl is the reward for winning the conference. In the Pac-10, their goal isn't complete without winning the Rose Bowl. That's not to say that Big Ten teams approach the Rose Bowl without an intense desire to win. But at Ohio State, we were conditioned all year long that Michigan was THE GAME. Half of our spring and summer camps were devoted to the Michigan game, and during the conference season, we spent a couple days each week preparing for them. Perhaps our preseason goal missed the mark by one game?"

ROSE BOWL GAME
1977
MICHIGAN vs. USC

THE 1977 ROSE BOWL
USC vs. MICHIGAN

JANUARY 1 · PASADENA, CALIFORNIA
official souvenir program $2

Charlie White, RB, USC

"On Game Day I wondered, 'how can I appear on TV, knowing Rickey was going to play the whole game unless he was hurt (never) or tired (impossible)?' It dawned on me when Coach Robinson was checking his headset— I would stand next to him. All I could think about was being seen on TV by my relatives and friends. My head wasn't in the game. Meanwhile during our first series of plays, Rickey's bell got rung. I saw the trainers running out on the field to help assist him back to the sidelines. Coach was yelling out my name, 'Charlie White! Charlie White!' Wouldn't you know, I couldn't find my helmet? It had fallen down in a gutter area beneath the benches. I was horrified. I wanted to be on national TV, but not like this. I found my helmet just as the commercial timeout was over."

USC TROJANS
HEAD COACH: JOHN ROBINSON
1976 RECORD: 10-1 (7-0) PAC-8 CHAMPIONS

DATE	OPPONENT	RESULT
Sep 11	Missouri	L 25-46
Sep 18	at Oregon	W 53-0
Sep 25	at Purdue	W 31-13
Oct 2	Iowa	W 55-0
Oct 9	at Washington St.	W 23-14
Oct 23	Oregon State	W 56-0
Oct 30	California	W 20-6
Nov 6	at Stanford	W 48-24
Nov 13	Washington	W 20-3
Nov 20	at UCLA	W 24-14
Nov 27	Notre Dame	W 17-13

Michigan rolled into Pasadena with the top-ranked offense and defense in the country and two-points shy of an undefeated season. Standing in their way of a possible national championship were the USC Trojans with designs of their own on the holy grail of college football. The winner of this contest hoped that undefeated Pittsburgh would falter in their bowl game later that day with once-beaten Georgia.

The game was filled with ferocious hitting from the start and USC's star tailback Ricky Bell left early in the first period after being injured. Freshman Charles White replaced Bell and would ultimately prove that Troy's cupboard would be filled with running back talent for at least the next few years. Both teams swapped touchdowns in the second period, but USC had a 1-point advantage thanks to Walt Underwood's block of the Michigan extra point.

SCORE BY QUARTERS	1 - 2 - 3 - 4	FINAL SCORE
MICHIGAN	0 - 6 - 0 - 0	6
USC	0 - 7 - 0 - 7	14

UNIVERSITY OF MICHIGAN WOLVERINES
HEAD COACH: BO SCHEMBECHLER
1976 RECORD: 10-1 (7-1) BIG TEN CHAMPIONS

DATE	OPPONENT	RESULT
Sep 11	Wisconsin	W 40-27
Sep 18	Stanford	W 51-0
Sep 25	Navy	W 70-14
Oct 2	Wake Forest	W 31-0
Oct 9	Michigan State	W 42-10
Oct 16	at Northwestern	W 38-7
Oct 23	at Indiana	W 35-0
Oct 30	Minnesota	W 45-0
Nov 6	at Purdue	L 14-16
Nov 13	Illinois	W 38-7
Nov 20	at Ohio State	W 22-0

PRESS BOX FACTS

USC RB Ricky Bell was the top pick in the 1977 NFL Draft. Fellow Trojans Marvin Powell and Gary Jeter were also first round picks. USC led all college teams with 14 players drafted by the NFL that year.

John Robinson, Head Coach, USC

"If you asked me which team I'd rather play in the Rose Bowl I would say Michigan because of their outstanding tradition. There's nothing like USC playing Michigan in the Rose Bowl. They have the two best university fight songs and the best football programs with a constant stream of quality players every year. Of course, my first Rose Bowl as head coach at USC was vs. Michigan. They were exceptionally strong, their offense and defense were both ranked first in the nation. I'll never forget when Ricky Bell and Michigan's top defensive player slammed into each other early in the first quarter—BAM! That game was memorable for the sheer physical nature of the teams and for coming down to the wire."

Defense ruled in the second half with the Wolverines managing just four first downs and the Trojans managing to sustain a few more drives. The decisive drive of the game culminated when White scored from seven yards out with three minutes remaining. Michigan then put together its best series of plays in the second half and managed to move the ball to the USC 17-yard line before running out of downs. White led all rushers with 114 yards on 32 carries and Michigan's Rob Lytle closed out his career with 67 yards on 18 carries. Vince Evans was 14-of-21 for 181 yards, and his favorite receiver, Shelton Diggs had 8 grabs for 98 yards, including an incredible ball-bouncing-off-the-helmet reception. Pitt went on to beat Georgia in the night game to remain undefeated and #1 and USC finished #2.

Left top: USC's Vince Evans passes under heavy pressure. Left center: Trojan tailback Charles White bursts through a hole in the Michigan defense. Lower left: USC flanker Shelton Diggs actually caught this ball after it bounced off his helmet. Top right: Wolverine RB Rob Lytle eludes Trojan tacklers for a big first half gain. Middle right: Michigan QB Rick Leach is collared in the pocket by USC's Gary Jeter. Bottom right: Richard N. Frank with Bo Schembechler at the Lawry's Beef Bowl.

ROSE BOWL GAME
1978
MICHIGAN vs. WASHINGTON

the 1978 Rose Bowl
JANUARY 2 / PASADENA, CALIFORNIA

WASHINGTON vs. MICHIGAN
Official Souvenir Program $2.50

Warren Moon, Q.B, Washington

"During our Beef Bowl event waiters came around with huge carts and served unbelievable cuts of meat right at our table. As a college student who was used to dining on fast food and racing to the dorm before the dining hall closed to feast on scraps, that experience was very new to me.. When we came through the tunnel of the Rose Bowl onto the field I was completely blown away by the beauty of the day. It was a perfect 72 degrees with a sea of purple and gold on one side of the stadium and blue and gold on the other. It's still the most electrifying moment in my sports career... The most vivid moment was coming out of the locker room and seeing the look on my mom's face and how proud I had made her that day. That's a look I will never forget."

UNIVERSITY OF WASHINGTON HUSKIES
HEAD COACH: DON JAMES
1977 RECORD: 7-4 (6-1) PAC-8 CHAMPIONS

DATE	OPPONENT	RESULT
Sep 10	Mississippi State	L 18-27
Sep 17	San Jose State	W 24-3
Sep 24	at Syracuse	L 20-22
Oct 1	at Minnesota	L 17-19
Oct 8	at Oregon	W 54-0
Oct 15	Stanford	W 45-21
Oct 22	Oregon State	W 14-6
Oct 29	at UCLA	L 12-20
Nov 5	at California	W 50-31
Nov 12	USC	W 28-10
Nov 19	Washington State	W 35-15

Left top: Washington QB Warren Moon passes in the first half. Bottom left: Warren Moon serves Coach Don James at the Lawry's Beef Bowl while Mrs. James looks on. Right top center: Michigan QB Rick Leach fakes a handoff to RB Stanley Edwards. Top right: Wolverine RB Russell Davis fights for yardage against Husky Antonwaine Richardson . Bottom right: Michigan and Washington before the snap in the Husky red zone during second half action.

Michigan was a solid favorite for this game and they demonstrated why in the fourth quarter with a spirited rally. The only problem is Washington had already built a 24-0 lead midway through the third period. Michigan gave the Huskies excellent field position early in the game that led to two short touchdown runs by Warren Moon. Washington's Steve Robbins added a 30 yard field goal to make it 17-0 at the break.

The Wolverines drove all the way to the Washington 3-yard line in the third quarter but were thwarted by a stiff defensive effort. Several plays later, Moon connected with Spider Gaines for a 28-yard scoring play that appeared to ice the game for the Huskies. But Michigan chose to fight back instead of wilting. Wolverine QB Rick Leach got the hot hand and fired a 76-yard TD pass to Curt Stephenson to make it 24-7. Robbins added another field goal to make it 27-7 heading into the fourth frame.

Michigan stormed back on four Leach completions and Russell Davis scored on a 2-yard run to make it 24-14. A couple changes of possession later and Leach hit Stanley Edwards for a 32-yard touchdown. The kick failed and the score was 27-20.

The Wolverine D was doing its job and getting the ball back to Leach and Co. but the Huskies loaded up against the passing game and intercepted passes on two late drives by Michigan. The last interception was a diving defensive gem at the Husky 8-yard line by linebacker Michael Jackson. That's how close Michigan came to tying this game up. It really was a tale of two quarterbacks and two halves of great football. Moon ended up 12-23, 188 yards, 1 TD and Leach was 14-27, 239 yards, and 2 TDs. Gaines had 4 grabs, 122 yards, 1 TD

SCORE BY QUARTERS	1 - 2 - 3 - 4	FINAL SCORE
MICHIGAN	0 - 0 - 7 - 13	20
WASHINGTON	7 - 10 - 10 - 0	27

 UNIVERSITY OF MICHIGAN WOLVERINES
HEAD COACH: BO SCHEMBECHLER
1977 RECORD: 10-1 (7-1) BIG TEN CHAMPIONS

DATE	OPPONENT	RESULT
Sep 10	at Illinois	W 37-9
Sep 17	Duke	W 21-9
Sep 24	Navy	W 14-7
Oct 1	Texas A&M	W 41-3
Oct 8	at Michigan State	W 24-14
Oct 15	Wisconsin	W 56-0
Oct 22	at Minnesota	L 0-16
Oct 29	Iowa	W 23-6
Nov 5	Northwestern	W 63-20
Nov 12	at Purdue	W 40-7
Nov 19	Ohio State	W 14-6

PRESS BOX FACTS

Warren Moon wasn't selected in the NFL draft, so he signed with the Edmonton Eskimos of the Canadian Football League in 1978. He led Edmonton to six consecutive Grey Cup championships. He went on to play for the NFL's Oilers, Vikings and Seahawks and retired ranked third all-time in NFL passing yardage and fifth in touchdown passes.

Rick Leach,
QB, Michigan

"There's nothing like the Rose Bowl with the stadium set in the valley and the mountains in the background. The game starts in the daytime and ends with the sun setting and the stadium lights on during the final minutes of the fourth quarter. We were fortunate to be there three years in a row. In the game against Washington we were down by 17 points at half and then 24 points early in the third quarter. That had never happened to us before. The Huskies had a great team and an incredible group of athletes. We came out in the second half with the mindset that we had nothing to lose. We opened up our game and started mixing things up and throwing more. It felt good to know that we made it a game in the end."

ROSE BOWL GAME
1979
MICHIGAN vs. USC

The 1979 ROSE BOWL

USC VS. MICHIGAN
January 1/Pasadena, California/Official Souvenir Program /$2.50

**John Robinson,
Head Coach, USC**

"Bo and I became friends and I often visited him in the spring. He had a large photo in his office of Charles White fumbling the ball on that infamous goal line dive in the 1979 Rose Bowl. I would point to the photo and laugh, raising my arms to signal 'Touchdown!' Bo would reply, 'Get outta here and go back to Southern California, you SOB!' Then I would admit it wasn't a TD. We barely won that one. Michigan had the momentum late in the game. They shut down our passing and I was concerned about our punting. We were close to our 20, and it was 3rd and 7. I called a fullback draw, a play we rarely used. Lynn Cain popped it for about 20 yards and we ran the clock down from that point. I'm just glad that game didn't go on much longer."

USC TROJANS
HEAD COACH: JOHN ROBINSON
1978 RECORD: 11-1 (6-1) PAC-10 CHAMPIONS

DATE	OPPONENT	RESULT
Sep 9	Texas Tech	W 17-9
Sep 16	at Oregon	W 37-10
Sep 23	at Alabama	W 24-14
Sep 29	Michigan State	W 30-9
Oct 14	at Arizona State	L 7-20
Oct 21	Oregon State	W 38-7
Oct 28	California	W 42-17
Nov 4	at Stanford	W 13-7
Nov 11	Washington	W 28-10
Nov 18	at UCLA	W 17-10
Nov 25	Notre Dame	W 27-25
Dec 2	at Hawaii	W 21-5

Top left: Trojan QB Paul McDonald drops back to pass in the first half. Bottom left: Michigan QB Rick Leach is stopped by USC defenders. Top right: Press photo of the infamous "goal line fumble" by Charles White that was ruled a touchdown. Middle right: L.A. TV sports anchor Stu Nahan interviews Michigan freshman Ed Muransky as he is about to break the mythical Lawry's Beef Bowl record. A 1979 Rose Princess is amused with the banter. Lower right: Freshman cohort Bubba Paris took this photo of Muransky at the Lawry's Beef Bowl.

There probably isn't a Michigan fan that saw this game that will ever forget the disputed touchdown that gave USC its winning margin. Early in the second quarter, with the ball resting on the 3-yard line, Trojan tailback Charles White got the call and before he hit the line of scrimmage he dove through the heart of the Wolverine defense. Ron Simpkins stripped the ball from White as he was airborne. Jerry Meter appeared to have recovered the fumble on the 1-yard line for Michigan. However, the line judge ruled the play a touchdown saying White had crossed the goal line before losing the ball. To this day, still photographs and videotape replays have never substantiated the official's call.

SCORE BY QUARTERS	1 - 2 - 3 - 4	FINAL SCORE
MICHIGAN	0 - 3 - 7 - 0	10
USC	7 - 10 - 0 - 0	17

UNIVERSITY OF MICHIGAN WOLVERINES
HEAD COACH: BO SCHEMBECHLER
1978 RECORD: 10-1 (7-1) BIG TEN CHAMPIONS

DATE	OPPONENT	RESULT
Sep 16	Illinois	W 31-0
Sep 23	at Notre Dame	W 28-14
Sep 30	Duke	W 52-0
Oct 7	Arizona	W 21-17
Oct 14	Michigan State	L 15-24
Oct 21	at Wisconsin	W 42-0
Oct 28	Minnesota	W 42-10
Nov 5	at Iowa	W 34-0
Nov 11	at Northwestern	W 59-14
Nov 18	Purdue	W 24-6
Nov 25	at Ohio State	W 14-3

Ed Muransky,
DL, Michigan

"Bubba Paris and I were two happy freshmen eating together at the 1978 Lawry's Beef Bowl. After we had enjoyed our fourth plate of prime rib, mashed potatoes, corn and Yorkshire pudding, Bubba asked what the record was, and they said 7 cuts. Bubba continued for 3 more cuts, and I continued for four, totally under the Bo Schembechler radar screen. When they delivered the 8th cut to me, the media started to gather around my table, Bo walked by and let me know what he was thinking without ever saying a word. Afterward, a Paris-Muransky night out ended with some pizza. The next morning in practice, Bo made an example of Bubba and me. We never ran so much in our lives as we did that day. We were in every play of scrimmage and then we ran sprints."

Still, this was a game the Wolverines could have won. Michigan's defense was stout and relentless, allowing White only 99 yards on 32 carries, well below his average. In fact, the Trojans only managed 23 yards in the air and 157 total yards, certainly not the type of stats that win games. USC, on the other hand, was resourceful when they had to be. Ronnie Lott and Dennis Smith both intercepted Rick Leach (10-21, 137 yards) in the first half and the Trojans cashed those picks in for 10 points on their way to a 17-3 halftime lead. Michigan's only first half score came on a 36-yard field goal by Greg Willner. Halfway through the third period Leach connected with Roosevelt Smith for a 44-yard touchdown to cut the margin to seven. Both defenses hung tough the rest of the game and the score remained 17-10 at the gun.

1980
1989

ROSE BOWL GAME
1980
OHIO STATE vs. USC

Rose Bowl
USC VS. OHIO STATE

Brad Budde, OG, USC

"When I think back on my experiences playing in three Rose Bowl Games, the word that comes to mind is PASSION. There is no better word to describe the people who love this violent sport and yet are civilized enough to appreciate the pageantry of the Rose Bowl Parade and a fine meal at Lawry's. The Rose Bowl means many things, but one thing is for certain, it is our game. It is what unites us all with the memories of heartache, hope, and miracles."
See Epilogue for entire recollection.

PRESS BOX FACTS

Trojans
SC

USC TROJANS
HEAD COACH: JOHN ROBINSON
1979 RECORD: 11-0-1 (6-0-1) PAC-10 CHAMPIONS

DATE	OPPONENT	RESULT
Sep 8	at Texas Tech	W 21-7
Sep 15	at Oregon State	W 42-5
Sep 22	Minnesota	W 48-14
Sep 29	at LSU	W 17-12
Oct 6	Washington State	W 50-21
Oct 13	Stanford	T 21-21
Oct 20	at Notre Dame	W 42-23
Oct 27	at California	W 24-14
Nov 3	Arizona	W 34-7
Nov 10	at Washington	W 24-17
Nov 24	UCLA	W 49-14

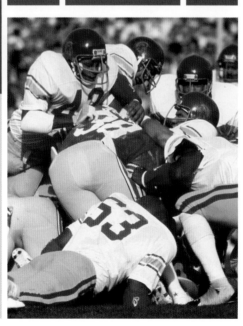

Ohio State head coach Earl Bruce shocked the Buckeye faithful in his first year by beating Michigan, winning the Big Ten title and a berth in the Rose Bowl with an unblemished record, #1 ranking in the polls, and a shot at the national title. It was the fifth time the Buckeyes and Trojans had met within a span of ten Rose Bowl Games and nearly every time a national championship was within the grasp of one or both teams.

SCORE BY QUARTERS	1	-	2	-	3	-	4	FINAL SCORE
OHIO STATE	0	-	10	-	3	-	3	16
USC	3	-	7	-	0	-	7	17

OHIO STATE UNIVERSITY BUCKEYES
HEAD COACH: EARL BRUCE
1979 RECORD: 11-0 (8-0) BIG TEN CHAMPIONS

DATE	OPPONENT	RESULT
Sep 8	Syracuse	W 31-8
Sep 15	at Minnesota	W 21-17
Sep 22	Washington State	W 45-29
Sep 29	at UCLA	W 17-13
Oct 6	Northwestern	W 16-7
Oct 13	Indiana	W 47-6
Oct 20	Wisconsin	W 59-0
Oct 27	Michigan State	W 42-0
Nov 3	at Illinois	W 44-7
Nov 10	Iowa	W 34-7
Nov 17	at Michigan	W 18-15

USC jumped out to a 10-0 lead but the Bucks scrapped their way back to tie the score before halftime thanks to a Vlade Janakievski field goal and a 67-yard TD pass from Art Schlichter to Gary Williams. Both defensive units cancelled each other out with ferocious goal line stands in the first half. Defense continued to rule the game with Ohio State managing a pair of Janakievski field goals that put them up 16-10 in the final period. With 5:31 to play and the ball on their own 17-yard line, the Trojans embarked on an eight-play 83-yard drive to glory. Heisman Trophy winner Charles White carried six times during the drive for 70 of those yards including the game-winning touchdown behind offensive lineman Anthony Munoz. White finished with a Rose Bowl record 247 rushing yards on 39 carries.

Top left: Trojan tailback Charles White explodes through Buckeye line in the second half. Bottom left: USC defenders wrap up Ohio State ball carrier. Top right: QB Art Schlichter fakes to Calvin Murray and hands off to Tyrone Hicks. Middle right: Schlichter hands off to Murray. Bottom right: Lawry's carver Andy Hunter serves Ohio State coach Earl Bruce, Rose Queen Julie Raatz, and QB Art Schlichter at the Lawry's Beef Bowl.

Vlade Janakievski, PK, Ohio State

"We beat UCLA in the Coliseum earlier that season and on the flight home the pilot flew over the Rose Bowl. Everyone talked about coming back to play there on January 1, and sure enough, we made that second trip to California. It was an amazing atmosphere and everything was 1st class. We got to meet Sammy Davis, Jr. at Lawry's and Frank Sinatra at the Rose Bowl luncheon. As a college kid it was so cool! The most pressure I ever felt was in the Rose Bowl because it was for the national title and every kick was so important. When USC went ahead by one point with 90 seconds to go, I thought, 'This is it, I'm going to have a chance to win the game with another kick.' It would have been a dream come true, but the clock ran out before I got that opportunity."

ROSE BOWL GAME

1981

MICHIGAN vs. WASHINGTON

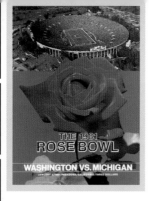

THE 1981 ROSE BOWL
WASHINGTON VS. MICHIGAN

SCORE BY QUARTERS	1	2	3	4	FINAL SCORE
MICHIGAN	0	7	10	6	23
WASHINGTON	0	6	0	0	6

Don James, Head Coach, Washington

"My favorite pre-game recollection was the police escort from Anaheim to the bowl site. All roads were cleared for us and as we got close to Pasadena, we were picked up with helicopter escorts. As we got closer to the stadium, the excitement began to grow as we saw fans from both teams and tailgaters lining the streets. When the Rose Bowl came into sight, and as the excitement grew, the feeling was unbelievable and it was a feeling that equals nothing I had ever felt before."

UNIVERSITY OF WASHINGTON HUSKIES
HEAD COACH: DON JAMES
1980 RECORD: 9-2 (6-1) PAC-10 CHAMPIONS

DATE	OPPONENT	RESULT
Sep 13	Air Force	W 50-7
Sep 20	Northwestern	W 45-7
Sep 27	Oregon	L 10-34
Oct 4	at Oklahoma St.	W 24-18
Oct 11	at Oregon State	W 41-6
Oct 18	at Stanford	W 27-24
Oct 25	Navy	L 10-24
Nov 1	Arizona State	W 25-0
Nov 8	Arizona	W 45-22
Nov 15	at USC	W 20-10
Nov 22	at Washington St.	W 30-23

Top left: Washington coach Don James during 2nd quarter action. Middle left: The Huskies return to the field for the start of the second half led by #1 Tony Alvarado and #23 Vince Newsome. Bottom left: UW cheerleaders. Top right: #72 Ed Muransky revs up the Michigan fans. Center right: Wolverines force Husky fumble. Lower right: Lawry's chef Lee Davis and Rose Queen Leslie Kawai serve Michigan QB John Wangler.

How good was this Michigan team? Good enough to bring Bo Schembechler his first Rose Bowl win in six appearances. The Wolverines' only two losses were at the beginning of the season to bowl-bound teams by a total of five points. By the end of the year, the Michigan defense was playing as well as any other unit in the country. They came into the Rose Bowl without having given up a touchdown in 18 consecutive quarters against a line-up of Illinois, Indiana, Wisconsin, Purdue and archrival Ohio State.

After this Rose Bowl Game it would stretch to 22 quarters in a row because Washington was only able to come away with two Chuck Nelson field goals. However, it didn't appear that the streak would last past the first half as the Huskies picked up 269 of their 374 total yards in the first two quarters. They had their chances to reach the end zone, the best one coming on their second drive of the game, but RB Toussiant Tyler was

stopped at the 1-yard line on fourth down. Midway through the second quarter, Washington was driving again when Kyle Stevens fumbled. Center Mike Reilly recovered the ball while it was still in the air and scored, but the play was whistled dead by the officials.

Butch Woolfolk put Michigan in the lead with a six-yard TD run before halftime, and the Wolverines stayed in command the rest of the way. Ali Haji-Sheikh contributed a chip shot field goal after an 83-yard drive and John Wangler hit Anthony Carter for a seven-yard TD to give Michigan a 17-6 lead heading into the final period. Stan Edwards punched across the goal from the 1-yard line with just a few minutes remaining to close out the scoring. Woolfolk ended with 182 yards rushing on 26 carries and Carter caught five passes for 68 yards, plus 33 more yards on four carries to provide Michigan's offensive juice. Husky QB Tom Flick was 23-39, 282 yards but gave up 2 picks.

UNIVERSITY OF MICHIGAN WOLVERINES
HEAD COACH: BO SCHEMBECHLER
1980 RECORD: 9-2 (8-0) BIG TEN CHAMPIONS

DATE	OPPONENT	RESULT
Sep 13	Northwestern	W 17-10
Sep 20	at Notre Dame	L 27-29
Sep 27	South Carolina	L 14-17
Oct 4	California	W 38-13
Oct 11	Michigan State	W 27-23
Oct 18	at Minnesota	W 37-14
Oct 25	Illinois	W 45-14
Nov 1	at Indiana	W 35-0
Nov 8	at Wisconsin	W 24-0
Nov 15	Purdue	W 26-0
Nov 22	at Ohio State	W 9-3

Ed Muransky,
DL, Michigan

"My junior year, we're flying out to the 1981 Rose Bowl and Bo made it a point to come back and talk to Bubba Paris and me. He wanted to let us know that my record from a couple years earlier would not be in jeopardy because we were going to be sitting with him at the Lawry's Beef Bowl. He said he was going to limit each of us to two cuts of prime rib."

PRESS BOX FACTS

1980 marked the first year that Michigan had won the Big Ten title outright since 1971. Wolverine Don Bracken's 73-yard punt in the first quarter set a modern day Rose Bowl record.

ROSE BOWL GAME

1982

IOWA vs. WASHINGTON

THE 1982 ROSE BOWL

WASHINGTON vs. IOWA

Steve Pelleur,
QB, Washington

"The pageantry and rich history of the event, and the beauty of the stadium at game time are things that stay with you forever. I recall there was a lot of excitement for Iowa because they hadn't been to the Rose Bowl in a long time. They had a huge following—half the state of Iowa was there in yellow and black. One of my favorite memories during the game was handing off to Jacque Robinson on a sprint draw play and seeing the hole open up off to the right. He burst through the hole before it closed up, made a couple guys miss in the secondary, and then he was off to the races."

W

UNIVERSITY OF WASHINGTON HUSKIES
HEAD COACH: DON JAMES
1981 RECORD: 9-2 (6-2) PAC-10 CHAMPIONS

DATE	OPPONENT	RESULT
Sep 12	Pacific	W 34-14
Sep 19	Kansas State	W 20-3
Sep 26	at Oregon	W 17-3
Oct 3	Arizona State	L 7-26
Oct 10	at California	W 27-26
Oct 17	Oregon State	W 56-17
Oct 24	at Texas Tech	W 14-7
Oct 31	Stanford	W 42-31
Nov 7	at UCLA	L 0-31
Nov 14	USC	W 13-3
Nov 21	Washington St.	W 23-10

Don James' Huskies returned to the Rose Bowl determined to avenge the previous year's loss to Michigan. Iowa was making its first trip to Pasadena in 23 years and was a slight favorite to win, but five turnovers would prove too much for the Hawkeyes to overcome.

Both teams battled to a scoreless tie in the first 15 minutes of the game with Washington knocking on the door twice in field goal range but failing to put any points on the board. Freshman Husky running back Jacque Robinson picked up 34 yards on a 65-yard drive in the second quarter and capped it off with a 1-yard TD burst to break the deadlock. Then, just seconds before halftime, fullback Vince Cosby culminated another drive with a 1-yard TD. The Huskies went for two but the pass failed making it 13-0 at the midway mark.

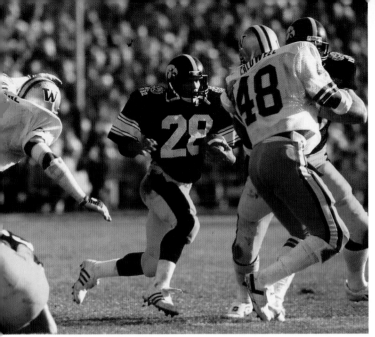

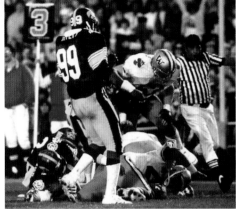

SCORE BY QUARTERS	1	2	3	4	FINAL SCORE
IOWA	0	0	0	0	0
WASHINGTON	0	13	0	15	28

The third quarter was scoreless. Iowa made its deepest penetration of the game during the period, only to see their drive come to a screeching halt when Washington linebacker Ken Driscoll intercepted. The Huskies put the game out of reach about five minutes into the fourth quarter when Robinson broke free for a 34-TD run. Washington found pay dirt again on their next possession to close out the scoring. The Huskies owned a modest advantage in total yards over Iowa (328-264) led by Robinson's 142 yards on 20 carries and QB Steve Pelleur's 142 yards on 15 of 29 passing. In the end, three interceptions and two fumbles doomed a very good Iowa team against an equally good, opportunistic Washington squad.

UNIVERSITY OF IOWA HAWKEYES
HEAD COACH: HAYDEN FRY
1981 RECORD: 8-3 (6-2) BIG TEN CHAMPIONS

DATE	OPPONENT	RESULT
Sep 12	Nebraska	W 10-7
Sep 19	at Iowa State	L 12-23
Sep 26	UCLA	W 20-7
Oct 3	at Northwestern	W 64-0
Oct 10	Indiana	W 42-28
Oct 17	at Michigan	W 9-7
Oct 24	Minnesota	L 10-12
Oct 31	at Illinois	L 7-24
Nov 7	Purdue	W 33-7
Nov 14	at Wisconsin	W 17-7
Nov 21	Michigan St.	W 36-7

Top left: Washington's Jacque Robinson on his way to a 34-yard score behind #31 Chris James in the 4th quarter. Lower left: Husky QB Steve Pelleur. Lower inside left: 1982 Rose Queen Kathryn Potthast makes a special appearance on Bob Hope's All-America TV special with USC's Marcus Allen. Top right: Iowa RB Phil Blatcher cuts off his block to evade #61 Ray Cattage and #48 Tony Caldwell. Far right: Game action. Lower right: Iowa coach Hayden Fry plays chef and serves two of his players at the Lawry's Beef Bowl.

Hayden Fry,
Head Coach, Iowa

"One of the rewards of winning the Big Ten title and a berth in the Rose Bowl is to be able to escape the winter snow for a while. The first thing I noticed when we arrived in Southern California was the fantastic hospitality of the Rose Bowl staff and volunteers. They are an incredible organization. It meant so much to our team to have over 20,000 Hawkeye supporters cheering us on (even though the only thing we won was the fabulous Lawry's Beef Bowl). I'll never forget that my quarterback fell in love with the Rose Queen."

ROSE BOWL GAME
1983
UCLA vs. MICHIGAN

The 1983 ROSE BOWL

UCLA vs. MICHIGAN

SCORE BY QUARTERS	1 - 2 - 3 - 4	FINAL SCORE
MICHIGAN	0 - 0 - 7 - 7	14
UCLA	7 - 3 - 7 - 7	24

Tom Ramsey, QB, UCLA

"As the last 2 minutes were winding down, the offense was at mid-field with a 24-14 lead and a first down, and a TV time-out had just been called. I told the guys in the huddle, 'look around here, catch a visual 360 degree of this place, we'll never be standing here again in this moment, and hopefully we won't forget it.' The sheer magnitude of the moment hit me while I glanced full-circle. The 104,000 plus spectators were still in their seats, and considering the TV audience as well, it was daunting. It was really the first time I let myself come out of 'the zone' of the game itself."

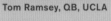

UCLA BRUINS
HEAD COACH: TERRY DONAHUE
1982 RECORD: 9-1-1 (5-1-1) PAC-10 CHAMPIONS

DATE	OPPONENT	RESULT
Sep 11	Long Beach St.	W 41-10
Sep 18	at Wisconsin	W 51-26
Sep 25	at Michigan	W 31-27
Oct 2	at Colorado	W 34-6
Oct 9	Arizona	T 24-24
Oct 16	Washington St.	W 42-17
Oct 23	at California	W 47-31
Oct 30	Oregon	W 40-12
Nov 6	at Washington	L 7-10
Nov 13	Stanford	W 38-35
Nov 20	USC	W 20-19

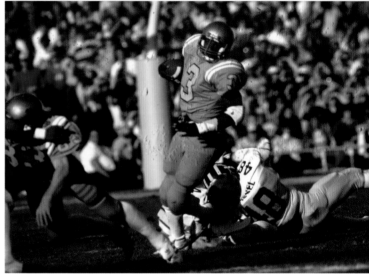

The 1983 Rose Bowl Game played on January 1, 1983 was the third meeting between Michigan and UCLA in 366 days. The Wolverines bested the Bruins 33-14 in the Bluebonnet Bowl on December 31, 1981 and lost at home to UCLA on September 25, 1982, 27-31.

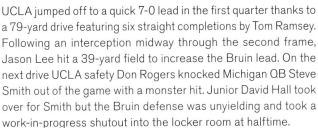

UCLA jumped off to a quick 7-0 lead in the first quarter thanks to a 79-yard drive featuring six straight completions by Tom Ramsey. Following an interception midway through the second frame, Jason Lee hit a 39-yard field to increase the Bruin lead. On the next drive UCLA safety Don Rogers knocked Michigan QB Steve Smith out of the game with a monster hit. Junior David Hall took over for Smith but the Bruin defense was unyielding and took a work-in-progress shutout into the locker room at halftime.

The Wolverines regrouped during the break and marched 55 yards for a touchdown in the third period on a Hall pass to fullback Eddie Garrett from a yard out. UCLA immediately took the momentum back and drove 71 yards before Danny Andrews capped the drive with a 9-yard touchdown run. Down by ten again, the Wolverines took over deep in their own territory but Hall was picked by Bruin linebacker Blanchard Montgomery who returned it 11 yards to put the game out of reach. Still, Michigan didn't give up and Hall connected with Dan Rice for a 1-yard touchdown to make the score respectable. For the second year in a row, UCLA took home the roses.

Ramsey was 18 of 25 for 162 yards. TE Paul Bergmann was his favorite target with 6 receptions for 48 yards. Only 27 total yards in penalties were assessed in the entire game (Michigan, 17 yards and UCLA, 10 yards).

	UNIVERSITY OF MICHIGAN WOLVERINES
M	HEAD COACH: BO SCHEMBECHLER
	1982 RECORD: 8-3 (8-1) BIG TEN CHAMPIONS

DATE	OPPONENT	RESULT
Sep 11	Wisconsin	W 20-9
Sep 18	at Notre Dame	L 17-23
Sep 25	UCLA	L 27-31
Oct 2	Indiana	W 24-10
Oct 9	Michigan State	W 31-17
Oct 16	at Iowa	W 29-7
Oct 23	at Northwestern	W 49-14
Oct 30	Minnesota	W 52-14
Nov 6	at Illinois	W 16-10
Nov 13	Purdue	W 52-21
Nov 20	Ohio State	L 14-24

Top left: #89 Mike Barbee #40 Karl Morgan #85 Lee Knowles. Middle left: UCLA's Kevin Nelson breaks free for gain. Lower left: Rose Queen Suzanne Gillaspie teases Bruin QB Tom Ramsey with prime rib at the Lawry's Beef Bowl. Top right: Second half action. Top far right: Bruin Danny Andrews cuts away from Michigan's #13 Keith Bostic in the 2nd half. Bottom right: Game time Rose Bowl Stadium panorama.

David Hall, QB, Michigan

"My second Rose Bowl (1983 game) was my junior year and I got to play more in that game than I had yet played in college after our starting QB was injured. We fought the best we could and closed to within 3 points in the third quarter before losing to a very good UCLA team 24-14. The Rose Bowl is an awesome college football experience and our team's special event dinner at Lawry's was a highlight of the Rose Bowl week activities."

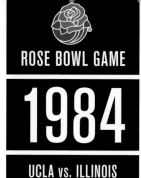

ROSE BOWL GAME
1984
UCLA vs. ILLINOIS

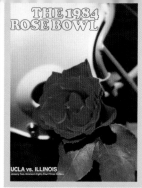

SCORE BY QUARTERS	1	2	3	4	FINAL SCORE
ILLINOIS	0	3	0	6	9
UCLA	7	21	10	7	45

Paul Bergmann,
TE, UCLA

"We went 0-3-1 to start the '83 season. It seemed like some of our coaches were ready to throw in the towel on the team, but our offensive coordinator Homer Smith didn't see it that way. I was one of the team captains and I knew the team had not given up. We went on a 6-1 run to finish the regular season, won the Pac-10 title and returned to the Rose Bowl with a 6-4-1 record. We were huge underdogs vs. a great 10-1 Illinois team, but I knew we were going to win. Homer had put together a masterpiece of an offensive game plan."

UCLA BRUINS
HEAD COACH: TERRY DONAHUE
1983 RECORD: 6-4-1 (6-1-1) PAC-10 CHAMPIONS

DATE	OPPONENT	RESULT
Sep 3	at Georgia	L 8-19
Sep 17	Arizona State	T 26-26
Sep 24	at Nebraska	L 10-42
Oct 1	Brigham Young	L 35-37
Oct 8	at Stanford	W 39-21
Oct 15	at Washington St.	W 24-14
Oct 22	California	W 24-16
Oct 29	Washington	W 27-24
Nov 5	at Oregon	W 24-13
Nov 12	at Arizona	L 24-27
Nov 19	at USC	W 27-17

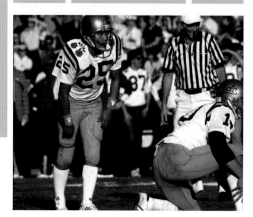

The Fighting Illini returned to the Rose Bowl Game for the first time in twenty years, highly ranked and sizable favorites over UCLA. After a season opening loss to Missouri, Illinois defeated Stanford and then blazed their way through the entire Big Ten schedule to finish the regular season at 10-1. The reigning Rose Bowl champions, UCLA came to play with a 6-4-1 record that was incredibly deceiving. To put the Bruins' record into perspective, three of their losses came early in the season to outstanding bowl-bound teams with a combined record of 33-3-1: Georgia (10-1-1) Nebraska (12-1) and Brigham Young (11-1). Their other two blemishes occurred in conference play with Arizona (7-3-1) and Arizona State (6-4-1).

PRESS BOX FACTS

The Big Ten Conference played a round robin schedule in 1983 where all the schools played each other. Illinois went 9-0 in conference play to earn the 1984 Rose Bowl berth. To this day, Illinois is the only school to defeat every Big Ten conference opponent in the same year.

UNIVERSITY OF ILLINOIS FIGHTING ILLINI
HEAD COACH: MIKE WHITE
1983 RECORD: 10-1 (9-0) BIG TEN CHAMPIONS

DATE	OPPONENT	RESULT
Sep 10	Missouri	L 18-28
Sep 17	Stanford	W 17-7
Sep 24	Michigan State	W 20-10
Oct 1	Iowa	W 33-0
Oct 8	Wisconsin	W 27-15
Oct 15	Ohio State	W 17-13
Oct 22	Purdue	W 35-21
Oct 29	Michigan	W 16-6
Nov 5	Minnesota	W 50-23
Nov 12	Indiana	W 49-21
Nov 19	Northwestern	W 56-24

Mike White,
Head Coach, Illinois

"Unfortunately, because of the results of the game it was one of those experiences that you would like to forget, or at least the game itself. The opportunity to bring an Illinois team to Pasadena after some 20 years since they had been there was a tremendous advantage for the alumni, school, and the players. I had a lot of players from California playing for me at Illinois, and being from California myself made it special. The Tournament of Roses provides a first class event that is second to none. This is what college football is all about, it shows accomplishment and success and we were happy to be a part of it."

The Bruins knew they had survived a murderous schedule and they carried a steady confidence into the game, led by All-American safety Don Rogers. Only 43 seconds had ticked off the game clock when Rogers intercepted a Jack Trudeau pass that quickly led to a Rick Neuheisel-to-Paul Bergmann 10-yard scoring toss. The Illini defense stiffened the remainder of the period and Chris White banged in a 41-yarder to make it 7-3. The second period was a killer for Illinois. Following White's FG, Bruin Kevin Nelson rushed for 28 yards and a score. Rogers intercepted again and Karl Dorrell was on the receiving end of Neuheisel's second TD pass. It was 21-3 UCLA and Neuheisel was far from finished. Before the half ended he hit Mike Young for 53 yards and another score.

Neuheisel remained hot after the break and connected with Dorrell again, this time for a 15-yard TD. Jason Lee added a 29-yard field goal and after three quarters, the score was 38-3. Touchdowns were traded in the final period for a final of 45-9. Neuheisel was 22 of 31, 298 yards and 4 TDs. His counterpart Trudeau was 23 of 39 for 178 yards, and 3 INTs.

ROSE BOWL GAME

1985

OHIO STATE vs. USC

Ted Tollner,
Head Coach, USC

"When I think about the Rose Bowl, the memories that come flooding back include the bus ride down through the canyon, and then as you get closer to the stadium, passing by thousands of fans lining the road in their team colors, the anticipation for the game beginning to swell. It's an unbelievable feeling. The weather was beautiful that day, and it was thrilling to walk on the field for pre-game warm-ups and feel the excitement we had for the game because many people questioned if we could hang with Ohio State after a couple late season losses. Near game's end, the sun was setting. It was a beautiful sight. Having been the underdog, the celebration with the fans at the trophy ceremony, and then back in the locker room afterward as a team—those are the things that really stand out."

USC TROJANS
HEAD COACH: TED TOLLNER
1984 RECORD: 8-3 (7-1) PAC-10 CHAMPIONS

DATE	OPPONENT	RESULT
Sep 8	Utah State	L 8-19
Sep 22	at Arizona State	W 6-3
Sep 29	LSU	L 3-23
Oct 6	at Washington St.	W 29-27
Oct 13	at Oregon	W 19-9
Oct 20	Arizona	W 17-14
Oct 27	California	W 31-7
Nov 3	at Stanford	W 20-11
Nov 10	Washington	W 16-7
Nov 17	at UCLA	L 10-29
Nov 24	Notre Dame	L 7-19

Top left: USC's Timmie Ware leaps past Buckeye DL Thomas Johnson. Left center: Trojan RB Fred Crutcher tries to slip through a hole in the line. Lower left: USC coach Ted Tollner with his wife and Richard R. Frank at the Lawry's Beef Bowl. Top right: Ohio State's Keith Byars. Bottom right: ESPN covering the OSU sidelines during the first half.

Five years removed from their last Rose Bowl meeting and ten years after the rivalry had reached its apex, Ohio State and USC came to Pasadena to do battle for the last time in the 20th century. The Buckeyes had no problem chewing up yardage by ground or through the air, rolling up 403 total yards to USC's 261, but the Trojan defense forced several turnovers and made the big stops when necessary.

SCORE BY QUARTERS	1 - 2 - 3 - 4	FINAL SCORE
OHIO STATE	3 - 3 - 3 - 8	17
USC	10 - 7 - 3 - 0	20

OHIO STATE UNIVERSITY BUCKEYES
HEAD COACH: EARL BRUCE
1984 RECORD: 9-2 (7-2) BIG TEN CHAMPIONS

DATE	OPPONENT	RESULT
Sep 8	Oregon State	W 22-14
Sep 15	Washington St.	W 44-0
Sep 22	Iowa	W 45-26
Sep 29	at Minnesota	W 35-22
Oct 6	at Purdue	L 23-28
Oct 13	Illinois	W 45-38
Oct 20	at Michigan State	W 23-20
Oct 27	at Wisconsin	L 14-16
Nov 3	Indiana	W 50-7
Nov 10	at Northwestern	W 52-3
Nov 17	Michigan	W 21-6

Early in the game Ohio State reached the USC 4-yard line but came up empty. Ohio State QB Mike Tomczak was intercepted three times and twice the Trojans converted those picks into touchdowns. Meanwhile USC QB Tim Green was efficient and error-free in the air. He completed 13 of 25 passes for 128 yards and his two TD passes both came in the first half to help USC build a 17-6 lead they would never relinquish.

The kicking games for both teams were exceptional and played a significant role in the final score. USC punted seven times for a 42.1-yard average and the Buckeyes countered with four punts for a 47.8-yard average. Steve Jordan nailed two 51-yard field goals for USC and Rich Spangler accounted for more than half of Ohio State's points and all of their scoring output in the first 45 minutes of the contest with field goals of 21, 46 and 52 yards.

Tomczak finished with 290 yards passing on 24 of 37 attempts and his favorite target, freshman receiver Cris Carter hauled in nine passes for 172 yards, including an 18-yard TD catch in the final period. Star running back Keith Byars logged 109 yards on 23 carries for the Buckeyes but half of that yardage came off one carry early in the game.

PRESS BOX FACTS

USC's win over Ohio State gave the Pac-10 Conference a 20-19 record and its first lead in the Rose Bowl series with the Big Ten Conference. It was the Pac-10's 13th victory in the last 15 games.

Jim Lachey, OL, Ohio State

"No matter were you play, you are going to have to take your jersey off somewhere for the last time and it was very special to me that my last college game was at the Rose Bowl. I recall being about 5 years old and watching Rex Kern in those great Rose Bowl games in the late Sixties, and then in the Seventies seeing the Buckeyes and Archie Griffin playing four years in a row. That's all we ever heard about as kids growing up and that was our goal every year when I was at Ohio State. My senior year we were outright Big Ten champions and it was a dream come true to go to Pasadena and be a part of that great Rose Bowl tradition and participate in all the events like the Lawry's Beef Bowl and Disneyland."

BIG TEN CONFERENCE

ROSE BOWL GAME
1986
IOWA vs. UCLA

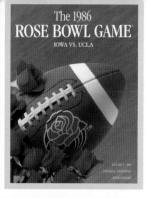

The 1986
ROSE BOWL GAME
IOWA vs. UCLA

SCORE BY QUARTERS	1 - 2 - 3 - 4	FINAL SCORE
IOWA	7 - 3 - 7 - 11	28
UCLA	10 - 14 - 7 - 14	45

Eric Ball, RB, UCLA

"While the team was gathering in the tunnel just before we were to enter the field I took a quick look out at the stadium and all I could see was this sea of black and yellow clad Iowa fans. I had never seen the Rose Bowl stadium entirely filled in every section and I was amazed. I was never one of the rah-rah guys before the game when we gathered but at that moment it hit me as to how big of a game it would be! When we finally charged onto the field I could see the entire stadium and the Bruins fans that had showed up. All of my adrenaline was surging and I was more than ready to play!"

UCLA BRUINS
HEAD COACH: TERRY DONAHUE
1985 RECORD: 8-2-1 (6-2) PAC-10 CHAMPIONS

DATE	OPPONENT	RESULT
Sep 7	at Brigham Young	W 27-24
Sep 14	at Tennessee	T 26-26
Sep 21	San Diego St.	W 34-16
Sep 28	at Washington	L 14-21
Oct 5	Arizona State	W 40-17
Oct 12	at Stanford	W 34-9
Oct 19	at Washington St.	W 31-30
Oct 26	California	W 34-7
Nov 9	at Arizona	W 24-19
Nov 16	Oregon State	W 41-0
Nov 23	at USC	L 13-17

The fourth-ranked and favored Hawkeyes presented a formidable challenge to the Bruins' Rose Bowl winning streak with Chuck Long directing the Iowa offense and linebacker Larry Station anchoring the defense. But UCLA always seemed to relish its underdog roles in the Rose Bowl. Four out their five appearances since 1966 were as underdogs and the Bruins had won them all. The key in each of their previous four wins had been forcing turnovers and capitalizing on them. This game would be no different as they recovered four fumbles and picked

UNIVERSITY OF IOWA HAWKEYES
HEAD COACH: HAYDEN FRY
1985 RECORD: 10-1 (7-1) BIG TEN CHAMPIONS

DATE	OPPONENT	RESULT
Sep 14	Drake	W 58-0
Sep 21	Northern Illinois	W 48-20
Sep 28	at Iowa State	W 57-3
Oct 5	Michigan State	W 35-31
Oct 12	at Wisconsin	W 23-13
Oct 19	Michigan	W 12-10
Oct 26	at Northwestern	W 49-10
Nov 2	at Ohio State	L 13-22
Nov 9	Illinois	W 59-0
Nov 16	at Purdue	W 27-24
Nov 23	Minnesota	W 31-9

off one pass. Despite replacing injured QB David Norrie with junior Matt Stevens and star RB Gaston Green with redshirt freshman Eric Ball, UCLA took a 24-10 halftime lead to the locker room after three Ball TD runs of 30, 6 and 40 yards and a John Lee 42-yard field goal.

In the second half, Stevens passed for a score to Mike Sherrard and ran for another on his way to a very respectable 16 of 26 for 189 yards and one interception. Ball ripped off another TD run of 32 yards in the fourth period and finished with 227 yards on 22 carries and 4 TDs. His 227-yard rushing output was the second highest total in Rose Bowl history at the time.

Iowa's Long was sacked four times and gave up one pick, but he displayed his Heisman worthiness completing 29 of 37 passes for 319 yards and a score. Ronnie Harmon grabbed more than a third of Long's completions logging 11 receptions for 102 yards to go with his 55 yards on 14 carries. The Hawkeyes could have really made a game of this had they not coughed up the pigskin four times. As it was, they hung with the Bruins in the second half, but were never able to close the margin to less than 14 points.

Top left: Bruin RB Eric Ball bursts past Hawkeye #9 Ken Sims in 1st half action. Left center: Richard N. Frank with UCLA coach Terry Donahue, Mrs. Donahue, and Rose Queen Aimee Richelieu at the Lawry's Beef Bowl. Lower left: Eric Ball racing toward his 4th TD of the game. Top center: Hawkeye QB Chuck Long drops back to pass in 3rd quarter action. Top right: Iowa All-American LB Larry Station sheds a block.

Larry Station, LB, Iowa

I feel a great sense of accomplishment and satisfaction in making it to the RoseBowl. I had received All-American and All-Big Ten individual honors, but I had yet to experience the thrill of playing in the Rose Bowl. Playing in the Rose Bowl was my dream from the time I decided to attend the University of Iowa. Earning the right to play in the Rose Bowl my senior year made my college football career complete. During one of the linebacker meetings a couple of days before the Rose Bowl Game, linebacker coach Barry Alvarez told us that 20 years from now we would look back at this Rose Bowl experience with a lot more appreciation for what we achieved. I understood what he was saying, but I didn't quite believe how much more appreciation I would have. Twenty years later I can say that he was definitely right!

PRESS BOX FACTS

Iowa's Chuck Long was the runner-up in the 1985 Heisman Trophy voting to Auburn RB Bo Jackson, but he won the Davey O'Brien Award as the top quarterback in the nation and the Maxwell Award as the nation's outstanding college football player.

ROSE BOWL GAME

1987

MICHIGAN vs. ARIZONA STATE

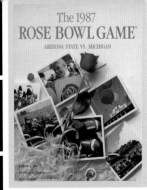

The 1987 ROSE BOWL GAME
ARIZONA STATE VS. MICHIGAN

SCORE BY QUARTERS	1 - 2 - 3 - 4	FINAL SCORE
MICHIGAN	8 - 7 - 0 - 0	15
ARIZONA STATE	0 - 13 - 6 - 3	22

Dan Villa, OL, Arizona State

"I come from Nogales, Arizona, a border town of only 15,000 people. I didn't know it was possible for 100,000 people to be in one place. I had seen the Rose Bowl on TV, but it's much bigger in real life. Even to this day, as I watch the Rose Bowl, I can still see myself in the end zone on New Year's Day 1987, just before ASU was introduced, staring in amazement at the crowd. It is one of my fondest memories."

ARIZONA STATE SUN DEVILS
HEAD COACH: JOHN COOPER
1986 RECORD: 9-1-1 (5-1-1) PAC-10 CHAMPIONS

DATE	OPPONENT	RESULT
Sep 13	Michigan State	W 20-17
Sep 20	SMU	W 30-0
Sep 27	Washington State	T 21-21
Oct 4	at UCLA	W 16-9
Oct 11	at Oregon	W 37-17
Oct 18	at USC	W 29-20
Oct 25	Utah	W 52-7
Nov 1	Washington	W 34-21
Nov 8	California	W 49-0
Nov 15	Wichita State	W 52-6
Nov 22	at Arizona	L 17-34

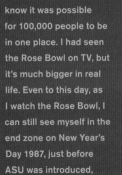

Top left: Sun Devil QB Jeff Van Raaphorst. Left center: ASU head coach John Cooper with a tough 4th period decision. Lower left: Van Raaphorst looks downfield for an open receiver. Top right: Michigan QB Jim Harbaugh scores in the second period. Right center: Wolverine RB Jamie Morris breaks free for an 18-yard TD in the first quarter. Bottom right: Harbaugh passing under pressure from ASU's #93 Trace Armstrong and #58 Larry McGlothen.

When you think of trick plays in college football you don't immediately think of the Michigan Wolverines. Maybe that's why their trick 2-point conversion worked so easily in the first quarter of this game. After moving into scoring position rather easily on its first possession of the game, Michigan scored first on an 18-yard touchdown run by Jamie Morris. On the PAT attempt, kicker Mike Gillette took the snap and passed to Gerald White. Arizona State was caught totally off-guard because the rest of the Michigan team was huddled off to the side where the play action took place.

The Sun Devils put three points on the board in the second period on a 37-yard field goal by Kent Bostrom, but the Wolverines stormed back and scored again on a 2-yard run by QB Jim Harbaugh. Gillette added the PAT and Michigan led 15-3. ASU's Bostrom kicked a 27-yard field goal midway in

PRESS BOX FACTS

The Wolverines won their 32nd Big Ten football championship and Bo Schembechler became the all-time winningest head coach in Michigan history with his 166th victory in 1986.

Jamie Morris, RB, Michigan

"It was so great to be a part of the Rose Bowl Game tradition. My brothers all played for Syracuse but I wanted to play for Michigan because it seemed like they always played in the Rose Bowl. My brother Joe told Bo about me when he played for him in the East-West Shrine Game. It was tough at first because I was so eager as a freshman to demonstrate my abilities. My favorite play was the Counter Trap. I was so anxious I kept going in front of the quarterback to get the handoff instead of behind him. I recall Bo saying, 'Son, you will not be here very long,' and 'The next time I recruit a 5'6" tailback, somebody shoot me!' Thank goodness for my position coach who helped put all of Bo's comments into perspective for me."

	UNIVERSITY OF MICHIGAN WOLVERINES HEAD COACH: BO SCHEMBECHLER 1986 RECORD: 11-1 (7-1) BIG TEN CHAMPIONS

DATE	OPPONENT	RESULT
Sep 13	at Notre Dame	W 24-23
Sep 20	Oregon State	W 31-12
Sep 27	Florida State	W 20-18
Oct 4	at Wisconsin	W 34-17
Oct 11	Michigan State	W 27-6
Oct 18	Iowa	W 20-17
Oct 25	at Indiana	W 38-14
Nov 1	Illinois	W 69-13
Nov 8	at Purdue	W 31-7
Nov 15	Minnesota	L 17-20
Nov 22	at Ohio State	W 26-24
Dec 6	at Hawaii	W 27-10

the period and on their last possession of the half, the Sun Devils ate up the remaining four minutes on the clock with a 60-yard drive capped off by a Jeff Van Raaphorst to Bruce Hill touchdown pass. Michigan's lead had been whittled to 2 points by halftime.

The second half was all Arizona State. They drove 80-yards on their first possession in the third quarter and Van Raaphorst again connected with Hill for the score. The two-point conversion failed, but it didn't matter. Michigan never scored again. ASU's Bostrom added a 25-yard field goal in the fourth period for the final score. Van Rapphorst finished with 16 of 30 passing for 193 yards and the two scores to Hill. Daryl Harris added 109 yards rushing to the Sun Devil attack. Harbaugh was 13 of 23 for 172 yards but he threw three costly picks.

ROSE BOWL GAME
1988
MICHIGAN STATE
vs. USC

The 74th Rose Bowl Game
USC vs Michigan State

Tim Ryan, DL, USC

"After we lost in the rain at Notre Dame we were down on ourselves and we had to regroup and come back and play four tough conference games including the season closer against a really great UCLA team led by Troy Aikman. Everyone expected UCLA to win that year, so it was really sweet to knock the Bruins out of it and earn the Rose Bowl berth for ourselves. We were so jacked to have made it to the Rose Bowl and we were anxious to get revenge on MSU for beating us earlier in the season. We played really tight the first half and Lorenzo White just chewed us up. We shut them down the second half and gave ourselves a chance to win. It was like two different games."

USC TROJANS
HEAD COACH: LARRY SMITH
1987 RECORD: 8-3 (7-1) PAC-10 CHAMPIONS

DATE	OPPONENT	RESULT
Sep 7	at Michigan State	L 13-27
Sep 19	Boston College	W 23-17
Sep 26	at California	W 31-14
Oct 3	Oregon State	W 48-14
Oct 10	at Oregon	L 27-34
Oct 17	at Washington	W 37-23
Oct 24	at Notre Dame	L 15-26
Oct 31	Washington State	W 42-7
Nov 7	Stanford	W 39-24
Nov 14	Arizona	W 12-0
Nov 21	UCLA	W 17-13

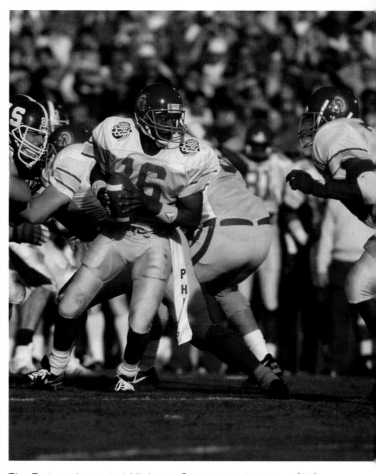

The Trojans dominated Michigan State in total yardage (410-276) and first downs (21-11) but five turnovers, including a fumble and an interception on the last two drives of the game sealed USC's fate. After yielding a field goal to USC on their second drive of the game, the Spartans responded with a 76-yard drive that ate up much of the first period clock. Lorenzo White capped the drive with a 5-yard touchdown run. Michigan State added another TD by White in the second quarter after Bobby McAllister hooked up with Andre Rison to cover 55 yards on that drive. The Spartans led 14-3 at halftime. It was the first Rose Bowl since 1975 that USC had not held the lead at the midway mark.

Rodney Peete led the Trojan charge in the second half and cut the Spartan lead to four with a 33-yard strike to Kevin Henry. It was the only scoring in the third period and set up an exciting fourth quarter finish. Michigan State's John Langeloh nailed a

SCORE BY QUARTERS	1 - 2 - 3 - 4	FINAL SCORE
MICHIGAN STATE	7 - 7 - 0 - 6	20
USC	3 - 0 - 7 - 7	17

MICHIGAN STATE UNIVERSITY SPARTANS
HEAD COACH: GEORGE PERLES
1987 RECORD: 8-2-1 (7-0-1) BIG TEN CHAMPIONS

DATE	OPPONENT	RESULT
Sep 7	USC	W 27-13
Sep 19	at Notre Dame	L 8-31
Sep 26	Florida State	L 3-31
Oct 3	at Iowa	W 19-14
Oct 10	Michigan	W 17-11
Oct 17	at Northwestern	W 38-0
Oct 24	Illinois	T 14-14
Oct 31	at Ohio State	W 13-7
Nov 7	Purdue	W 45-3
Nov 14	Indiana	W 27-3
Nov 21	at Wisconsin	W 30-9

George Perles, Head Coach, Michigan State

"One day at practice before the game we were visited by Charlie Wedemeyer. Charlie had been an outstanding senior quarterback at MSU in 1968 and played in the East-West Shrine Game as well as the Hula Bowl. In 1977, he was diagnosed with Lou Gehrig's Disease. Charlie was in a wheelchair and struggled to breathe through a tube. Yet, with the help of his wife, Lucy—who spoke for him—he was a highly successful high school football coach in California through 1985. Charlie was as inspirational as they come. Speaking to our team through Lucy, he inspired them to go beyond what they thought were their own limits and play the best game of their lives. Perhaps the victory belongs to Charlie as much as anyone!"

40-yard field goal early in the last period to make it 17-10. USC responded with an 80-yard drive that culminated with another Peete-to-Henry TD connection to tie the score. Just over eight minutes remained in the game with the score knotted at 17 and there was still plenty of turbulent action left.

Under a heavy third down rush, McAllister scrambled and found Rison open downfield giving the Spartans the ball on the USC 34-yard line. Blake Ezor carried the ball six straight times to set up a 36-yard Langeloh field goal. The Trojans stormed back and advanced to the MSU 30-yard line only to lose the ball on a fumble off the snap. After forcing a Spartan punt, USC had one more chance but Peete's desperation pass was intercepted deep in MSU territory to ice the game. White finished with 113 yards rushing on 35 carries, and McAllister averaged over 30 yards per completion (4 of 7, 128 yards) with most of that coming on two huge passes to Rison (2 receptions, 91 yards).

Top left: Trojan QB Rodney Peete prepares to hand off to his tailback. Lower left: Peete passing behind solid protection from #71 Brent Parkinson. Bottom left: USC's Dave Cadigan and Rodney Peete with Rose Queen Julie Jeanne Myers at the Lawry's Beef Bowl. Top right: Spartan RB Lorenzo White scores from five yards out in the first quarter. Right center: Michigan State's Percy Snow puts the big hit on a USC ball carrier. Lower right: Spartan receiver Andre Rison pulls down a pass for a big gain.

ROSE BOWL GAME
1989
MICHIGAN vs. USC

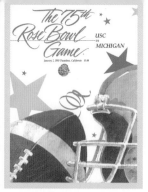

The 75th Rose Bowl Game
USC vs MICHIGAN

SCORE BY QUARTERS	1 - 2 - 3 - 4	FINAL SCORE
MICHIGAN	3 - 0 - 6 - 13	22
USC	0 - 14 - 0 - 0	14

Tim Ryan, DL, USC

"We came into the 1989 Rose Bowl Game with our heads held low because we had essentially lost the national championship against Notre Dame a month earlier in the Coliseum. We were ranked #2 and ND came in ranked #1. The hype for that game was unbelievable and the letdown afterward was enormous. It took a lot of willpower for everyone to get charged back up for the Michigan game. Michigan was an excellent team and the '89 Rose Bowl was like the year before against MSU, two different games. We dominated the first half and Michigan dominated in the second half. It was a big game for Coach Smith because he was a disciple of Michigan coach Bo Schembechler."

USC TROJANS
HEAD COACH: LARRY SMITH
1988 RECORD: 10-1 (8-0) PAC-10 CHAMPIONS

DATE	OPPONENT	RESULT
Sep 1	at Boston College	W 34-7
Sep 10	at Stanford	W 24-20
Sep 24	Oklahoma	W 23-7
Oct 1	at Arizona	W 38-15
Oct 8	Oregon	W 42-14
Oct 15	Washington	W 28-27
Oct 29	at Oregon State	W 41-20
Nov 5	California	W 35-3
Nov 12	at Arizona State	W 50-0
Nov 19	at UCLA	W 31-22
Nov 26	Notre Dame	L 10-27

Top left: USC QB Rodney Peete dives for a second quarter TD. Bottom left: Peete decides to take off after his pocket collapsed. Top right: Michigan coach Bo Schembechler early in the fourth period. Right center: Wolverine RB Leroy Hoard and USC's #53 Delmar Chesley. Bottom right: Leroy Hoard breaks loose for a 61-yard gain in the fourth period.

Michigan's Leroy Hoard became the first running back to gain over 100 yards rushing against USC in the season, capping it off with two fourth quarter touchdown to give Bo Schembechler the win over former assistant coach Larry Smith. The Wolverines jumped out to the lead with a 49-yard field goal by Mike Gillette near the end of the first period, but it was short-lived. The Trojans picked up two touchdowns off short runs by QB Rodney Peete in the second quarter and the score at half was USC 14, Michigan 3.

In the opening minutes of the second half, Demetrius Brown led a Michigan drive highlighted by his 22-yard scramble and 6-yard TD pass to Chris Calloway. The 2-point conversion failed

UNIVERSITY OF MICHIGAN WOLVERINES
HEAD COACH: BO SCHEMBECHLER
1988 RECORD: 8-2-1 (7-0-1) BIG TEN CHAMPIONS

DATE	OPPONENT	RESULT
Sep 10	at Notre Dame	L 17-19
Sep 17	Miami (FL)	L 30-31
Sep 24	Wake Forest	W 19-9
Oct 1	at Wisconsin	W 62-14
Oct 8	Michigan State	W 17-3
Oct 15	Iowa	T 17-17
Oct 22	at Indiana	W 31-6
Oct 29	at Northwestern	W 52-7
Nov 5	Minnesota	W 22-7
Nov 12	Illinois	W 38-9
Nov 19	at Ohio State	W 34-31

Chris Calloway,
WR, Michigan

"As an athlete it means a lot to me to have played in the Rose Bowl because it was always a goal of ours at Michigan to win the Big Ten title and earn the invitation to play in Pasadena. I was fortunate we were able to play in the Rose Bowl Game three of my four years. Coach Schembechler was a great coach, disciplinarian, motivator, and educator. He really emphasized our schoolwork and made sure we were staying on track. When I was underperforming as a freshman in the classroom, he threatened to make me swim back to Chicago across Lake Michigan. Knowing he cared helped me work harder to make the transition from high school to college level studies."

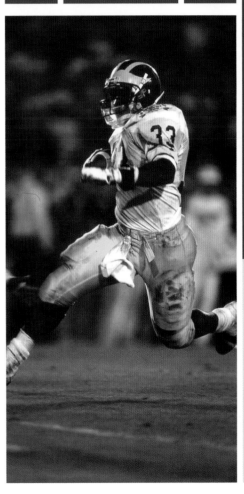

PRESS BOX FACTS

The Trojans have never been defeated three consecutive times in the Rose Bowl. In fact, they have only suffered back-to-back Rose Bowl defeats once in the 116-year history of USC football.

but the Wolverines had secured the momentum. Near the end of the third period, Michigan launched a crushing 92-yard TD drive that left them one point ahead of USC after another 2-point try failed.

The Trojans weren't able to sustain enough offense to do any damage in the second half and with just over five minutes to go in the game, Leroy Hoard broke loose on a 61-yard run that put Michigan inside USC's ten-yard line. After running the clock down an extra three minutes, Hoard smashed in from the 1-yard line on a fourth and goal situation. Hoard ended up with 142 yards on 19 carries and 2 TDs.

1990
1999

ROSE BOWL GAME
1990
MICHIGAN vs. USC

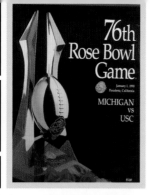

76th Rose Bowl Game
January 1, 1990
Pasadena, California
MICHIGAN vs USC

Larry Smith,
Head Coach, USC

"It was our third straight trip to Pasadena and I felt more pressure to win than ever before. I had a lot of confidence in the talent, experience, and leadership of our squad. All season they had the attitude we were going to win this time around. However, I was getting pretty uptight a few days before the game. Tim Ryan came to me and said, 'Coach, we're ready to play, we should take it easier.' I took his advice and lightened the remaining practices. On game day I was in the locker room talking with the players and I spotted a set of golf clubs hanging on the wall. 'Who the hell brought these in the locker room?' I asked. 'I did, Coach,' replied Gary Wellman. I hesitated before reacting, recalling what Tim had said about the team being loose and ready. Of course they were."

USC TROJANS
HEAD COACH: LARRY SMITH
1989 RECORD: 8-2-1 (6-0-1) PAC-10 CHAMPIONS

DATE	OPPONENT	RESULT
Sep 4	Illinois	L 13-14
Sep 16	Utah State	W 66-10
Sep 23	Ohio State	W 42-3
Sep 30	at Washington State	W 18-17
Oct 7	Washington	W 24-16
Oct 14	at California	W 31-15
Oct 21	at Notre Dame	L 24-28
Oct 28	Stanford	W 19-0
Nov 4	Oregon State	W 48-6
Nov 11	at Arizona	W 24-3
Nov 18	UCLA	T 10-10

In a re-match of the previous year, Michigan and USC followed much of the same script from that game through the first three quarters. The Trojans' scoring came off a 1-yard run by QB Todd Marinovich followed by a Quin Rodriguez field goal. Michigan countered with a J.D. Carlson field goal to make it a 10-3 game in favor of USC at the half.

The Wolverine defensive unit limited USC to just 27 total yards in the third quarter while their offense finally started to click. Allen Jefferson scored on the second drive of the period from two yards out to tie the game at 10. Just as in the 1989 game, the final period was poised to provide plenty of drama.

One of the most unlikely selections from Michigan's playbook could have helped win this game with just under six minutes to go. Instead, it had an opposite effect. On fourth and two from the Michigan 46-yard line, Wolverine punter Chris Stapleton faked a punt and gained 24 yards to the USC 30. However, a holding penalty was called, nullifying the first down. An unsportsmanlike conduct penalty was tacked on as well, pushing Michigan back to its own 21 and forcing a punt. Energized by the bizarre turn of events, USC marched 75 yards in 13 plays with Ricky Ervins scoring on a 14-yard run to clinch the victory. Ervins ended up with 126 yards on the ground and Leroy Hoard had 121 for the Wolverines.

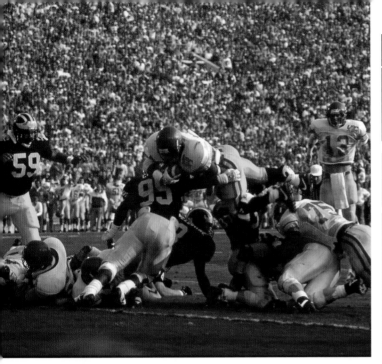

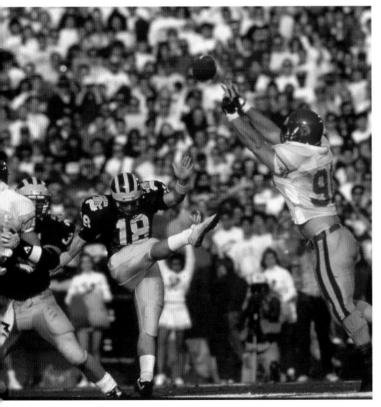

SCORE BY QUARTERS	1 - 2 - 3 - 4	FINAL SCORE
MICHIGAN	0 - 3 - 7 - 0	10
USC	0 - 10 - 0 - 7	17

UNIVERSITY OF MICHIGAN WOLVERINES
HEAD COACH: BO SCHEMBECHLER
1989 RECORD: 10-1 (8-0) BIG TEN CHAMPIONS

DATE	OPPONENT	RESULT
Sep 16	Notre Dame	L 19-24
Sep 23	at UCLA	W 24-23
Sep 30	Maryland	W 41-21
Oct 7	Wisconsin	W 24-0
Oct 14	at Michigan State	W 10-7
Oct 21	at Iowa	W 26-24
Oct 28	Indiana	W 38-10
Nov 4	Purdue	W 42-27
Nov 11	at Illinois	W 24-10
Nov 18	at Minnesota	W 49-15
Nov 25	Ohio State	W 28-18

Bo Schembechler, Head Coach, Michigan

"Regarding the controversial holding penalty called on us during the fake punt play we ran, Junior Seau later told me at a golf tournament: 'Coach, that was no penalty.' I wish the head referee would have come to the same conclusion. I retired because the physicians thought I wouldn't last much longer when I reached the age of 60. Now, I'm 76 years old and a doctor at UM is writing a book about my heart problems titled, 'The Heart of a Champion.' He said to me, 'After having a heart attack at age 39, you should not be alive. Medically speaking, you are a miracle.'"

Top left: USC's Ricky Ervins scored the winning TD on a 14-yard run late in the 4th quarter. Left: Ervins hauls in one of his 5 receptions. Top right: Michigan's D, led by #99 Randy Stark, stops USC's Leroy Holt short of pay dirt. Far right: Wolverine QB Michael Taylor drops back to pass in the pocket. Bottom right: UM punter Chris Stapleton barely gets off his punt under heavy pressure from #99 Tim Ryan and #90 Dan Owen.

PRESS BOX FACTS

Glenn "Bo" Schembechler retired after the 1990 Rose Bowl with a career record at Michigan of 194-48-5. He ranks number one among all coaches in Rose Bowl history with the most appearances (10).

ROSE BOWL GAME

1991

IOWA vs. WASHINGTON

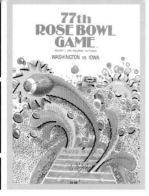

**Charles Mincy,
DB, Washington**

"My 9 years in the NFL included playoff games, Monday Night games and an AFC Championship but nothing compares to the Rose Bowl! My mom made me go to church when I was a child and while there I would daydream over and over about scoring a touchdown in the Rose Bowl. In my dream I would pick off a pass and run down the sideline and dive over some people into the end zone. I got my chance in 1991. Iowa's quarterback audibled and I knew what to expect. I jumped the route, caught the ball and ran it down the sideline into the end zone. It was just as I imagined except I was on the other side of the field in my dream and I didn't have to dive over the Iowa dudes. I just outran them! Thanks Mom for Church!"

**UNIVERSITY OF WASHINGTON HUSKIES
HEAD COACH: DON JAMES
1990 RECORD: 9-2 (7-1) PAC-10 CHAMPIONS**

DATE	OPPONENT	RESULT
Sep 8	San Jose State	W 20-17
Sep 15	at Purdue	W 20-14
Sep 22	USC	W 31-0
Sep 29	at Colorado	L 14-20
Oct 6	at Arizona State	W 42-14
Oct 13	Oregon	W 38-17
Oct 20	at Stanford	W 52-16
Oct 27	California	W 46-7
Nov 3	Arizona	W 54-10
Nov 10	UCLA	L 22-25
Nov 17	at Washington State	W 55-10

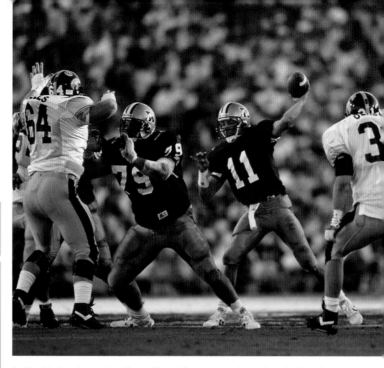

In the highest-scoring Rose Bowl Game ever, Iowa battled back from a 33-7 halftime deficit to Washington to pull within 13 points (39-26) with five minutes to go. Both teams reached the end zone once more before the fireworks were over. Fourteen of the Huskies' early points came directly off turnovers in the first half. Andy Mason blocked a punt in the first quarter and Dana Hall scooped it up and rambled in from 27 yards out. With less than five minutes off the clock, Washington held a 10-0 lead. Iowa cut the lead to three in the second quarter when Nick Bell scooted in from 15 yards out. It was the closest the Hawkeyes would get to Washington the rest of the game.

After Travis Hanson added his second field goal, Charles Mincy picked off a Matt Rodgers pass and raced 37 yards down the sideline for the score. QB Mark Brunell scored on a 5-yard run and then passed 22 yards to Mario Bailey for another tally to provide a commanding 26-point lead at the half. The Hawkeyes scored first in the third period on a Rodgers 7-yard TD run, but the Huskies responded with a score of their own on Brunell's impressive 20-yard run. Fifteen minutes remained and four more scores—three by the Hawkeyes—helped keep the fans in their seats until the end.

SCORE BY QUARTERS	1	2	3	4	FINAL SCORE
IOWA	0	7	7	20	34
WASHINGTON	10	23	6	7	46

UNIVERSITY OF IOWA HAWKEYES
HEAD COACH: HAYDEN FRY
1990 RECORD: 8-3 (6-2) BIG TEN CHAMPIONS

DATE	OPPONENT	RESULT
Sep 15	Cincinnati	W 63-10
Sep 22	Iowa State	W 45-35
Sep 29	at Miami (FL)	L 21-48
Oct 6	at Michigan State	W 12-7
Oct 13	Wisconsin	W 30-10
Oct 20	at Michigan	W 24-23
Oct 27	Northwestern	W 56-14
Nov 3	at Illinois	W 54-28
Nov 10	Ohio State	L 26-27
Nov 17	Purdue	W 38-9
Nov 24	at Minnesota	L 24-31

PRESS BOX FACTS

The previous Rose Bowl record for most points scored by both teams was 79 points in the 1963 Rose Bowl Game: USC (42) and Wisconsin (37).

Iowa led in total yards 454 to 385, but five turnovers took their toll, especially the blocked punt and interception that were returned for scores in the first half. Husky RB Greg Lewis led all rushers with 128 yards on 19 carries. Brunell was 14 of 24, 163 yards, with 1 INT, 2 rushing TDs and 2 passing scores. Rodgers finished 15 of 34, 196 yards, 3 picks, 2 rushing TDs, and 1 passing TD to Mike Saunders, who led all receivers with 5 grabs for 99 yards.

Top left: Washington QB Mark Brunell gets a pass off before Iowa's #31 John Derby gets to him. Left center: Andy Mason blocks an Iowa punt in the first quarter. Bottom left: Rose Queen Cara Rullman feeds Mark Brunell at the Lawry's Beef Bowl. Top right: Hawkeye Mike Saunders grabs one of his 5 receptions despite Husky defender Walter Bailey's attempt to thwart the catch. Right center: Iowa's Matt Rodgers finds an open receiver. Far right: Iowa head coach Hayden Fry.

Mike Saunders, RB, Iowa

"Like any college football team, when you get 100 guys away from the focus and intensity of a practice or game there tends to be a lot of laughing and joking around. The day before the game we went to Rose Bowl Stadium for a photo shoot and a walk-around. The horseplay continued as we walked through the tunnel, but when we reached the entrance to the field, you could have heard a pin drop. Everyone was in awe. We were staring at hallowed ground. As kids, we had all dreamed of playing on that field, and yet nobody wanted to be the first one to step foot on it. We all felt a deep respect for the players and coaches who had competed on that field before us. As I look back now, I still feel a great sense of pride for being a part of that tradition."

ROSE BOWL GAME

1992

MICHIGAN vs. WASHINGTON

Steve Emtman, DL, Washington

"From the first day of training camp and throughout the season, our goal was the Rose Bowl and our sights were set on Pasadena. Our theme was 'Nothing but Roses.' We had a big rose painted above our locker room doors, and every time we passed through those doors for practices or games, each player would touch that rose and think about our team goal. It was a bittersweet feeling after we won the Rose Bowl. Here we were, an elated group of guys who had just accomplished the goal we worked so hard to achieve, and yet, realizing it was the last time we would be together in that capacity. I don't think anyone wanted to leave the field after the game. We just wanted to let it all sink in and enjoy the pride of that accomplishment right there—together—with each other and our fans."

UNIVERSITY OF WASHINGTON HUSKIES
HEAD COACH: DON JAMES
1991 RECORD: 11-0 (8-0) PAC-10 CHAMPIONS

DATE	OPPONENT	RESULT
Sep 7	at Stanford	W 42-7
Sep 21	at Nebraska	W 36-21
Sep 28	Kansas State	W 56-3
Oct 5	Arizona	W 54-0
Oct 12	Toledo	W 48-0
Oct 19	at California	W 24-17
Oct 26	Oregon	W 29-7
Nov 2	Arizona State	W 44-16
Nov 9	at USC	W 14-3
Nov 16	at Oregon State	W 58-6
Nov 23	Washington State	W 56-21

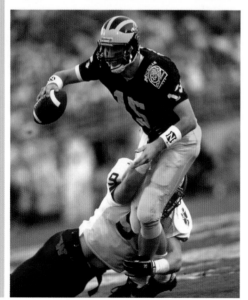

Michigan managed to hang tough through the first half against Washington's top ranked defense and explosive offense, but the Huskies thoroughly dominated the game beyond the midway mark. Led by Outland Trophy winner Steve Emtman, Washington engineered five QB sacks and limited Michigan's potent offense to 205 total yards. The Wolverines' Heisman Trophy winner, Desmond Howard, was held to one 35-yard reception in the second quarter. Already behind 7-0, Howard's catch led to Walter Smith's 9-yard TD grab from Elvis Grbac to tie the score in the second period. Travis Hanson added two field goals to give the Huskies a 13-7 halftime lead.

The only scoring in the third period came off a dominating 80-yard touchdown drive that culminated with a 5-yard TD toss from Billy Joe Hobert to Mark Bruener. Hobert also hit Aaron Pierce for the two-point conversion to make it 21-7, Huskies. Early in the fourth period at the close of another drive, Hobert found Pierce in the back of the end zone for a 2-yard touchdown. Michigan turned the ball over on their next drive when they failed on a fourth-and-one attempt at their own 38-yard line. Back-up quarterback Mark Brunell hit Mario Bailey on the first play following the turnover to make it 34-7. Freshman RB Tyrone Wheatley registered a few points of respect for the Wolverines when he cut loose on a 53-yard touchdown run late in the game.

Aside from Wheatley's long run, Washington's smothering defense held Michigan to 19 net yards on the ground. The QB duo of Hobert and Brunell generated a passing game that was 25 of 42 for 281 yards. Pierce (7 receptions, 86 yards) and Bailey (6 catches, 126 yards) were their main targets.

SCORE BY QUARTERS	1 - 2 - 3 - 4	FINAL SCORE
MICHIGAN	0 - 7 - 0 - 7	14
WASHINGTON	0 - 13 - 8 - 13	34

UNIVERSITY OF MICHIGAN WOLVERINES
HEAD COACH: GARY MOELLER
1991 RECORD: 10-1 (8-0) BIG TEN CHAMPIONS

DATE	OPPONENT	RESULT
Sep 7	at Boston College	W 35-13
Sep 14	Notre Dame	W 24-14
Sep 28	Florida State	L 31-51
Oct 5	at Iowa	W 43-24
Oct 12	at Michigan State	W 45-28
Oct 19	Indiana	W 24-16
Oct 25	at Minnesota	W 52-6
Nov 2	Purdue	W 42-0
Nov 9	Northwestern	W 59-14
Nov 16	at Illinois	W 20-0
Nov 23	Ohio State	W 31-3

Desmond Howard, WR/Return Specialist, Michigan

"We had already clinched the Big Ten title and the Rose Bowl berth, but the rivalry with Ohio State is so powerful—it's a must-win game to consider the season a success. The Buckeyes told everyone they intended to keep me from catching any touchdown passes. They were doing a pretty good job keeping me out of the end zone until I was able to break loose on a 93-yard punt return. When I reached the end zone I spontaneously struck the Heisman 'pose.' I understand ABC Sports' Keith Jackson at that moment said, 'Hellooo Heisman!' Any time you score on special teams it's an added bonus—especially when it comes at a turning point in the game. That touchdown gave us some breathing room and forced Ohio State to play catch-up. It was an honor to represent the Big Ten in the Rose Bowl, despite our lackluster performance."

Top left: Washington's Donald Jones brings down Wolverine Ricky Powers in the second half. Bottom left: Husky All-American Steve Emtman sacks Elvis Grbac. Top right: Heisman Trophy winner Desmond Howard returns a punt in the first half. Right center: Emtman and #57 Tyrone Rodgers pressure Grbac in first half action. Lower right: Richard N. Frank with Desmond Howard and Michigan coach Gary Moeller.

ROSE BOWL GAME
1993
MICHIGAN vs. WASHINGTON

79th
Rose Bowl Game
January 1, 1993 Pasadena, California
WASHINGTON vs MICHIGAN

Lincoln Kennedy, OT, Washington

"Over time I have realized what a tremendous accomplishment it was to make it to the Rose Bowl three years in a row—and then to have won the national championship one of those years. When we were in school, our goal was to win the Pac-10 title and the Rose Bowl Game. There were so many classic match-ups in the Rose Bowl back then between Big Ten and Pac-10 teams, and you had Keith Jackson with that great voice of his calling the game. It's one of the greatest traditions in college football. Ty Wheatley and I had lockers next to each other in the pros and I had the opportunity to block for him. We used to go back and forth with each other about the '92 and '93 Rose Bowl games. I had the rings to prove our success, and he would talk about preventing our 3-peat."

UNIVERSITY OF WASHINGTON HUSKIES
HEAD COACH: DON JAMES
1992 RECORD: 9-2 (6-2) PAC-10 CHAMPIONS

DATE	OPPONENT	RESULT
Sep 5	at Arizona State	W 31-7
Sep 12	Wisconsin	W 27-10
Sep 19	Nebraska	W 29-14
Oct 3	USC	W 17-10
Oct 10	California	W 35-16
Oct 17	at Oregon	W 24-3
Oct 24	Pacific	W 31-7
Oct 31	Stanford	W 41-7
Nov 7	at Arizona	L 3-16
Nov 14	Oregon State	W 45-16
Nov 21	at Washington State	L 23-42

Several records fell in this shootout re-match between Michigan and Washington as the Huskies tried to win a record third straight Rose Bowl Game. The Wolverines jumped off to a 17-7 lead early in the second period following a 49-yard TD pass from Elvis Grbac to Tony McGee and a 56-yard touchdown run by Tyrone Wheatley. The Huskies responded with two Mark Brunell touchdown passes, the first one covering 64 yards to Jason Shelley and the second one 18 yards to Mark Bruener. Washington's quick strike capability allowed them to take a 21-17 lead into the halftime break.

The second half was just as much a see-saw affair as the first. Wheatley cut loose off a Steve Everitt block and romped 88 yards for the score. The Huskies came right back and notched ten quick points thanks to Napoleon Kaufman's 1-yard touchdown smash and a 44-yard Travis Hanson field goal. Before the third period ended, Wheatley scored again, this time on a 24-yard run. The score was knotted at 31 heading into the fourth quarter but the Wolverines appeared to have the momentum.

Michigan's game-winning score came midway through the period. They had driven 65 yards and were faced with third down and a couple yards to go from the Washington 15-yard line.

SCORE BY QUARTERS	1 - 2 - 3 - 4	FINAL SCORE
MICHIGAN	10 - 7 - 14 - 7	38
WASHINGTON	7 - 14 - 10 - 0	31

UNIVERSITY OF MICHIGAN WOLVERINES
HEAD COACH: GARY MOELLER
1992 RECORD: 8-0-3 (6-0-2) BIG TEN CHAMPIONS

DATE	OPPONENT	RESULT
Sep 12	at Notre Dame	T 17-17
Sep 19	Oklahoma State	W 35-3
Sep 26	Houston	W 61-7
Oct 3	Iowa	W 52-28
Oct 10	Michigan State	W 35-10
Oct 17	at Indiana	W 31-3
Oct 24	Minnesota	W 63-13
Oct 31	at Purdue	W 24-17
Nov 7	at Northwestern	W 40-7
Nov 14	Illinois	T 22-22
Nov 21	at Ohio State	T 13-13

Elvis Grbac, QB, Michigan

"1993 was like night and day compared to the '92 game for our returning players. We worked extra hard through the off-season and felt like we were going to win the conference and return to the Rose Bowl. We were excited to face Washington again. Our '92 game plan tried to do too much to counter Washington's great D-line, so we simplified the game plan for '93, running a smaller number of plays off different formations. The two-tight end set worked best because we were able to spring Ty Wheatley past their linebacker and isolate him against a safety. I'll never forget the winning drive. Ty had been sidelined with cramps, so we shifted into a 2-minute offense. Many of us were 5th year seniors and the feeling in the huddle was like 'we've been here before, and we're ready to do it.' We had incredible confidence."

Grbac hit McGee about 12 yards downfield and McGee powered the ball in for six over a Husky defender. It proved to be the only score of the quarter for either team and foiled Washington's attempt at a three-peat. Wheatley ended up with 235 yards on just 15 carries and the Grbac-to-McGee connection produced 6 receptions and 117 yards. Grbac ended up 17-30, 175 yards and Brunell was 18 of 30 for 308 yards. Shelley had 3 receptions for 100 yards and Bruener had 4 grabs for 85 yards.

Top left: Husky QB Mark Brunell hands off to #8 Curtis Bogan in first half action. Upper left: Washington's Lincoln Kennedy being interviewed at the Lawry's Beef Bowl by Los Angeles TV sports anchor Jim Hill. Bottom left: UW's D-line surges at the snap. Top right: QB Elvis Grbac passing behind a solid wall of protection. Right center: Ty Wheatley heading toward one of his TDs. Bottom right: Michigan TE Tony McGee powers over Washington defender Jaime Fields for the winning score.

ROSE BOWL GAME

1994

UCLA vs. WISCONSIN

SCORE BY QUARTERS	1 - 2 - 3 - 4	FINAL SCORE
UCLA	3 - 0 - 0 - 13	16
WISCONSIN	7 - 7 - 0 - 7	21

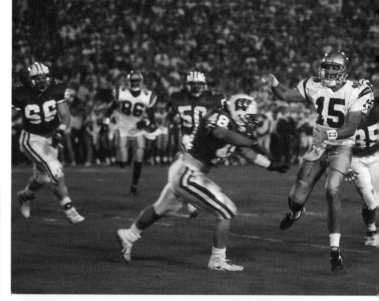

Terry Donahue,
Head Coach, UCLA

It was counter to any Rose Bowl experience I had ever gone through. We had always had at least fifty percent of our fans in the stadium, sometimes sixty percent, but when we came out onto the field for the game and EIGHTY percent of the Rose Bowl was in red, it was disappointing to our players and coaches. All of a sudden you don't feel like you are playing in Pasadena anymore, you feel like you're playing in Madison. It was surprising.

UCLA BRUINS
HEAD COACH: TERRY DONAHUE
1993 RECORD: 8-3 (6-2) PAC-10 CHAMPIONS

DATE	OPPONENT	RESULT
Sep 4	California	L 25-27
Sep 18	Nebraska	L 13-14
Sep 25	at Stanford	W 28-25
Sep 30	San Diego State	W 52-13
Oct 9	Brigham Young	W 68-14
Oct 16	Washington	W 39-25
Oct 23	at Oregon State	W 20-17
Oct 30	Arizona	W 37-17
Nov 6	at Washington State	W 40-27
Nov 13	Arizona State	L 3-9
Nov 20	at USC	W 27-21

Top left: Bruin QB Wayne Cook is pressured by Badger Pete Monty late in the fourth quarter. Left center: Badger RB Brent Moss is dragged down by Bruin LB Jamir Miller. Lower left: J.J. Stokes picks up huge yards after one of his receptions. Top right: QB Darrell Bevell calling signals at the line. Right center: RNF with Rose Queen Erica Beth Brynes, Badger lineman Joe Panos, and coach Barry Alvarez. Lower right: Moss cuts back against over-pursuit by UCLA DB Carl Greenwood.

Wisconsin football had suffered through one of the longest droughts in the Big Ten's association with the Rose Bowl Game. Thirty-one years had passed since Badger-mania had invaded Pasadena, California. Whether or not the 70,000 plus Badger fans had anything to do with UCLA's six turnovers is debatable, but no one could argue that Rose Bowl Stadium certainly had the look and feel of a Wisconsin home game. Nevertheless, the Bruins moved the ball with little difficulty from the start and Bjorn Merten chipped in a 27-yard field goal to assume the only lead they would have the rest of the game.

UNIVERSITY OF WISCONSIN BADGERS
HEAD COACH: BARRY ALVAREZ
1993 RECORD: 9-1-1 (6-0-2) BIG TEN CHAMPIONS

DATE	OPPONENT	RESULT
Sep 4	Nevada	W 35-17
Sep 11	at SMU	W 24-16
Sep 18	Iowa State	W 28-7
Sep 25	at Indiana	W 27-15
Oct 9	Northwestern	W 53-14
Oct 16	at Purdue	W 42-28
Oct 23	at Minnesota	L 21-28
Oct 30	Michigan	W 13-10
Nov 6	Ohio State	T 14-14
Nov 20	at Illinois	W 35-10
Dec 5	Mich. St. (at Tokyo)	W 41-20

Barry Alvarez,
Head Coach, Wisconsin

"The driver (a former UCLA student body president) that was assigned to my family and me told us five days prior to our 1994 Rose Bowl Game that the stadium would be full of red. I asked him what he meant. He said the UCLA fans would rather sell their tickets to Wisconsin fans, buy a new TV, and watch the game at home. When our team took the field in Pasadena (which is the most beautiful of all venues in sports) it was a sea of red and we therefore called it Camp Randall West."

Despite rolling up 500 total yards in the game, turnovers—six of them—constantly thwarted promising UCLA drives. Wisconsin was quick to capitalize and Brent Moss banged in a pair of short runs in each of the first two quarters to give the Badgers a 14-3 halftime lead. After a scoreless third quarter, Ricky Davis pulled UCLA within five with a nice 12-yard run, and Merten added the PAT to make it 14-10.

While Bruin QB Wayne Cook (28-43, 288 yards) and J.J. Stokes were consuming yardage through the air, Wisconsin's running game was matching them yard-for-yard on the ground. The Badgers worked their way down to the 21-yard line where QB Darrell Bevell, unable to find any receivers open in the end zone, escorted the ball in for the security score. The Bruins didn't give up and cut the lead to five with a short Cook-to-Mike Nguyen TD toss. The 2-point conversion pass failed, but UCLA regained possession with just over minute to go and moved quickly down to the Wisconsin 18-yard line before time expired. Stokes set school and Rose Bowl records with 14 receptions for 176 yards. Moss paced the Badger running attack with 158 yards on 36 carries.

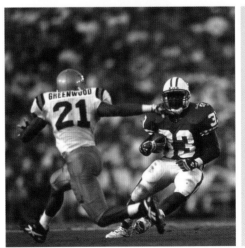

PRESS BOX FACTS

Two Rose Bowl-winning quarterbacks in the 1990s, Wisconsin's Darrell Bevell and USC's Brad Otton (1996 Rose Bowl) interrupted their college studies and football careers to serve voluntary church missions for two years.

BIG TEN CONFERENCE

ROSE BOWL GAME
1995
PENN STATE vs. OREGON

Danny O'Neil,
QB, Oregon

"Among many special memories from my Rose Bowl experience is the aura of the game itself. The Goodyear blimp covering the action from overhead, the stadium filled to capacity with both team's colors, and Keith Jackson calling the game on TV for a worldwide audience; just knowing that I was part of such a coveted bowl game is an honor. It meant a lot to have my family and friends there to share in the experience, and even my pastor there to pray with me before kick-off. Another impression that has stayed with me over the years is the massive effort by hundreds of Tournament of Roses volunteers involved in making our pre-game experience so memorable. We were treated like royalty at all of the activities such as Disneyland, Lawry's, and the Rose Bowl luncheon. They do a fantastic job!"

UNIVERSITY OF OREGON DUCKS
HEAD COACH: RICH BROOKS
1994 RECORD: 9-3 (7-1) PAC-10 CHAMPIONS

DATE	OPPONENT	RESULT
Sep 3	Portland State	W 58-16
Sep 10	at Hawaii	L 16-36
Sep 17	Utah	L 16-34
Sep 24	Iowa	W 40-18
Oct 1	at USC	W 22-7
Oct 8	at Washington State	L 7-21
Oct 15	California	W 23-7
Oct 22	Washington	W 31-20
Oct 29	Arizona	W 10-9
Nov 5	Arizona State	W 34-10
Nov 12	at Stanford	W 55-21
Nov 19	at Oregon State	W 17-13

Top left: Duck QB Danny O'Neil passes over the leaping #52 Willie Smith. Left center: Rose Bowl Stadium field the day before the game. Lower left: Josh Wilcox making one of his 11 receptions. Top right: Penn State's Ki-Jana Carter breaks free from Oregon's Troy Bailey for one of his big gains. Right center: Nittany Lion defense stuffs a Duck ball carrier. Far right: Penn State coach Joe Paterno.

The Rose Bowl Game had rarely seen the likes of the aerial bombardment that Oregon unleashed on the undefeated Big Ten champion Nittany Lions. QB Danny O'Neil's New Year's Day hailstorm broke five Rose Bowl offensive records: most passes completed (41) most attempts (61) most passing yards (456) most plays (74) and total offense (436 yards). The Ducks' game plan made for some happy receivers, too, notably Josh Wilcox (11 receptions, 135 yards, 1 TD) and Cristin McLemore (10, 90 yards, 1 TD).

If any team could withstand such an assault from the air, Penn State could. The Nittany Lions were battle-tested tough and knew their way around the big game scene. Led by two All-Americans on the offensive side of the ball, Penn State paced the nation in scoring with 47.8 points per game. They also had more on the line than just pride. Ranked #2 in the country, they had a shot at the national championship if Nebraska faltered in their bowl game. Less than four minutes into the game, All-

SCORE BY QUARTERS	1 - 2 - 3 - 4	FINAL SCORE
PENN STATE	7 - 7 - 14 - 10	38
OREGON	7 - 0 - 7 - 6	20

American running back Ki-Jana Carter (21 carries, 156 yards, 3 TDs) busted loose for an 83-yard touchdown on PSU's first play from scrimmage to establish a balanced attack that would end up yielding 228 yards on the ground and 202 more in the air.

Most fans don't recall this game was tied 14-14 midway through the third period. That's when Penn State opened the floodgates, perhaps blurring our perceptions of the first 40 minutes of the game. Ambrose Fletcher set up a 17-yard Carter score with a 72-yard kickoff return, and then Chuck Penzenik picked off his second pass of the game and returned it 44 yards to set up another Carter touchdown. The scoreboard was quiet for the space of 12 minutes before the N-Lions tacked on 10 more points to put the game out of reach at 38-14. Oregon managed one more score late in the fourth, but it was purely cosmetic. Penn State had reached zenith with a convincing victory, a perfect 12-0 record, and a Rose Bowl trophy to carry back to Happy Valley. The national championship, however, proved elusive.

PENN STATE UNIVERSITY NITTANY LIONS
HEAD COACH: JOE PATERNO
1994 RECORD: 11-0 (8-0) BIG TEN CHAMPIONS

DATE	OPPONENT	RESULT
Sep 3	at Minnesota	W 56-3
Sep 10	USC	W 38-14
Sep 17	Iowa	W 61-21
Sep 24	Rutgers	W 55-27
Oct 1	at Temple	W 48-21
Oct 15	at Michigan	W 31-24
Oct 29	Ohio State	W 63-14
Nov 5	at Indiana	W 35-29
Nov 12	at Illinois	W 35-31
Nov 19	Northwestern	W 45-17
Nov 26	Michigan State	W 59-31

Joe Paterno, Head Coach, Penn State

"I can't tell you how much going to the Rose Bowl means to me personally as well as to our people in Pennsylvania. There's an enthusiasm for Penn State football as a result of going to Pasadena that I can't describe. Over the years, I talked to 20, maybe 25, coaches who had been to different bowl games and to a man they told me that nothing compared with the Rose Bowl experience. Now that I'm here, I believe them. Nothing approaches it. Like they say, it's The Granddaddy of them all."

ROSE BOWL GAME

1996

USC vs. NORTHWESTERN

USC TROJANS
HEAD COACH: JOHN ROBINSON
1995 RECORD: 8-2-1 (6-1-1) PAC-10 CHAMPIONS

DATE	OPPONENT	RESULT
Sep 9	San Jose State	W 45-7
Sep 16	Houston	W 45-10
Sep 23	at Arizona	W 31-10
Sep 30	Arizona State	W 31-0
Oct 7	at California	W 26-16
Oct 14	Washington State	W 26-14
Oct 21	at Notre Dame	L 10-38
Oct 28	at Washington	T 21-21
Nov 4	Stanford	W 31-30
Nov 11	Oregon State	W 28-10
Nov 18	UCLA	L 20-24

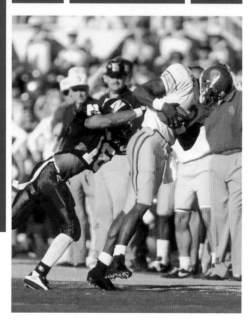

The Northwestern Wildcats were *the* Cinderella sports story of 1995, and perhaps the entire decade. Beginning with a monumental upset of 28-point favorite Notre Dame at South Bend (their first victory over the Irish since 1962) the 'Cats proceeded to sweep away forty-six years of Rose Bowl-less frustration with a perfect run through the Big Ten Conference schedule to win the coveted invitation to Pasadena. Northwestern's improbable journey also included wins over Michigan and Iowa for the first time since 1965 and 1973, respectively.

Nearly 50,000 NU fans poured into the Rose Bowl only to see their beloved Wildcats fall behind 14 points at halftime to the Rose Bowl tradition-rich USC Trojans. Playing without team captain and All-American linebacker Pat Fitzgerald, the Bednarik and Nagurski Award winner as best defensive player in the nation, Northwestern's highly rated defense (12.7 ppg, +1.82 turnover margin) struggled to find a neutralizing solution for the electrifying QB/WR duo of Brad Otton and Keyshawn Johnson.

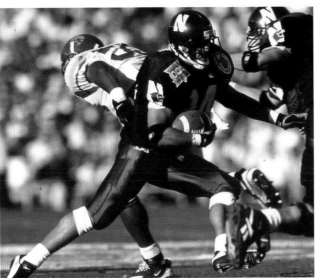

SCORE BY QUARTERS	1 - 2 - 3 - 4	FINAL SCORE
USC	7 - 17 - 7 - 10	41
NORTHWESTERN	7 - 3 - 16 - 6	32

NORTHWESTERN UNIVERSITY WILDCATS
HEAD COACH: GARY BARNETT
1995 RECORD: 10-1 (8-0) BIG TEN CHAMPIONS

DATE	OPPONENT	RESULT
Sep 2	at Notre Dame	W 17-15
Sep 16	Miami (Ohio)	L 28-30
Sep 23	Air Force	W 30-6
Sep 30	Indiana	W 31-7
Oct 7	at Michigan	W 19-13
Oct 14	at Minnesota	W 27-17
Oct 21	Wisconsin	W 35-0
Oct 28	at Illinois	W 17-14
Nov 4	Penn State	W 21-10
Nov 11	Iowa	W 31-20
Nov 18	at Purdue	W 23-8

Top left: Trojan QB Brad Otton passes behind excellent protection. Left center: USC's Delon Washington tries to reach the end zone in first half action. Lower left: USC's Keyshawn Johnson hauls in a pass defended by #16 Chris Martin. Top right: Northwestern receiver D'Wayne Bates looks for more yardage after a catch against #34 Ryan Tyiska. Right center: Wildcat RB Darnell Autry darts through a seam in the USC line for a gain.

Pat Fitzgerald,
LB, Northwestern

"My fondest memory is walking through the tunnel for the first time toward the field a few days before the game. The tunnel was dark but at the end you could see the bright California sunshine and a small glimpse of the playing surface. As a kid growing up in Chicago you dream of playing in the Granddaddy, and when I saw the end zone painted purple and NORTHWESTERN spelled out in white it was no longer a dream, it was reality. Words cannot describe my emotions at that time—and we had not even played the game yet!"

PRESS BOX FACTS

Tie games were eliminated in Division I-A and went into effect with the 1996 regular season. Bowl games were allowed to implement the tie-breaker system for 1995 contests and the tie-breaker was first used in the Las Vegas Bowl, where Toledo edged Nevada 40-37 in overtime.

The solution turned out to be the Wildcat offense, which was able to match USC almost blow-for-blow with offensive weapons Darnell Autry (32 carries, 110 yards, 3 TDs) QB Steve Schnur (23-39, 336 yards) and D'Wayne Bates (7 grabs, 145 yards). Unfortunately, the offense missed two field goals, had one TD called back on a penalty, and committed two turnovers that resulted in touchdowns for the Trojans. Daylon McCutcheon returned a Brian Musso fumble 53 yards for a TD in the second period, and USC converted Jesse Davis' 41-yard interception return into a score early in the fourth period after Northwestern had taken the lead at 32-31. The Wildcats outgained the Trojans in total yardage, 520 to 475, but in the end, too many offensive miscues and USC's air game (Otton: 29-44, 391 yards, 2 TDs & Johnson: 12 catches, 216 yards, 1 TD) were too much to overcome.

ROSE BOWL GAME

1997

OHIO STATE vs. ARIZONA STATE

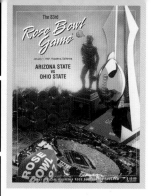

The 83rd
Rose Bowl Game

ARIZONA STATE
vs
OHIO STATE

Jake Plummer,
QB, Arizona State

"It was bittersweet because it kind of capped off a historical year that was really unbelievable. Our team was full of unselfish quality guys who all banded together throughout the year. It was a sweet season but it ended on a bad note. We wish we could have won it, but it was a season I'll never forget, and a game I'll never forget. The Rose Bowl, we all watched it growing up. It's 'The Granddaddy of them All' and we saw many, many games there, and to be playing in it finally—and Arizona State hadn't been in it for a long time, since they won it in '87—it was a huge game. A lot of the guys on our team were from California, but wherever you're from you've watched it growing up so it was huge to be playing in it."

ARIZONA STATE UNIVERSITY SUN DEVILS
HEAD COACH: BRUCE SNYDER
1996 RECORD: 11-0 (8-0) PAC-10 CHAMPIONS

DATE	OPPONENT	RESULT
Sep 7	Washington	W 45-42
Sep 14	North Texas	W 52-7
Sep 21	Nebraska	W 19-0
Sep 28	Oregon	W 48-27
Oct 5	Boise State	W 56-7
Oct 12	at UCLA	W 42-34
Oct 19	USC	W 48-35
Oct 26	at Stanford	W 41-9
Nov 2	at Oregon State	W 29-14
Nov 9	California	W 35-7
Nov 23	at Arizona	W 56-14

Top left: OL Orlando Pace and TE #89 D.J. Jones pass protect while ASU's #42 Pat Tillman blitzes in second half action. Left: Line of scrimmage action in the first half. Top right: Buckeye QB Joe Germaine passing from the pocket. Right center: OSU's David Boston celebrates his TD reception in the first quarter. Lower right: Sun Devil QB Jake Plummer wrapped up by LB Andy Katzenmoyer.

Ohio State held the Sun Devils to their lowest point total of the season with a dominating defense led by freshman linebacker Andy Katzenmoyer (3 sacks, 5 tackles for loss and one interception) leading the way. ASU's Jake "The Snake" Plummer was contained for most of the game and the Sun Devil running game ended up yielding just 75 yards on 41 carries.

The teams were deadlocked at halftime thanks to a first quarter 9-yard TD pass from the Bucks' Stanley Jackson to David Boston and Plummer's 25-yard scoring strike to Ricky Boyer in the second period. Arizona State took the lead in the third period on a 37-yard FG by Robert Nycz, but Ohio State snatched the lead right back moments later on a 72-yard touchdown pass from back-up QB Joe Germaine to Demetrious Stanley. It was the longest TD pass in the Buckeyes' bowl history.

The final quarter started slowly but turned out to be a barnburner. As the game clock reached the two-minute mark, Plummer made two incredible plays that appeared to give ASU the Rose

In memory of Patrick Daniel Tillman,
November 6, 1976–April 22, 2004
The Pat Tillman Foundation,
PO Box 20053, San Jose, California, 95160
www.pattillmanfoundation.net

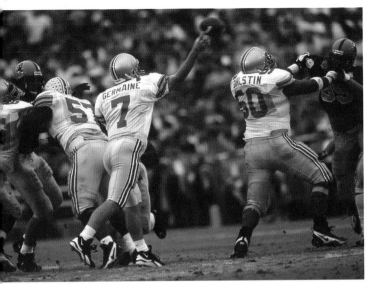

SCORE BY QUARTERS	1 - 2 - 3 - 4	FINAL SCORE
OHIO STATE	7 - 0 - 7 - 6	20
ARIZONA STATE	0 - 7 - 3 - 7	17

 OHIO STATE UNIVERSITY BUCKEYES
HEAD COACH: JOHN COOPER
1996 RECORD: 10-1 (7-1) BIG TEN CHAMPIONS

DATE	OPPONENT	RESULT
Sep 7	Rice	W 70-7
Sep 21	Pittsburgh	W 72-0
Sep 28	at Notre Dame	W 29-16
Oct 5	Penn State	W 38-7
Oct 12	Wisconsin	W 17-14
Oct 19	at Purdue	W 42-14
Oct 26	at Iowa	W 38-26
Nov 2	Minnesota	W 45-0
Nov 9	at Illinois	W 48-0
Nov 16	at Indiana	W 27-17
Nov 23	Michigan	L 9-13

Bowl Trophy and very likely, the national title. On fourth down, "The Snake" connected with Lenzie Jackson on a 29-yard pass that set up first-and-goal inside the Ohio State 10. Two plays later, on third-and-goal from the 11-yard line, he scrambled his way into the end zone for the go-ahead score. With 1:30 remaining, the Buckeyes set off on a miracle 12-play, 65-yard drive, helped out in large part by two third-down catches and two pass interference penalties. With just 19 seconds left on the clock, Germaine found David Boston open in the end zone for a 5-yard winning score.

**Joe Germaine,
QB, Ohio State**

"I grew up in Mesa, AZ and my family had ASU season football tickets. Some of my fondest memories as a kid were listening to the post-game radio show with my Dad on our drive home after a big win. It's pretty ironic that one of my favorite memories as a college player would occur against the Sun Devils. With 1:40 to go in the '97 Rose Bowl, we had the ball trailing ASU 17-14. As I stepped into the huddle for that last drive, the look in my teammates' eyes gave me instant confidence and we proceeded to march down the field in pursuit of victory. With few precious seconds remaining and the ball on ASU's 5-yard line I connected with David Boston for the winning score. We had won the Rose Bowl against a mighty Sun Devil squad—the same team I rooted for as a kid!"

ROSE BOWL GAME

1998

MICHIGAN vs. WASHINGTON STATE

Jason McEndoo, OL, Washington State

"We had one last shot starting at our 7-yard line with :29 seconds left. After two incomplete passes we still believed we could win it. On third down, Leaf completed a 46-yard rainbow pass to Nian Taylor at the Michigan 47. The call came in from the sideline: '590 Hook and Ladder.' We were surprised because we hadn't run that particular play all season. Desperate times call for desperate measures. Leaf completed the pass to Love Jefferson, who lateraled to Jason Clayton, who went out of bounds at the Michigan 26. The clock showed :02 seconds. We hustled to the line to spike the ball but the time expired. I remember pleading with the ref in disbelief after he blew his whistle to end the game while the Wolverines' bench came running out to celebrate. It is one of those moments that will be etched in my mind forever."

WASHINGTON STATE UNIVERSITY COUGARS
HEAD COACH: MIKE PRICE
1997 RECORD: 10-1 (7-1) PAC-10 CHAMPIONS

DATE	OPPONENT	RESULT
Aug 30	UCLA	W 37-34
Sep 13	at USC	W 28-21
Sep 20	at Illinois	W 35-22
Sep 27	Boise State	W 58-0
Oct 4	at Oregon	W 24-13
Oct 18	California	W 63-37
Oct 25	Arizona	W 35-34
Nov 1	at Arizona State	L 31-44
Nov 8	LA-Lafayette	W 77-7
Nov 15	Stanford	W 38-28
Nov 22	at Washington	W 41-35

Like father, like son. Thirty-one years after Bob Griese led Purdue to a victory in the Rose Bowl, his son Brian was in Pasadena on New Year's Day leading the Michigan Wolverines to a win over the Washington State Cougars. Like Purdue's close 14-13 win over USC in 1967, this was a nail-biter, too. The game was tied 7-7 at halftime, and Michigan held a 14-13 advantage after three periods. Trailing by five points with less than 30 seconds to play, Washington State moved sixty-seven yards to the Michigan 26-yard line before time ran out.

The Cougars took the lead early in the game on a six-play scoring drive culminating with Ryan Leaf's 15-yard TD toss to Kevin McKenzie. It was only the third touchdown Michigan had given up in the first period all year. The Wolverines responded with a 53-yard touchdown pass from Griese to Tai Streets in the second quarter to tie the game at the half. After stopping Michigan's second half opening drive, the Cougars drove 99 yards for the go-ahead score on Michael Tinis' 14-yard reverse run. Michigan blocked the extra point attempt and then Griese engineered an 80-yard drive capped off by a 58-yard TD pass to Streets to retake the lead after three periods.

The momentum clearly in their favor, Michigan chewed up over twelve minutes of the fourth quarter on two drives. The first drive covered 14 plays and five and a half minutes, the score coming off Griese's third touchdown pass of the game, this one to Jerame Tuman covering 23 yards. Following a Cougar field goal that tightened the score to 21-16, the Wolverines launched

SCORE BY QUARTERS	1 - 2 - 3 - 4	FINAL SCORE
MICHIGAN	0 - 7 - 7 - 7	21
WASHINGTON STATE	7 - 0 - 6 - 3	16

UNIVERSITY OF MICHIGAN WOLVERINES
HEAD COACH: LLOYD CARR
1997 RECORD: 11-0 (8-0) BIG TEN CHAMPIONS

DATE	OPPONENT	RESULT
Sep 13	Colorado	W 27-3
Sep 20	Baylor	W 38-3
Sep 27	Notre Dame	W 21-14
Oct 4	at Indiana	W 37-0
Oct 11	Northwestern	W 23-6
Oct 18	Iowa	W 28-24
Oct 25	at Michigan State	W 23-7
Nov 1	Minnesota	W 24-3
Nov 8	at Penn State	W 34-8
Nov 15	at Wisconsin	W 26-16
Nov 22	Ohio State	W 20-14

Jon Jansen, OL, Michigan

"I've tried to put into words what it means and what it is like to be a part of Rose Bowl history. It can't possibly be done. I spent my whole life dreaming and working towards one goal: Win a Big Ten Championship and win the Rose Bowl. It is one goal, because one doesn't mean as much without the other. I have no way of explaining the joy and ultimate feeling of success that comes with the successful completion of such a goal. There is a bond that can never be broken among the teammates who attain this goal. It is a bond that only becomes stronger with time because you realize how difficult it was to attain."

a 16-play drive covering nearly seven minutes that left WSU without enough time to reach the end zone again. Griese was 18 of 30 for 251 yards and 3 TDs. Streets accounted for two of those touchdowns and finished with 4 receptions for 127 yards. Leaf was 17 of 35 for 331 yards and one score. His lone interception came at the hands of Heisman Trophy winner Charles Woodson. Michigan finished the season 12-0 and undefeated and untied for the first time since the 1948, splitting the national championship with Nebraska.

Top center: Washington State QB Ryan Leaf is sacked by Wolverine LB Dhani Jones in the first half. Top left: A 1998 Rose Princess and two Cougar players at the Lawry's Beef Bowl. Lower left: Ryan Leaf poised to pass. Top right: Michigan receiver Tai Streets streaks toward his first TD and jubilant fans in end zone seats. Top far right: Charles Woodson returns a punt. Right center: QB Brian Griese, 1998 Rose Bowl Game MVP.

ROSE BOWL GAME
1999
WISCONSIN vs. UCLA

UCLA BRUINS
HEAD COACH: BOB TOLEDO
1998 RECORD: 10-1 (8-0) PAC-10 CHAMPIONS

DATE	OPPONENT	RESULT
Sep 12	Texas	W 49-31
Sep 19	at Houston	W 42-24
Oct 3	Washington State	W 49-17
Oct 10	at Arizona	W 52-28
Oct 17	Oregon	W 41-38
Oct 24	at California	W 28-16
Oct 31	Stanford	W 28-24
Nov 7	at Oregon State	W 41-34
Nov 14	at Washington	W 36-24
Nov 21	USC	W 34-17
Dec 5	at Miami (FL)	L 45-49

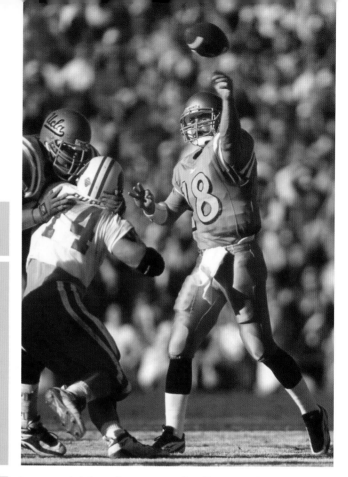

In a re-match from five years earlier, there was keen interest in how UCLA's high-scoring offense (40.5 points per game) would match up against a smothering Wisconsin defense that had limited seven opponents to 7 points or less during the season. The Bruins' offense didn't disappoint (538 total yards) and neither did the Badgers' (497) as both teams ended up combining for a Rose Bowl record of most yards gained (1,035 yards).

The bulk of the scoring took place in the first half with Wisconsin holding a 24-21 lead at the break. The Badgers were grinding up most of their yardage on the ground with Ron Dayne taking the pigskin to the market three times on runs of 54, 7 and 10 yards respectively. UCLA preferred to air it out and Cade McNown launched scoring strikes of 38 yards to Jermaine Lewis and 41 yards to Danny Farmer. Freddie Mitchell also got into the act with a 61-yard bomb to Durell Price on a halfback option. Wisconsin added a 40-yard field goal to round out the first half fireworks.

SCORE BY QUARTERS	1 - 2 - 3 - 4	FINAL SCORE
WISCONSIN	7 - 17 - 7 - 7	38
UCLA	7 - 14 - 7 - 3	31

Taking up where he left off, Dayne punched in his fourth TD of the day from 22 yards out in the third period. UCLA countered with Lewis' second score of the day, this time on a 12-yard run. Less than a minute into the final frame, Jamar Fletcher picked off a McNown pass near midfield and raced 46 yards for the score. After a Bruin field goal cut the deficit to seven, UCLA got the ball back with less than two minutes to go. McNown and Co. managed to drive to the Badger 47-yard line, but Wisconsin's defense came up with a sack on fourth down to seal the victory. Dayne ended up with 246 yards rushing, one shy of the Rose Bowl record, and McNown was 19 of 34 for 340 yards passing. Badger QB Mike Samuel had 65 yards on 13 carries and passed for 154 more yards. Danny Farmer (7 catches, 142 yards) was McNown's favorite target.

UNIVERSITY OF WISCONSIN BADGERS
HEAD COACH: BARRY ALVAREZ
1998 RECORD: 10-1 (7-1) BIG TEN CHAMPIONS

DATE	OPPONENT	RESULT
Sep 5	at San Diego St.	W 26-14
Sep 12	Ohio	W 45-0
Sep 19	UNLV	W 52-7
Sep 26	Northwestern	W 38-7
Oct 3	at Indiana	W 24-20
Oct 10	Purdue	W 31-24
Oct 17	at Illinois	W 37-3
Oct 24	at Iowa	W 31-0
Nov 7	Minnesota	W 26-7
Nov 14	at Michigan	L 10-27
Nov 21	Penn State	W 24-3

Top left: UCLA QB Cade McNown goes deep in the first half. Lower left: Bruin receiver Freddie Mitchell fights for possession with Badger CB Jamar Fletcher near the goal line in the first half. Far left: Bruin Kris Farris served by a trio of Rose Princesses at the Lawry's Beef Bowl. Top right: Badger RB Ron Dayne darts through a seam in the line. Right center: Wisconsin's QB Mike Samuel is hit by a Bruin lineman as he passes the ball.

Ron Dayne, RB, Wisconsin

"The Rose Bowl is such a huge game to play in. I remember a lot of Badger red at both our games because we have a big fan following. The whole experience was just fun. My strongest memory was being named the MVP two years in a row and receiving the crystal rose. I still try to watch it every year, even if I don't know anyone playing in the game. We didn't get to see the Rose Parade (in person) but we got to see it on TV, so that is a big part of my Rose Bowl memory, too."

ROSE BOWL GAME
2000
WISCONSIN vs. STANFORD

Todd Husak, Q.B. Stanford

"Both personally and as a team, the Rose Bowl was a culmination of so much hard work and overcoming adversity. We were picked to finish 8th in the Pac-10, we got crushed in our opening game to Texas. We had a bunch of no-names and over-achievers on our squad. Stanford was the only scholarship offer I received and consensus All-American Troy Walters had one other offer—quite a difference from the teams we played. It was also the first time Stanford had played in Pasadena on New Year's Day in 28 years. To be able to go back home to southern California (I'm from Long Beach) and be a part of something as meaningful and tradition-rich as the Rose Bowl Game with that group of guys was the most rewarding part of the experience."

STANFORD CARDINAL
HEAD COACH: TY WILLINGHAM
1999 RECORD: 8-3 (7-1) PAC-10 CHAMPIONS

DATE	OPPONENT	RESULT
Sep 4	at Texas	L 17-69
Sep 11	Washington State	W 54-17
Sep 18	at Arizona	W 50-22
Sep 25	UCLA	W 42-32
Oct 2	San Jose State	L 39-44
Oct 16	Oregon State	W 21-17
Oct 23	at USC	W 35-31
Oct 30	at Washington	L 30-35
Nov 13	at Arizona State	W 50-30
Nov 20	California	W 31-13
Nov 27	Notre Dame	W 40-37

This game figured to be as much of an offensive display as the previous year's Rose Bowl since Stanford was averaging 37.2 points per game and Wisconsin was scoring at a 35.6 ppg clip. The points never materialized, though. Aside from Ron Dayne's 200 yards rushing and Todd Husak's 258 yards passing, the most notable aspect of the game was that there were no turnovers committed by either team. No pass interceptions, no fumbles. Zero. That's practically unheard of in post-season bowl competition where turnover margins frequently dictate who takes home the trophy.

However, there were two muffed kicks on Stanford's part that might have altered the outcome. The first was a botched extra point in the second quarter after Kerry Carter scored on a one-yard run to put the Cardinal up 9-3. The second kicking snafu occurred in the third period after Dayne had scored on a 4-yard run to help Wisconsin take a one-point lead, 10-9. Stanford mounted an impressive drive aided by a Husak-to-DeRonnie Pitts 30-yard pass completion that advanced to the Badger six-yard line before stalling. Mike Biselli was called on to retake the lead with a 23-yard field goal attempt. Once again, an errant center snap affected the ball placement and Badger Mike Echols blocked the kick.

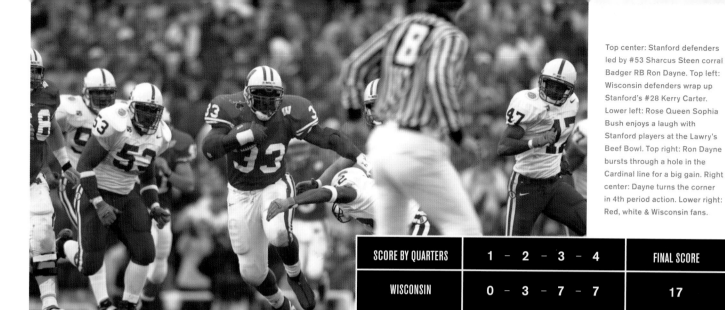

SCORE BY QUARTERS	1 - 2 - 3 - 4	FINAL SCORE
WISCONSIN	0 - 3 - 7 - 7	17
STANFORD	0 - 9 - 0 - 0	9

Wisconsin added to their lead in the final period on a Brooks Bollinger 1-yard sneak. Still in the game with only an 8-point deficit, Husak led Stanford into Badger territory with about a minute left before a fourth-down sack put this one in the history books. The Badgers became the first Big Ten team ever to win the Rose Bowl Game two years in a row, and the first Big Ten team to win three Rose Bowl games within the span of six years. Dayne's 200 yards gave him 446 yards on 61 carries for his Rose Bowl career, just 14 yards shy of the record set by USC's Charles White in three Rose Bowl games (1977-79-80, 103 carries).

UNIVERSITY OF WISCONSIN BADGERS
HEAD COACH: BARRY ALVAREZ
1999 RECORD: 9-2 (7-1) BIG TEN CHAMPIONS

DATE	OPPONENT	RESULT
Sep 4	Murray St.	W 49-10
Sep 11	Ball State	W 50-10
Sep 18	at Cincinnati	L 12-17
Sep 25	Michigan	L 16-21
Oct 2	at Ohio State	W 42-17
Oct 9	at Minnesota	W 20-17
Oct 16	Indiana	W 59-0
Oct 23	Michigan State	W 40-10
Oct 30	at Northwestern	W 35-19
Nov 6	at Purdue	W 28-21
Nov 13	Iowa	W 41-3

Jamar Fletcher, DB, Wisconsin

"Since it was our second year in a row at the Rose Bowl, we felt more comfortable. It gave us a second chance to see all the sights and experience all the things we didn't get to the previous year before. Coming into the 1999 game we felt disrespected. All the talk was about UCLA. Against Stanford, it was a completely different situation. All the talk was about us, and how we were expected to win big. I'm sure Stanford felt like they weren't getting any respect. They played us very tough. It was huge to get that win with so much pressure on us."

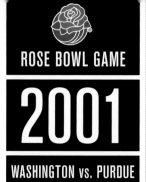

ROSE BOWL GAME
2001
WASHINGTON vs. PURDUE

THE 87TH ROSE BOWL GAME
TEAM 1 VS TEAM 2

SCORE BY QUARTERS	1 - 2 - 3 - 4	FINAL SCORE
WASHINGTON	14 - 0 - 6 - 14	34
PURDUE	0 - 10 - 7 - 7	24

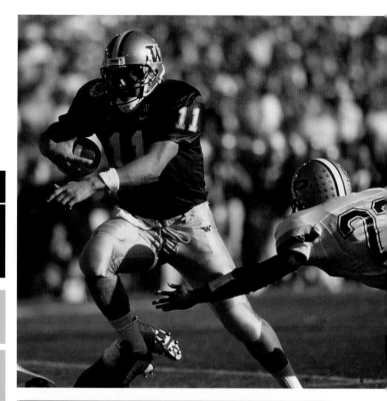

Marques Tuiasosopo, QB, Washington

"One of my favorite memories of the Rose Bowl was when Chad Ward, Larry Triplett, and myself were walking out to midfield for the coin toss. It was an amazing sight. There wasn't an empty seat in the stadium, the atmosphere was buzzing, and then these Air Force jets came screaming over our heads. The crowd went wild and I got goose bumps. It was the loudest stadium of fans I have ever experienced—and then it hit me that this was the Big Time."

UNIVERSITY OF WASHINGTON HUSKIES
HEAD COACH: RICK NEUHEISEL
2000 RECORD: 10-1 (7-1) PAC-10 CHAMPIONS

DATE	OPPONENT	RESULT
Sep 2	Idaho	W 44-20
Sep 9	Miami (FL)	W 34-29
Sep 16	at Colorado	W 17-14
Sep 30	at Oregon	L 16-23
Oct 7	at Oregon State	W 33-30
Oct 14	at Arizona State	W 21-15
Oct 21	California	W 36-24
Oct 28	at Stanford	W 31-28
Nov 4	Arizona	W 35-32
Nov 11	UCLA	W 35-28
Nov 18	at Washington State	W 51-3

PURDUE UNIVERSITY BOILERMAKERS
HEAD COACH: JOE TILLER
2000 RECORD: 8-3 (6-2) BIG TEN TRI-CHAMPIONS

DATE	OPPONENT	RESULT
Sep 2	Central Michigan	W 48-0
Sep 9	Kent State	W 45-10
Sep 16	at Notre Dame	L 21-23
Sep 23	Minnesota	W 38-24
Sep 30	at Penn State	L 20-22
Oct 7	Michigan	W 32-31
Oct 14	at Northwestern	W 41-28
Oct 21	at Wisconsin	W 30-24 OT
Oct 28	Ohio State	W 31-27
Nov 11	at Michigan State	L 10-30
Nov 18	at Indiana	W 41-13

Washington QB Marques Tuiasosopo shook off an injury to his throwing shoulder in the second half to lead the Huskies to two fourth quarter touchdowns and a 34-24 victory over Purdue and the vaunted Boilermaker passing attack. Purdue had fallen behind 14-0 early in the game, but rallied to tie the score at 17 in the third quarter. Drew Brees was 23 of 39 for 275 yards and two scoring passes to Vinny Sutherland. Sutherland had 7 grabs for 88 yards and 68 more yards on kick-off returns including a 51-yarder that he nearly broke for pay dirt.

The Huskies dedicated their game performance to Curtis Williams, a fifth-year senior safety from Fresno, who was paralyzed from the neck down during Washington's conference game at Stanford two months earlier. Teammates wore his initials on their jerseys and Williams spent several minutes with them in an emotional locker room before the game. Coach Rick Neuheisel joined a rare circle of coaches who had also tasted victory in the Rose Bowl as players. Tuiasosopo was named MVP of the game, finishing 16 of 22, 138 yards, 1 TD, and 75 yards rushing on 15 carries for another score.

Top left: Washington QB Marques Tuiasosopo cuts to evade Purdue DB Chris Clopton. Left center: Husky TE Jerramy Stevens finds a seam in Purdue's zone while #16 Gilbert Gardner closes in. Lower left: Rose Parade Grand Marshal Tom Brokaw with Tournament of Roses President Lorne J. Brown. Top right: Purdue QB Drew Brees looks downfield while #54 Rob Turner tries to give him more time to throw. Far right: TE Tim Stratton lifts up WR Vinny Sutherland after one of his TDs. Lower right: Drew Brees answers questions from the media at the Lawry's Beef Bowl.

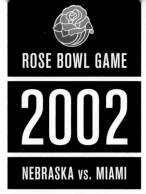

ROSE BOWL GAME

2002

NEBRASKA vs. MIAMI

THE 88TH ROSE BOWL GAME
NATIONAL CHAMPIONSHIP

2002

$10

NEBRASKA VS. OKLAHOMA

SCORE BY QUARTERS	1 - 2 - 3 - 4	FINAL SCORE
NEBRASKA	0 - 0 - 7 - 7	14
MIAMI	7 - 27 - 0 - 3	37

Pete Fiutak's "Stream of Consciousness Notes" live blog on collegefootballnews.com, referring to Keith Jackson's ABC Sports television commentary with Miami leading the 2002 Rose Bowl 34-0 at halftime

"Jackson: 'The mountain is pretty big right now for the Nebraska Cornhuskers.' Dude, that's nothing compared to the rock you're going to have to climb to come up with enough filler material for the second half."

UNIVERSITY OF NEBRASKA CORNHUSKERS
HEAD COACH: FRANK SOLICH
2001 RECORD: 10-1 (7-1) BIG12

DATE	OPPONENT	RESULT
Aug 25	TCU	W 21-7
Sep 1	Troy	W 42-14
Sep 8	Notre Dame	W 27-10
Sep 15	Postponed vs. Rice	
Sep 20	Rice	W 48-3
Sep 29	at Missouri	W 36-3
Oct 6	Iowa State	W 48-14
Oct 13	at Baylor	W 48-7
Oct 20	Texas Tech	W 41-31
Oct 27	Oklahoma	W 20-10
Nov 3	at Kansas	W 51-7
Nov 10	Kansas State	W 31-21
Nov 23	at Colorado	L 36-62

Top left: Nebraska RB Dahrran Diedrick fights his way through Miami defenders. Left center: Rose Parade Grand Marshal Regis Philbin escorted by Tournament of Roses President Ron Okum and his wife Nan during pre-game festivities. Lower left: Cornhusker cheerleaders and band members at halftime. Top right: Miami QB Ken Dorsey looks for an open receiver in the end zone. Top far right: Hurricane cheerleader. Middle far right: Heisman Trophy-winning QB Eric Crouch finds himself boxed in by Miami's Howard Clark. Lower right: Miami WR Andre Johnson hauls in a sideline pass.

It was the first Rose Bowl Game since 1946 to feature teams other than the traditional match-up of Big Ten and Pac-10 champions, and it created quite an uproar among fans because the Oregon Ducks were ranked #2 in both the coaches and sportswriters polls at the end of the regular season. The Bowl Championship Series (BCS) computers didn't process it that way, though, and pitted their #2 rated Nebraska vs. Everyone's #1 Miami.

UNIVERSITY OF MIAMI HURRICANES
HEAD COACH: LARRY COKER
2001 RECORD: 11-0 (7-0) BIG EAST CHAMPIONS

DATE	OPPONENT	RESULT
Sep 1	at Penn State	W 33-7
Sep 8	Rutgers	W 61-0
Sep 15	Postponed vs. Washington	
Sep 27	at Pittsburgh	W 43-21
Oct 6	Troy State	W 38-7
Oct 13	at Florida State	W 49-27
Oct 25	West Virginia	W 45-3
Nov 3	Temple	W 38-0
Nov 10	at Boston College	W 18-7
Nov 17	Syracuse	W 59-0
Nov 24	Washington	W 65-7
Dec 1	at Virginia Tech	W 26-24

The Hurricanes didn't care about the new brew of BCS hullabaloo. They were still steaming about the BCS computers leaving them out of the national championship game the previous year and felt like they had a score to settle. By halftime, they had amassed a 34-point lead over the Cornhuskers, dominating in every phase of the game.

QB Ken Dorsey completed 22 of 35 passes for 362 yards and 3 TDs, Andre Johnson hauled in 7 passes for 199 yards and two scores, and Clinton Portis picked up 104 yards on 20 carries as Miami rolled up 472 total yards. Nebraska's Heisman Trophy-winning QB Eric Crouch ran 22 times for 114 yards and completed 5 of 15 passes for 62 yards, but the Husker option was bottled up most of the game and finished with 259 total yards.

ROSE BOWL GAME

2003

OKLAHOMA vs. WASHINGTON STATE

Rien Long,
DE, Washington State

"After polishing off three huge cuts of prime rib at the Beef Bowl, I was told there wasn't any more. I was dismayed. Wasn't this a contest to see who could eat more beef between the Cougars and the Sooners? At that moment, I was asked to take a photo with Jason Gesser and the Rose Queen. I happily agreed, and there in the adjacent room where the pictures were to be taken I noticed a couple of silver carts. I sat down at the table with a suspicious eye on the silver carts, and of course, one eye on the Queen. Sure enough, they flipped up the lids on the carts and to my astonishment I saw several racks of prime rib. They proceeded to carve a couple slices and set them on plates in front of us as props in the photos. Need-less to say, I was pretty perturbed of a limit being placed on us because I was still hungry."

WASHINGTON STATE UNIVERSITY
HEAD COACH: MIKE PRICE
2002 RECORD: 10-2 (7-1) PAC-10 CHAMPIONS

DATE	OPPONENT	RESULT
Aug 31	Nevada	W 31-7
Sep 7	Idaho	W 49-14
Sep 14	at Ohio State	L 7-25
Sep 21	Montana State	W 45-28
Sep 28	at California	W 48-38
Oct 5	USC	W 30-27
Oct 12	at Stanford	W 36-11
Oct 26	at Arizona	W 21-13
Nov 2	Arizona State	W 44-22
Nov 9	Oregon	W 32-21
Nov 23	Washington	L 26-29
Dec 7	at UCLA	W 48-27

Top left: Washington State QB Jason Gesser lofts a pass downfield in the first half over the arms of #96 Lynn McGruder. Left center: Cougar defenders wrap up Oklahoma's Quentin Griffin. Lower left: Outland Trophy winner Rien Long and Jason Gesser pose with Rose Queen Alexandra Wucetich at the Lawry's Beef Bowl. Top right: Sooner QB Nate Hybl hands off to Quentin Griffin. Top far right: Sooner fan, obviously. Lower right: Personal photo mentioned in Chuck Long's recollection taken after the game: Chuck Long, Bob Stoops, Jonathan Hayes and Mike Stoops.

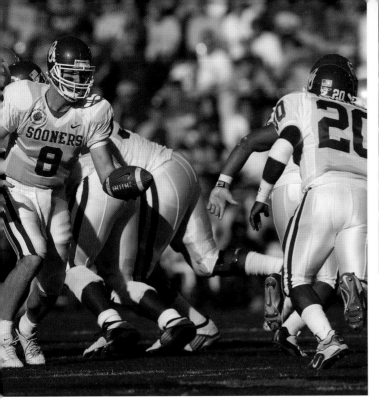

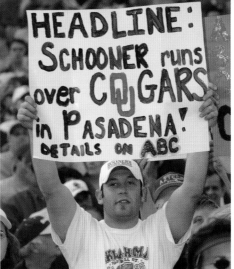

SCORE BY QUARTERS	1	-	2	-	3	-	4	FINAL SCORE
OKLAHOMA	3	-	14	-	3	-	14	34
WASHINGTON STATE	0	-	0	-	0	-	14	14

For the second year in a row, the Bowl Championship Series left the Rose Bowl without its traditional Big Ten/Pac-10 showdown. Led by QB Nate Hybl (19–29, 239 yards, 2 TDs) and RB Quentin Griffin (30 carries, 144 yards, 1 TD) the Sooners' first ever visit to the Rose Bowl was a smashing success. Oklahoma took a 27-0 lead into the middle of the fourth quarter until Jason Gesser connected with Jerome Riley on a 37-yard touchdown pass with just over six minutes to play. Sammy Moore returned a kickoff 89 yards for Washington State's final score. Washington State head coach Mike Price announced he was leaving for Alabama the week before the game and the Cougars' longtime defensive coordinator Bill Doba was named as his replacement.

UNIVERSITY OF OKLAHOMA SOONERS
HEAD COACH: BOB STOOPS
2002 RECORD: 11-2 (7-2) BIG 12 CHAMPIONS

DATE	OPPONENT	RESULT
Aug 30	at Tulsa	W 37-0
Sep 7	Alabama	W 37-27
Sep 14	Texas-El Paso	W 68-0
Sep 28	South Florida	W 31-14
Oct 5	at Missouri	W 31-24
Oct 12	Texas (at Dallas)	W 35-24
Oct 19	Iowa State	W 49-3
Nov 2	Colorado	W 27-11
Nov 9	at Texas A&M	L 26-30
Nov 16	at Baylor	W 49-9
Nov 23	Texas Tech	W 60-15
Nov 30	at Oklahoma State	L 28-38
Dec 7	Colorado (at Houston)	W 29-7

Chuck Long, Offensive Coordinator, Oklahoma

"Growing up in Big Ten country as kids, it was a dream come true to play for Iowa in the Rose Bowl. The final outcome of the '82 and '86 games still gnaw at my competitive spirit. But as former Hawkeyes, Bob and Mike Stoops, Jonathan Hayes, and myself all like to joke about how we had to get to the Big 12 as coaches to win the 'The Granddaddy of them all.' We made sure we took a photo of the four of us on the field after that 2003 Rose Bowl victory!"

ROSE BOWL GAME
2004
USC vs. MICHIGAN

USC vs. MICHIGAN
90th Rose Bowl Game
JANUARY 1, 2004

SCORE BY QUARTERS	1 - 2 - 3 - 4	FINAL SCORE
USC	7 - 7 - 14 - 0	28
MICHIGAN	0 - 0 - 7 - 7	14

Matt Leinart, QB, USC

"Michigan had just answered one of our scores with a touchdown, which could have changed the momentum. But on our next series, Norm Chow called for a trick play and it worked. I handed off to Hershel Dennis, who swept right, and then he tossed it back to Mike Williams on a reverse as I snuck out of the backfield. Mike threw a perfect pass to me and all I could think was, 'Don't drop it.' I was all alone along the left sideline and scored. That play sealed our victory and the photo of it was everywhere the next day. It's something I'll always remember."

Trojans
SC

USC TROJANS
HEAD COACH: PETE CARROLL
2003 RECORD: 11-1 (7-1) PAC-10 CHAMPIONS

DATE	OPPONENT	RESULT
Aug 30	at Auburn	W 23-0
Sep 6	BYU	W 35-18
Sep 13	Hawaii	W 61-32
Sep 27	at California	L 31-34, 3OT
Oct 4	at Arizona State	W 37-17
Oct 11	Stanford	W 44-21
Oct 18	at Notre Dame	W 45-14
Oct 25	at Washington	W 43-23
Nov 1	Washington State	W 43-16
Nov 15	at Arizona	W 45-0
Nov 22	UCLA	W 47-22
Dec 6	Oregon State	W 52-28

USC jumped out to a 21-0 lead and withstood a Michigan challenge in the second half to claim the 2004 Associated Press national title. Two Wolverine turnovers resulted in USC's two first half touchdowns. USC defensive lineman Shaun Cody blocked an attempted field goal on the Wolverines' opening possession and USC LB Lofa Tatupu grabbed a pass that bounced off Braylon Edwards' heel deep in Michigan territory near the end of the second quarter.

Both teams relied heavily on their air attacks when their rushing games sputtered. USC ended up with 68 yards on the ground and Michigan had 49. USC's Matt Leinart completed 23 of his 34 pass attempts for 327 yards and three touchdowns—two of those to Keary Colbert. Leinart also scored on the receiving end of a trick pass play from WR Mike Williams in the fourth quarter that turned the momentum in favor of the Trojans for good. Wolverine QB John Navarre was 27 of 46 for 271 yards and one TD but he was sacked nine times for 69 lost yards. His favorite target, Braylon Edwards, had 10 receptions for 107 yards.

UNIVERSITY OF MICHIGAN WOLVERINES
HEAD COACH: LLOYD CARR
2003 RECORD: 10-2 (7-1) BIG TEN CHAMPIONS

DATE	OPPONENT	RESULT
Aug 30	Central Michigan	W 45-7
Sep 6	Houston	W 50-3
Sep 13	Notre Dame	W 38-0
Sep 20	at Oregon	L 27-31
Sep 27	Indiana	W 31-17
Oct 4	at Iowa	L 27-30
Oct 10	at Minnesota	W 38-35
Oct 18	at Illinois	W 56-14
Oct 25	Purdue	W 31-3
Nov 1	at Michigan State	W 27-20
Nov 15	at Northwestern	W 41-10
Nov 22	Ohio State	W 35-21

Top left: Trojan QB Matt Leinart scores on a flea-flicker play in the third period. Left center: USC cheerleaders greet their players at the Lawry's Beef Bowl. Lower left: WR Keary Colbert snares his second TD reception. Top right: Michigan RB Chris Perry fights for more yardage against Trojan's #58 Roy Manning. Lower right: Michigan's Tyler Ecker and David Baas sing a duet at the Lawry's Beef Bowl.

John Navarre, QB, Michigan

"While we were waiting to be served at Lawry's we chanted for two of our players (infamous for their a capella style of singing) to go up to the podium and perform the National Anthem. Tyler Ecker and David Baas did a great job and gave everyone a good laugh. Later in the event, Jason Avant ended up getting booed off the stage because he sang so poorly."

ROSE BOWL GAME
2005
TEXAS vs. MICHIGAN

SCORE BY QUARTERS	1	2	3	4	FINAL SCORE
TEXAS	7	7	7	17	38
MICHIGAN	0	14	17	6	37

Texas Coach Mack Brown at the 2004 Lawry's Beef Bowl

"Mr. Frank and I had dinner at Lawry's in Dallas last year, and he said, 'You ought to come try our Beverly Hills restaurant some time.' Well, you probably didn't think I'd take your invitation so seriously, but here I am—and I brought the whole team with me!"

UNIVERSITY OF TEXAS LONGHORNS
HEAD COACH: MACK BROWN
2004 RECORD: 10-1 (7-1)

DATE	OPPONENT	RESULT
Sep 4	North Texas	W 65-0
Sep 11	at Arkansas	W 22-20
Sep 25	Rice	W 35-13
Oct 2	Baylor	W 44-14
Oct 9	at (2) Oklahoma	L 0-12
Oct 16	Missouri	W 28-20
Oct 23	at (23) Texas Tech	W 51-21
Oct 30	at Colorado	W 31-7
Nov 6	Oklahoma State	W 56-35
Nov 13	at Kansas	W 27-23
Nov 26	(22) Texas A&M	W 26-13

Michigan entered the 2005 Rose Bowl ranked first in college football all-time victories with 842 and Texas came in ranked fourth with 787 wins. Although it took more than 100 years for these elite programs to meet on the field, their first clash was a thriller. With flashbulbs popping throughout the stadium, Texas kicker Dusty Mangum sent a partially tipped, wobbly kick through the uprights as the final two seconds ticked off the clock to give the Longhorns a 38-37 victory.

The game had a colorful cast of heroes and record breakers. Texas quarterback Vince Young ran for 192 yards and four touchdowns while passing for 180 yards and another score on his way to receiving the Rose Bowl MVP award. Michigan's freshman quarterback Chad Henne tied a Rose Bowl record with four touchdown passes, three to All-American wide receiver Braylon Edwards, who shattered several Rose Bowl career receiving records. Michigan's Garrett Rivas kicked three field goals, the last a 42-yarder with 3:04 remaining to give Michigan a 37-35 lead, and Wolverine Steve Breaston set a Rose Bowl record with 315 total yards between pass receptions and dazzling kick returns.

Top left: A Longhorn lineman chows down at Lawry's Beef Bowl. Left center: Texas QB Vince Young races in for one of his 4 TDs. Top right: Rose Parade Grand Marshal Mickey Mouse flips the coin to determine who will receive the opening kick-off. Joining Tournament of Roses President Dave Davis in the circle are legendary retired coaches Darrell Royal of Texas and Bo Schembechler of Michigan and Michigan DB Marlin Jackson and Texas LB Derrick Johnson. Far right: Braylon Edwards secures the ball for one of his 3 TD receptions.

Lawry's issued the first ever Rose Bowl trading cards at the 2004 Beef Bowl events honoring 2005 Rose Bowl participants Michigan and Texas. These cards were designed and produced by custom-sportscards.com and limited to an issue of 1,000 cards per team.

The rear of each card features the respective team's 2004 schedule/results, coach's all-time record, all-time bowl record, Rose Bowl record, all-time victories, and the Lawry's Beef Bowl logo.

UNIVERSITY OF MICHIGAN WOLVERINES
HEAD COACH: LLOYD CARR
2004 RECORD: 9-2 (7-1) BIG TEN CO-CHAMPION

DATE	OPPONENT	RESULT
Sep 4	Miami (OH)	W 43-10
Sep 11	at Notre Dame	L 20-28
Sep 18	San Diego State	W 24-21
Sep 25	(11) Iowa	W 30-17
Oct 2	at Indiana	W 35-14
Oct 9	Minnesota	W 27-24
Oct 16	at Illinois	W 30-19
Oct 23	at Purdue	W 16-14
Oct 30	Michigan State	W 45-37
Nov 13	Northwestern	W 42-20
Nov 20	at (24) Ohio State	L 21-37

Michigan All-American receiver Braylon Edwards, autographing a 2004 Lawry's Beef Bowl program

"I'll bet this is probably gonna end up on E-Bay tomorrow morning, huh?"

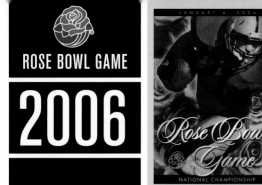

ROSE BOWL GAME

2006

Visit www.roadtotherosebowl.com after January 16 to download
the 2006 Rose Bowl Game information for this book

PRESS
BOX
FACTS

Visit www.roadtotherosebowl.com after January 16 to download
the 2006 Rose Bowl Game information for this book

1957

Ken Ploen, QB, Iowa

Playing in a Rose Bowl game representing the U. of Iowa was a boyhood dream growing up in Clinton, Iowa. The Iowa Hawkeye's had never represented the Big Ten in the Rose Bowl and to actually be there playing for Iowa didn't sink in until they opened our dressing room door and entered the tunnel leading to the field. That's when an unbelievable feeling went through me. It is indescribable, a feeling not felt prior to this game or since. You had to be part of this Iowa team to experience it.

Coach Evashevski's last words prior to the opening kick-off: "Give me 60 minutes of unrelenting pressure and you will have a lifetime to remember." The rest is history.

Randy Duncan, QB, Iowa

One of my great memories was the 1957 Rose Bowl when I was a sophomore. A West Coast writer was interviewing my teammates asking what they would like for Christmas. Invariably, everyone wanted a victory over Oregon State. I told the writer I wanted a date with Jayne Mansfield. She appeared at the Big Ten banquet and called me up to the podium. Being an unsophisticated kid from Iowa, I gave her a kiss that lasted for some time (at least I thought so). I gained instant admiration and envy from my teammates, and the picture of me kissing Jayne Mansfield hit the wire services. I received more mail and phone calls from that moment than from any game I ever played.

Left: University of Iowa press photo of QB Kenny Ploen. Right: Hawkeye QB Randy Duncan gets his Christmas wish at the Big Ten banquet and meets movie star Jayne Mansfield.

Ray Jauch, HB, Iowa

Where else in your life would you be able to meet Mickey Mouse, make a pass at Alice in Wonderland, date a Rose Bowl Princess, meet Louie Prima and Keely Smith, play football before more than 100,000 spectators, win the game and finish #1 in the country?

Willie Fleming, HB, Iowa

Rose Bowl memories? After breaking curfew one night before the game we were punished by running the same play against our defense about 10 times straight in the hot California sun—we were thoroughly trounced... I remember coming on the field through the tunnel and seeing the tens of thousands of people in the stands so close by, and wishing that we could hurry up and get the game started...I remember forming a lasting friendship with Joe Kapp that continues to this day... My most lasting memory is meeting my future wife and 45 years later we're still sharing some of those Rose Bowl moments.

Joe Kapp, QB/DB, California

Our Cal '59 Rose Bowl team was distinguished by its lack of apparent distinction. However, look closely and you see why the Pacific Coast Conference Champions overcame all challenges, and challengers.

We played the Big Ten's Iowa Hawkeyes with the smallest line (avg. 196 lbs.) in Rose Bowl modern times. We had lost our preseason all-American candidate, Bob Chiappone 6'4", 240 lbs. before the season even started. We played the split-T and lost to the Hawkeyes playing the wing-T. The Iowa lineman probably ate more pounds of Lawry's prime rib beef than our line weighed. Our team enjoyed the Lawry's dinner, but we Bears from Berkeley were more accustomed to the San Francisco Bay cuisine. Spenger's Sea Food, San Francisco's China Town, Kip's Hamburgers, La Val's Pizza, and Mexican food at Juan's.

When all of our intangibles-stamina-perseverance-intellect-courage-toughness and attitude failed us in the game of football, we took the tack that a team that plays together celebrates together. Win or lose, celebrate, commiserate, and get ready for the next challenge in life. Some of our players were unable to resist and returned to Lawry's for a post-game meal. Most of us stayed at our hotel, The Ambassador, and attempted to drown our pain and sorrow with room service.

When the bill arrived for the food and beverages, it became another barrier to success on that day, January 1, 1959. One of our players asked, "How do we pay for this?" And our illustrious captain, Jack Hart responded, "How do you spell ChiaPPONE?" That is how Bob was finally able to make a contribution to our team.

Our team enjoys the distinction of being the last Cal team to play in Pasadena on New Year's Day, and we look forward to another Lawry's Beef Bowl team party next year! The party is on Bob.

Left: Rose Princess Thea Corcoran, Iowa HB Ray Jauch, QB Randy Duncan and Rose Queen Pamela Prather enjoy dinner together at Frank Sennes' Moulin Rouge in Hollywood. Top right: 1959 Rose Bowl action. Right: University of California Football publicity photo of QB Joe Kapp.

1959

1960

Below left: 1960 Rose Bowl action. Lower left: Wisconsin governor Gaylord Nelson gets autographs from Badger football stars Dan Lanphear and Dale Hackbart at the annual Big 10 Alumni dinner in Los Angeles. Top center: Jim Bakken in the cockpit of the team's DC-7 en route to LA. Top right: 1960 Royal Court with actors John Forsythe and William Bendix at Revue Studios tour with Badger players. Top center: Badger players touring Western movie set featuring Doug McClure and William Bendix. Center right: 1960 Royal Court welcoming Badger players to Pasadena. Center left: Quarterbacks Dale Hackbart of Wisconsin and Bob Schloredt of Washington talk during a photo shoot at Disneyland.

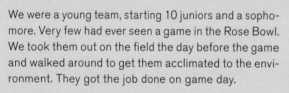

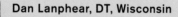

Jim Owens, Head Coach, Washington

We were a young team, starting 10 juniors and a sophomore. Very few had ever seen a game in the Rose Bowl. We took them out on the field the day before the game and walked around to get them acclimated to the environment. They got the job done on game day.

Dan Lanphear, DT, Wisconsin

The Rose Bowl was a phenomenal experience but we were not as mentally prepared as we should have been for the game. Here we were, a bunch of small-town kids playing college football in a sleepy, little Midwest college town. We rode a bus to many of our games. If we had to fly, it was on a DC-3 chartered from the Purdue University flight school fleet.

Contrast that with flying in a new DC-7 out to Los Angeles with real flight attendants. They even let us sit in the cockpit with the pilot. We were treated first class the entire time we were in Southern California. The Rose Queen and 1960 Royal Court greeted us at the airport, and there were luncheons and banquets to attend. We went to Disneyland, and dinners featuring Hollywood stars like Bob Hope and Dennis Morgan. This was all a huge deal to college kids from the Midwest. We were dazzled and distracted. It was easy to lose focus on the game, and we did.

We were also playing a very good Washington team that had better speed than we did. Back then Big Ten football wasn't geared toward playing catch-up football. It's one thing if the score is close, but we were embarrassed by the outcome and nobody really likes to talk about that game. We were a much better team than that.

Bob Schloredt, QB, Washington

How do you top winning two Rose Bowl games in a row? I ended up dating Carol Washburn, the 1961 Rose Bowl Queen for a year after the Minnesota game!

Bob Schloredt, QB, Washington

Ever since I was a freshman at UW, I had envisioned myself in a crucial punting situation with our back against the wall in the Rose Bowl. I actually practiced for this type of punt over and over for 4 years. Minnesota was driving in the second half and we stopped them on the 3-yard line with the score 17-7. Had they scored it could have been a 2 or 3-point game. Well, I got my chance to punt from the back of our end zone, and it was like déjà vu. I think it was a 55-yard punt and it was fielded so well by our cover men they lost even more yardage after the catch. The Golden Gophers never threatened after that.

Murray Warmath, Head Coach, Minnesota

Our boys had been away from home for two weeks [in California] preparing for the game and then the families and girlfriends arrived two nights before the game. I think we really lost our edge. We really got off to a slow start vs. Washington. They kicked a field goal and scored two touchdowns in the first half. We started to make a game of it in the second half, and we felt we could have won it if we would've played another quarter. But, Washington was a darn good team and we just didn't get clicking like we should have at the start.

Jim Owens, Head Coach, Washington

It was amazing that we made it back to the 1961 Rose Bowl because we had some key injuries during the year and played in some really tight games. But most of the seniors were starters and we were ready by game time.

Top left: Rose Queen Carol Washburn presents a Washington Huskies straw hat to Susie and Laurie Frank, daughters of Richard N. Frank, who looks on with Washington QB Bob Schoredt. Top center: Bob Schloredt punts for Washington in first half action of the 1961 Rose Bowl Game. Top right: 1961 game action.

Murray Warmath, Head Coach, Minnesota

When UCLA scored first with a field goal (just like Washington did in the 1961 Rose Bowl) I thought, "Oh shit, here we go again." But, we sucked it up and played well the rest of the game. We had learned from the previous year. It helped that we took the boys up to a monastery in the mountains before the game to eliminate the distractions and stay focused.

Above: 1962 game action.

"Bo" Schembechler, Assistant Coach, Ohio State

We were undefeated (with one tie to TCU at the beginning of the season) and we had won the Big Ten title outright. I was with Woody in Cleveland at an alumni function. We were in the pre-dinner cocktail party and a guy came in and told us that the faculty had just voted down the invitation to the Rose Bowl because they wanted to make a point that football wasn't more important than academics. Woody was fuming. "Get your coat, Bo." We walked out into the freezing cold night air. We walked and walked. He didn't say anything for a while. He looked in a few store windows, then we continued walking. Finally, he said, "Okay, let's go back." We went back into that alumni gathering and Woody made one of the most impassioned speeches I've ever heard about why the faculty's decision was wrong.

William F. "Bill" Barnes, Head Coach, UCLA

Minnesota Coach Murray Warmath was an assistant coach to General Robert Neyland at the University of Tennessee for several years. I played for Murray and Coach Neyland at Tennessee. It turned out that my UCLA team won the AAWU and we ended up playing in that 1962 Rose Bowl against Minnesota after Ohio State turned down the invitation. After Minnesota won the game I went over to congratulate Murray. We shook hands and he said, "I'm sorry it had to be you."

1963

Pat Richter, WR, Wisconsin

Once I ran into a fellow from Philadelphia and when I mentioned my name he looked a bit peeved, then he said "I remember you... you were in that Rose Bowl game... I was seven years old and my dad wouldn't let us eat until it was over." It was pretty late on the East Coast by the time the game finished.

Ron Carlson, DL, Wisconsin

After 40 plus years it is hard to distinguish between all of the special events of the Rose Bowl experience; the banquets, the Rose Parade floats, the Lawry's Beef Bowl, the game itself. Unfortunately, for Wisconsin, USC took advantage of the opportunities in the first half and we didn't, including a Trojan fumble we thought we had (which they scored on a play or two after that) and a Badger touchdown on the last play of the half that was called back. The second half was spectacular with the game ending in the dark under limited lighting. The last play of the game was a USC punt that we nearly blocked. I have watched the film many times, but Wisconsin has yet to score enough points to finish the comeback. Congratulations to USC for winning the game. It was a great game,

Top: Wisconsin QB Ron VanderKelen scrambles out of the pocket for more yards against USC. Above: 1963 game action.

between to excellent football teams. Win, lose, or draw, I am always proud to say I played in one of the most exciting Rose Bowl games ever.

Hal Bedsole, WR, USC

For over 40 years I've heard people say "Wow, what a great game!" But, we were disappointed. We had a great offense and an incredible defense. We only gave up 55 points in ten games prior to the Rose Bowl game. It felt horrible that somebody scored 37 points on us. We had already shut out Notre Dame, Iowa, Washington and UCLA that year. But when Coach McKay called off the dogs, it threw us out of our rhythm. The university had a party that night back at the hotel and none of the players showed up. The 1962 national champion USC team that played in the 1963 Rose Bowl was really the beginning of the modern era USC dynasty.

Pete Elliott, Head Coach, Illinois

We played at Washington the year before (1962 regular season) and they beat us. After the game some of the Huskies made remarks about the "Big Fat Big Ten." The December weather in Champaign the next year was pretty bad with a lot of snow. We couldn't practice much, so we moved indoors and ran, and ran and ran. The boys remembered what had been said the year before and they wanted to be in the best shape for the game. When the game was over, the entire team ran a triumphant victory lap around the field. It was something to see. When I was growing up the premiere game was the Rose Bowl. You had to be a champion to play in the Rose Bowl. There's no other bowl game that can compare.

1964

Left: Illinois head coach Pete Elliott autographs a football for Lawry's manager Sheldon Balzac while Mrs. Elliott looks on.

Bob Stiles, DB, UCLA

Before the game both teams walked on the field at the same time. Standing next to those behemoths felt kind of primal. Not only were they big and bad but they were ugly and that had to make them mean. I felt they should be four touchdown favorites, minimum. UCLA had never won a Rose Bowl game so hopes weren't screaming through the rooftops. Turned out to be a pretty nice day for the Bruins. An onside kick, interceptions, pass completions, split timing delivery of plays, both on offense and defense, all done according to Coach Prothro's game plan. The man was a genius. He certainly didn't have the guns on that team but he sure made the most of what showed up on the first day of practice. Perhaps two or three of those players could possibly play on a major college team of today, whereas, the entire team from the Spartans would be on scholarship at some major powerhouse. I would not want to have played them again.

1966

Gary Beban, QB, UCLA

It is always memorable to reach back to January 1,1966, even though my body still aches a bit from that day. You have to remember that there was a significant size differential between the 1965 UCLA Bruins and the Michigan State Spartans; the Spartans had the likes of Bubba Smith, Harold Lucas and George Webster's that made us feel like dwarfs. I remember thinking, "UCLA could eat the great Beef Bowl meal everyday for a year and we would still come out on the short end of the stats."

Above: Michigan State Spartans L-R, Bob Apisa, Clint Jones, Bubba Smith, Gene Washington and George Webster.

Charles "Bubba" Smith, DE, Michigan State

I never wanted to get to the Big Game and lose it. To me, that shows a lack of character. I just wanted to prepare and work on our game plan. I didn't understand the whole Disneyland aspect of the activities. After practice, you just want to get off your feet and find some shade. Here we were riding these little kiddie rides at Disneyland, and I kept saying to George (Webster) "Man, they're setting us up for the kill." In my way of thinking, you focus and prepare for the game. That's the most important thing. We just beat ourselves in the Rose Bowl. When we played UCLA earlier in the year, their offense didn't cross the 50-yard line the entire game on their own.

Bob Apisa, RB, Michigan State

When our team heard that UCLA had come back to beat USC, the news was somewhat of a letdown since we had already beaten the Bruins on our opening game of that undefeated season. We were anxious to play the Trojans and their Heisman Trophy-winning tailback Mike Garrett. We thought that it would be a walk in the park (which Duffy Daugherty had warned us repeatedly against) to the point that he moved the entire team to a monastery in the Sierra mountains a couple of days prior to the game to concentrate and "hone in" on the task at hand. Boy, were we in for a surprise. Duffy proved to be prophetic.

My ultimate dream as a youngster growing up in Honolulu, Hawaii was to play in "the Granddaddy of all bowl games," the Rose Bowl. Those dreams were fulfilled on Jan.1, 1966. I remember shortly after scoring on a 39-yard run earlier in the 4th quarter and we were going for the tying 2-point conversion with time running out, Duffy called my

Above: Michigan State Football publicity photo of RB Bob Apisa.

number on a option pitch with the game and undefeated season on the line. This was the ultimate "heady" stuff for a young sophomore in view of the national TV audience as well the international press who were present. As the play was executed, I immediately surveyed the defense and figured I would eventually meet up with the safety Bob Stiles around the two-yard line. I felt my momentum would carry him into the end zone, but I did not anticipate Jim Colletto busting through the right side to lend a hand. As we (Bob Stiles and I) collided all I heard was a roar from the crowd. I wasn't sure if it was because I made the touchdown or not. It was strange feeling not knowing because I was at the bottom of the pile. To my disappointment, I finally realized I was short of the goal line. It's a play that's been referred to throughout the years and has become a part of Rose Bowl folklore for the ages.

John Cooper, Asst. Coach, UCLA

Coach Prothro made one of the most brilliant calls ever in the '66 Rose Bowl. Early in the game, he called a play-action pass. Bubba Smith, Michigan State's All-World defensive end came crashing in to kill our great running back, Mel Farr. Bubba stuffed the fullback and tackled Mel Farr but quarterback Gary Beban still had the ball and completed a long pass to one of our receivers. For the rest of the game, Bubba Smith had to make that decision whether to stuff the off-tackle run, or try and contain Gary Beban. Tommy Prothro was one of the greatest football coaches that ever coached the game. I was president of the American Football Coaches Association and I recommended him for the Hall of Fame. They asked me what kind of coach he was. I simply said, "He took Oregon State to two Rose Bowl games." Coach Prothro was selected for the College Football Hall of Fame the next year.

1967

Leroy Keyes, RB/DB, Purdue

It was very special to represent our school in the Rose Bowl Game for the first time ever. Back then, if you didn't win the Big Ten Conference title you didn't play in a post-season bowl game. It was a huge honor to play against some of the great coaching legends in college football such as Woody Hayes, Duffy Daugherty, and Bump Elliott. You knew you deserved to go to the Rose Bowl when you made it through a conference with those coaches and their great teams. For a kid from the East Coast, just to be able to go out to Pasadena and enjoy the climate and be a part of that tradition, dress in that historic locker room, and play on that hallowed ground was unforgettable.

Bob DeMoss, Asst. Coach, Purdue

It was a great thrill to be coaching in a Rose Bowl game against USC because we were playing against one of my former teammates at Purdue, John McKay. The game had a strange feel to it since John had given us their offense a few years before. Naturally you remember the play of the game: The score was 14-13 and you know John is going for two. We are fortunate that George Catavolas, our safety, stepped in front of their receiver for an interception, with a little over a minute to go, and the rest is history. Two things stand out about Bob Griese in that Rose Bowl game. The first was his audible at the line of scrimmage calling for a pass that put us in scoring position. The other was the fact that he kicked both extra points, ultimately giving us the winning margin.

1968

Doug Crusan, DL, Indiana

Coach Pont switched me from the offensive line to the defensive line for my senior year and I lost the 35 pounds he had strongly suggested. I was much quicker at that new weight. We changed to a 4-4 defense with a lot of movement. That was one of the changes that helped us make the incredible turnaround from the year before. To go from 1-8-1 and last place in 1966 to 9-1 and Big Ten champions in 1967 was absolutely amazing. After losing all that weight and then being turned loose at the Lawry's Beef Bowl—that just wasn't fair. I didn't have that kind of appetite anymore! Walking onto that field for the coin toss was an experience I'll never forget. It was an honor to be out there representing Indiana University and the Big Ten Conference in the Rose Bowl. It was the culmination of a dream and a goal. I was also proud that I was representing my hometown of Monessen, Pennsylvania, where football and steel are king. We had a kick-off banquet at the beginning of the season and someone handed me a rose. A news cameraman snapped a photo of me smelling the rose. That turned out to be quite a premonition.

Top: Newspaper photo of Hoosier football player Doug Crusan smelling a rose someone handed him at the 1967 Indiana University Football Kick-off banquet. Left: Indiana University Football publicity photo of Doug Crusan, defensive lineman and team captain of the 1967 Hoosier team.

John Pont, Head Coach, Indiana

Above: Indiana Hoosier QB Harry Gonso horses around for the camera with a Lawry's waitress at the Lawry's Beef Bowl.

Aside from the unforgettable Game Day experience, there were many functions to attend that are part of the wonderful tradition of the Rose Bowl. It could be a bit tiring at times, but it was always enjoyable, especially for a university that had never been there before. Lawry's gave us such a great impression that we asked them to serve our boosters in the press box the next time we played at Northwestern. They did a superb job there, too. My wife, Sandy, and I had 3 children younger than ten years of age with us for the team's trip to Disneyland. The people mover she and I were on broke down and we sat high above everyone while our children were with several players on the ground. Sandy did worry about the children but they were in good hands with team members, some of them had babysat for us in the past. We were there for at least 2 hours and I must admit it was very peaceful. Sandy and I have a photo of us as a reminder of that experience.

Harold Mauro, C, Indiana

We were greeted at the airport Rose Queen Linda Strother and her Royal Court. Queen Linda gave Coach Pont a glass slipper. Was it Cinderella's? In between the double session practices that were intended to get the team used to the heat and Southern California smog, we had time to sightsee and make new friends. A trip to Disneyland found several of our players stuck on the tram, but being stranded for two hours and 35 feet above the ground with the Rose Queen and her Rose Princesses made the time pass very quickly. Christmas was spent two thousand miles from home but family and friends flew to Pasadena to be with the players and coaches. A Christmas Eve party was a University affair, with a special Hoosier Santa Claus, assistant coach Herb Fairfield. A Christmas Day party was given to the team by the Tournament of Roses organization. Gifts to the players included watches and binoculars. The official party of students, cheerleaders, alumni, band and fans arrived after Christmas and suddenly "Hoosiers" were everywhere! They really helped get us pumped up for the game.

1971

Jim Plunkett, QB, Stanford

Coach Ralston was brilliant at visualizing his messages. A week before the game, he gave us the night off on Christmas Eve. Before we went out, he gathered the team together and gave us a little pep talk. He had a brown paper grocery bag filled with one of his object lessons. He walked around to each player and gave everyone a Buckeye nut to show us how insignificant they were.

John Ralston, Head Coach, Stanford

Two things come to mind regarding our 1971 Rose Bowl game with Ohio State. Our coaching staff watched 16,000 feet of film and never saw Jim Stillwagon (Ohio State nose guard) in a bad play. We designed all our runs to have the play side guard assist our center, John Sande. At halftime, I approached Sande and asked him how he was coming with Stillwagon. His response was very quick, "Coach, I can handle him myself." The films of the game bore out his exactness. Jim Stillwagon only assisted on one tackle the entire game.

I will always remember a comment made by Randy Vataha, our outstanding receiver. We were ahead 20-17 late in the fourth quarter and moving the ball inside the Buckeye 20-yard line when Jim Plunkett dropped back to pass and found Vataha in the end zone for the touchdown. After the game, Randy's comment to the press was, "When Jim let go of the ball, I knew we had won the game." No thought at all of dropping the ball--super confidence.

David Tipton, DL, Stanford

Ohio State had a fullback named John Brockington, who was a stud even by today's standards. No one had stopped him all year and we were barely slowing him down. At a crucial moment, late in the game, Woody Hayes elected to go for it on fourth-and-one deep in our territory. The Thunder Chickens rose up with Ron Kadziel and Jeff Siemon hitting him first, then everyone else finishing the job. The look in Brockington's eyes was priceless! I don't think that had ever happened to him before. They were stopped short. This proved to be the turning point of the game. Despite being 17-point underdogs, we went on to beat the Buckeyes 27-17. It was a moment and a game that has had a profound effect on each of our lives.

Jim Stillwagon, NG, Ohio State

I like to say that we were a "horse and plough" team that became a John Deere tractor. Woody Hayes didn't want to read the directions to make it run, so he kept going back to the horse and plough, what he knew best. Some of the greatest games Ohio State ever played when I was there were played on our own practice field: Woody vs. Lou McCullough, our defensive coordinator.

As soon as we knew we were headed to the Rose Bowl Game, I suggested in a Captain's meeting with Woody that we go out one day earlier and let everyone relax—no taping on the plane as was our usual practice. Woody told his assistants that it was a great idea. I went back to my teammates and told them the good news: no taping on the plane, light practice in sweats, and then we'd be taking it easy the first day and get all the public relations things out of the way.

On the flight out to Southern California, one of the players alerted me that players were getting taped in the back of the plane. I went and asked Woody what was going on and he said it was raining in the practice area and he just wanted to protect the player's ankles.

After greeting the Rose Bowl Committee and Rose Queen and her Court at the Huntington Sheraton, we were on buses taped and headed for the practice field in East L.A.—and it wasn't raining out. We arrived at the practice field and all our equipment was laid out for a normal scrimmage practice. When I questioned

Woody again, he said this was all for the press. The players needed to wear the equipment to look bigger for the press photographers. We ended up having a full scrimmage practice and after that we ran 25 gassers (40-yard wind sprints).

After the practice, I confronted Lou McCullough. "Today you did more to demoralize us and possibly lose this game than anything else." Lou replied, "Woody made me do it."

Back at the hotel, the seniors called a private meeting and we voted to go home. Jan White, our All-American tight end offered to be the speaker for the group, but he backed out at the last second. As we went to open the door in the meeting room, he told me I would be the only one that could face Woody Hayes and do this, and he handed me the papers with the outline of the grievances that we discussed in the senior meeting. The rest of the team was in the room with Woody and the assistant coaches when our group of seniors walked in. In order to protect the younger guys from any ramifications of what we were going to do, we asked everyone to leave the room except for the senior players.

"Coach, the senior class had a meeting and we need to talk about some things," I said. I began to review the outline from the seniors' meeting and everything that had

Top: Ohio State goal line stand vs. Stanford. Above: Ohio State University Football game action publicity photo of two-time All-American nose guard Jim Stillwagon.

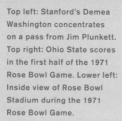

happened contrary to what we had discussed and told the team before we left Ohio. Everyone knew it wasn't the hard work that we objected to, it was the way we were being treated. Everything that had been agreed upon was being reneged, the rules began changing as soon as we got on the plane and kept changing after we landed. The seniors had voted and unanimously decided to go back home if things didn't change. Most of the seniors were vocal about how this Rose Bowl Game trip was supposed to be a reward for winning the Big Ten and not a punishment. All of the sudden, Woody yelled for a chalkboard. He moved from the center of the meeting room to the front with the chalkboard like all great leaders do. Then he started writing down all of the items we had mentioned, so he could begin to take charge of the situation. He agreed to make the changes and wrote it all down on the board. I said, "You can't take this grievance out on any single player on the field."

But Lou McCullough retorted, "I'll tell you this. This man has done more for you boys than anyone in the world and I can't believe you are doing this. If I catch one of you boys breaking one of these rules, I'll run you until your ass bleeds." Woody told him not to say that,

but the end result had already been put into motion. Woody came to me privately after the meeting and said, "If we lose this game, it's all your fault." I replied, "No. Like I said earlier, you did more to ruin us than anything else."

We went on to our spring-like training camp practices, but that special feeling was gone and people just went through the motions. Nothing really changed except the curfew was extended a couple of hours and we didn't have to travel en masse in vans. It seemed that the lovin' feeling was gone and the special energy that all great teams seem to possess had been lost.

Stanford ended up beating us that game because they out-played us and out-coached us for one hour that day. In my estimation this time, Woody and Lou had taken a #1 team and run it into the ground when it should have been enjoying its pinnacle of greatness. Ohio State lost the Rose Bowl before the opening kick-off but no one in the stands or on the sidelines knew it.

When the season was over, Woody called me into his office, thanked me for my leadership, and for my sacrifice playing nose guard on defense. He said I could've been drafted higher had I played the linebacker position. We were good friends to his death, and he asked me to talk to his other teams. He was a great American, a great person and a great coach. In my opinion, he just got so focused at times that he developed tunnel vision and lost sight of the big picture and didn't recognize the affects it had on other people around him. His great strength and weakness was his consistency and predictability.

Pete Lazetich, DT, Stanford

Our seniors decided the team should go on strike when we first arrived in Southern California because they were upset about some things like not having rental cars and enough free time to cruise the beach scene. We sat in the locker room that first day until Coach Ralston came in from the field. He listened carefully to the players' concerns and agreed to make some adjustments regarding these issues. Then Coach Ralston launched into an impassioned speech about how we wouldn't remember anything we did off the field twenty years from now, but we would remember what happened in the Rose Bowl Game on January 1, 1971. The team took the practice field with a new energy and focus to win the game.

Anthony Davis, RB, USC

My first Rose Bowl was my sophomore year when we were undefeated and had just wrapped the regular season with a huge victory over Notre Dame [AD scored 6 TDs in that game]. We were staying at the Hyatt Wilshire Hotel and had the option of getting taped up before the game at the hotel, so I had trainer Paul Williams tape up my right ankle there before we left for the stadium. When I was all suited up at the stadium for our pre-game drills my teammates couldn't help but break out in laughter. I had put a black sock on one foot and a white sock on the other. On top of that, I noticed my jock was still in my locker and then I remembered my left ankle still needed to be taped up—the one that needed it the most. I was just so caught up in thinking about the game that I hadn't paid attention to these other preparatory details. So, I had to strip all my gear off, get my left ankle taped and then get re-suited again. Every piece of USC clothing and equipment was marked with the Rose Bowl logo and our jersey number—even our jocks. I wanted to save everything after the game as my keepsakes, but you know what? My shoes, my wristbands, and even my jock were missing when I got out of the shower. Somebody out there still has my jockstrap from the 1973 Rose Bowl!

1973

USC star tailback Anthony Davis hands a team autographed Trojan football to Richard N. Frank at the Lawry's Beef Bowl.

1976

Top: UCLA Bruin QB John Sciarra passing in the 1976 Rose Bowl Game. Above: Close-up of the blazer worn by UCLA Bruins football players for 1976 Rose Bowl pre-game social activities.

John Sciarra, QB, UCLA

We lost to Ohio State earlier in the season, 41 - 20. Needless to say, we were 17-point underdogs going into the Rose Bowl game. I believe that the point spread was and is the biggest in Rose Bowl history. In any event, very few people gave us any chance to win the game. Coach Vermeil and his staff worked us extremely hard in preparing for the game. At one point during the first week of practice some of the players started to question the "high intensity" workouts. But those questions were soon laid to rest when Coach Vermeil made it very clear that any student-athlete that did not want to put forth the effort could leave the program and that he would find others to do the job. From that point on we were focused on one thing - win the game. I remember when we took the Rose Bowl field on New Year's Day and seeing more people than I had ever seen at any sporting event, over 105,000 Bruin and Buckeye fans. The powder blue and gold, together with the silver and red colors were truly amazing. We kept it close the first half, thanks to our defense. At halftime, Coach Vermeil scrapped the offensive game plan of running the option and decided to "pass first and run second." It was a great adjustment. The eight- man front the Buckeyes were presenting became vulnerable as we started to move the ball through the air. Everything started to click for the Bruins, we gained the momentum and the Buckeyes fell off balance. If there was ever a game where we put forth a "total team effort," the 1976 Rose Bowl game was it for us. Arguably, this Bruin victory may be the biggest upset in Rose Bowl history. The most memorable moments were watching Coach Hayes walk across the field to congratulate Coach Vermeil on our victory with just under a minute left on the game clock, and celebrating with my teammates and coaching staff in the locker room as I held one arm around my father.

John Sciarra, QB, UCLA

I happened to sit next to Wendell Tyler our star running back at the Lawry's Beef Bowl. Wendell had been playing the last few games with a broken hand and his hand was still in a soft cast. Wendell was upset because his cast prevented him from cutting his prime rib. Everyone at our table had a lot fun joking and teasing him about the great meal he was missing. Eventually, I cut his prime rib so he could enjoy with the rest of us.

Wendell Tyler, RB, UCLA

Both teams had met at a special event at Disneyland earlier in the week. Our entire team had to wear a dark blue sports jacket that had a rose sewn on the lapel and patch that read "U.C.L.A. 1976 Rose Bowl" on the front. Some of the Ohio State players called us "choirboys." I guess they must have felt pretty confident after beating us by a lot earlier in the season. At the end of the game one of the U.C.L.A. football players attempted to shake Woody Hayes' hand but he refused. Some player shouted, "You don't want to shake the choir boy's hand!"

Cornelius Greene, QB, Ohio State

How weird is this? Ten years after an undefeated and top-ranked Big Ten team [Michigan State] was poised to win the national championship with a Rose Bowl victory over UCLA, the Bruins turned the table again, this time on an undefeated Buckeye team on the verge of a national championship. The common thread? Both Big Ten teams stayed at a creepy monastery in the mountains before the game.

Ray Bell, LB, UCLA

I have two priceless memories from the 1976 Rose Bowl. First, seeing the pride and excitement on my mom and dad's faces when I gave them the tickets to attend college football's greatest bowl game. Second, my teammates and I hugging, shaking hands and literally going crazy on the field after beating the great Ohio State team led by legendary coach Woody Hayes.

Brad Budde, OG, USC
"The Miracle-Man of the 1980 Rose Bowl"

When I think back on my experiences playing in three Rose Bowl Games, the word that comes to mind is PASSION. There is no better word to describe the people who love this violent sport and yet are civilized enough to appreciate the pageantry of the Rose Bowl Parade and a fine meal at Lawry's. The Rose Bowl means many things, but one thing is for certain, it is *our game*. It is what unites us all with the memories of heartache, hope, and miracles.

I was a member of the USC Rose Bowl teams of 1977, 1978, and 1980. As I reminisce, I don't recall the final scores or even the speeches our coaches gave before each Big Game. What I do remember are the people who made an impact on my life. One person in particular made us all believe when we found it difficult to believe anymore. This is a true story of the "Miracle-Man" of the 1980 Rose Bowl.

After heeding the voice in my heart that told me, "go west young man, go west," I boarded a plane in my hometown of Kansas City and flew to Los Angeles to begin my career as a Trojan. I will never forget the first time I met my USC football roommate. Opening the door to my room, there was the biggest Mexican I had ever

seen. With his massive 6'6, 300 lb frame, he stood there smiling ear to ear, just one big, smiling friend.

Unfortunately, those smiles were short lived. While we were playing in successive Rose Bowls, my beloved roommate was on the sidelines with busted knees. Instead of causing pain with his dominating blocking abilities, he hid his own pain and heartache handing out water to thirsty teammates on the sidelines.

Top athletes, like successful people in other walks of life, tend to have a mindset that only good things will ALWAYS come their way. When road-bumps, or injuries, do come along, others easily abandon them to regain a false sense of control in their own lives. My roommate suffered such fair weather friends. However, heading into his senior year he had his eye on one thing only, and that was to play in his dream game. After recovering from two serious knee injuries, it seemed like his hardships were finally over.

During the first game of the 1980 Rose Bowl season, his senior year, he was carted off the field again. This was his third knee injury in four years. As we watched our fallen teammate leave the game, all the coaches and players felt sick inside. Doctors, coaches and players, it didn't matter, we all told him the same thing in different ways. Some of us told him to his face that he

Above left: Aerial view of the 1980 Rose Bowl Game. Above center: USC's All-American offensive guard Brad Budde. Above right: USC offensive tackle and future NFL Hall of Famer Anthony Munoz.

was crazy to think that he could rehab from another surgery and play in the Rose Bowl within a matter of months. Others were more cowardly, using body language or avoiding him altogether. But we were the ones with limitations. It has been said, "life is not a problem to solve as much it is a mystery to live."

Defying the predictions and assessments of the so-called experts, he and the special lady he married demonstrated a unique faith that allowed them to embrace the mystery of his athletic career. Despite the skepticism expressed by coaches and teammates, their faith enabled him to rehabilitate his knee just in time to play in the 1980 Rose Bowl.

Late in the fourth quarter, USC trailed Ohio State by six points with one last chance to score. They started their drive from deep in their own territory. As they marched steadily up the field, the sports announcers commented that, "SC's running game is overpowering the Buckeye defense mainly behind the big offensive tackle, number 77." When the Trojans crossed the goal line to win the game, the player making the key block was #77, "The Miracle-Man." His name is Anthony Munoz. Football fans will recognize that NFL Hall of Fame name right off the bat, but few know the story of his tumultuous college career. When you know the injuries he had to fight through to continue playing, his accomplishments are even more impressive.

The empowering story of "The Miracle-Man of the 1980 Rose Bowl" touches all our hearts because Anthony Munoz is what the Rose Bowl is all about. The Rose Bowl represents what is good about our world and what is good for our souls; it represents heartache, hope and yes, MIRACLES!

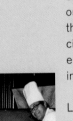

Top left: USC offensive tackle Anthony Munoz in action. Above: USC head coach John Robinson and tailback Charles White at the Lawry's Beef Bowl, then still referred to as the Lawry's Beef Scrimmage. Lower left: USC Football publicity photo of Coach John Robinson with #71 Brad Budde, #12 Charles White, and #77 Anthony Munoz.

John Robinson, Head Coach, USC

Anthony Munoz had rehabbed from a bad knee injury in record time to play in this game. Nobody really understands that lonely, desperate struggle when you are injured unless it happens to you. It is a very difficult time for an athlete to make it through rehab. Nobody thought Anthony would make it back but he worked his tail off to play in this game and he played like a monster. We were behind 16-10, not more than four minutes were left on the clock and we were 83 yards away. I just said, "Get the ball to Charlie White and run behind Munoz." They couldn't stop him and eight plays later he scored the winning TD. We got the ball back with 20 seconds left and Charlie pops loose and made it to the one-inch line. I decided to sit on the ball and we won by 1 point. Well, the point spread was 2-3 points in our favor and I never got so much hate mail my life. Tons of letters from people who were irate that we didn't go for the score to beat the point spread!

Butch Woolfolk, RB, Michigan

Someone just sent me a video copy of the game in June 2005. I'd never seen the game before. I watched it with my boys, and all the excitement and memories came flooding back to me. The celebration afterwards was incredibly sweet because there was so much tension going in. Coach Schembechler had never won in his previous five Rose Bowl games. Everyone expected us to win because we were playing some of the best football in the nation at the end of the season. Our defense was awesome. They had not given up a touchdown in 18 consecutive quarters, and the offense was clicking with the running and passing game and a great offensive line.

We had a big lead at the end of the game, but nobody was celebrating because we had been in that situation before. Nobody took anything for granted. We waited until the final tick of the clock and then we just went crazy. It felt so good to win that game.

We had a team party that night and I didn't get back to the hotel until about 1am in the morning. I got a call from a press person in Michigan and they wanted to pick up Coach Schembechler and me at 3am to be on NBC Today that morning. It was just the two of us in the limo and Bo was chewing on a big cigar and he was going over the play-by-play of the game. We did the show together and on the ride back I fell asleep. When we arrived at our hotel, he was still chewing on the cigar and talking about the game. He was overjoyed and relieved. And, despite my fatigue, I was so happy for him.

Above: 1981 Rose Bowl Game action.

Danny Andrews, RB, UCLA

With the score 10-7 and the momentum in Michigan's favor, we put together one of the best drives in UCLA football history. A 13-play, 80-yard drive ended with me diving into the end zone on a 9-yard run touchdown. I am blessed to have been a part of it. I will never forget looking up into the stands after the game and finding my parents among the 104, 000 people at the Rose Bowl, and seeing the pride on their faces. That is something I will cherish forever.

Terry Donahue, Head Coach, UCLA

As an assistant coach, making it to the Rose Bowl game is one of the pinnacle achievements in a coaching career. But, as a head coach, especially when your team wins the Rose Bowl, it solidifies your credibility in the coaching fraternity. It's a rare milestone in one's coaching career.

Mike White, Head Coach, Illinois

My favorite moment would probably have to be the morning of the game. Driving up on the Arroyo Seco that enters into the valley where the Rose Bowl is situated is a magnificent sight. I was sitting in the front of the bus and as we came up over the hill and saw the Rose Bowl Stadium, it almost brought tears to my eyes. It was an emotional moment. Illinois fans had been waiting 20 years to return to the Rose Bowl Game.

Above: UCLA head coach Terry Donahue signals instructions to his players on the field during the 1983 Rose Bowl Game. Left: Wide angle view inside Rose Bowl Stadium at the 1984 Rose Bowl Game between Illinois and UCLA.

Doug West, LB, UCLA

I acquired the nickname of "Tape Man" from the Bruin trainers because of my pre-game ritual where I would go off and tape my hands and wrists by myself. After having my ankles taped by one of the training staff before the 1983 Rose Bowl Game, I grabbed some tape and started my ritual. Ducky Drake and head trainer Larry Carter noticed this and told me to take a couple of extra wraps of tape because this was the Rose Bowl and you only get one shot at a game like this—you don't want to leave anything to chance.

The following year when we were getting ready to face Illinois, the same situation occurred. Larry Carter and Ducky Drake looked at each other and kind of smiled when Ducky said, "Well, I guess we were wrong, and you got another opportunity to play in the Granddaddy, so take that extra wrap of tape again because it may have made the difference." There is no way to tell if that was true, but we did go on to win our second Rose Bowl title in two years.

1986

Hayden Fry, Head Coach, Iowa

I will never forget seeing one of my assistant coaches and his brother walk into the lobby of our team hotel in only their underwear. They had been robbed at gunpoint two blocks away and were stripped of their clothes.

I invited one of my friends to give a short pre-game talk to our team. He was so highly motivated to speak to the team that he couldn't stop. We are probably the only team in the history of the Rose Bowl Game to receive two officials' warnings to get on the field for the kick-off.

1987

John Cooper, Head Coach, Arizona State

My fondest pre-game experience was when I was waiting with my team to take the field for the start of the game. You look up and see one hundred thousand plus fans evenly divided between the two schools, and you know the game is being shown around the world on TV... The thought I had was, "Man, I finally made it to the BIG TIME."

Mark Messner, DL, Michigan

It's amazing how much you want to win a game for someone like Bo. To be captain of one of the teams that gave Bo one of those very elusive Rose Bowl victories was one of the most meaningful accomplishments in my athletic career—to see the exuberance on his face after that win over USC brought absolute joy to me.

Tim Ryan, DL, USC

The 1990 Rose Bowl victory was the greatest feeling and that feeling has never left me to this day. I still have a photo on my office wall of Leroy Holt and myself holding up the Rose Bowl trophy on the field. The look on both of our faces is pure reality. I look at that every day and get a lot of motivation from it. The journey to get to that point was so incredibly difficult. We had transitioned into a new coach after a disappointing '86 season and needed four wins in a row to make the '88 Rose Bowl. We had to come back from that really tough loss against Notre Dame in '88 and almost pulled off the win in the '89 Rose Bowl. There were many opportunities to get soft, but we hung in there and supported each other and believed in each other.

Ricky Ervins, RB, USC

Our fourth game of the year we were playing Washington State on the road. They were a very good team. Nearly all of their starters were seniors and they were undefeated at the time. They were beating us 17-10 with three minutes remaining and we had the ball on our own 10-yard line. We looked into each other's eyes in the huddle and we knew we were going to get the job done—to score on that drive. We converted three first downs and then I lined up in the slot to the left and Todd Marinovich threw a flare to me that I took in for the score. The next play we lined up in the same formation and when the ball was hiked, everyone followed me and left Gary Wellman open for the two-point conversion. Watching that ball travel through the air was like watching a scene from a movie. We won 18-17. That was a key moment in our season. When I watch the tape of that game I get chills in my spine because I remember what it felt like to be in that huddle—to feel that bond and confidence with my teammates.

The 1989 Trojan team was so tight and so confident—not cocky—we were just confident in each other and as a team. I remember we were singing the Notre Dame fight song before the game when their band was playing and we were waiting to run onto the field. The Notre Dame players were shocked that we knew the words to their fight song. That was a really tough game to lose. When I watch the tape of that game I just about want to cry because we should have won it.

But that confidence we had in each other was the same feeling we took with us into the Rose Bowl. Michigan

Above: USC lineman Tim Ryan with Rose Queen Yasmine Delawari at the Lawry's Beef Bowl. Left: All-American defensive tackle Tim Ryan (#99) and Dan Owen (#90) pressure the Michigan punter in 1990 Rose Bowl Game action.

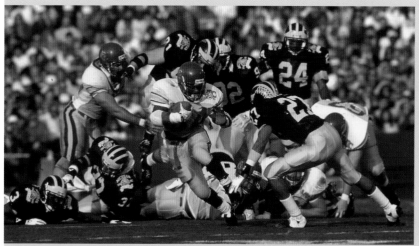

Left: USC tailback Ricky Ervins leaves a trail of Michigan defenders behind as he jukes his way down the field in the 1990 Rose Bowl Game. Right: The University of Southern California Trojans marching band performing at halftime of the 1990 Rose Bowl Game.

was an outstanding team, and we were in a similar situation late in the game. We were tied 10-10 with two minutes left, and it was third down and seven to go for the first down. We ran off-tackle to the left and I made the first down. The next play called was an 84 Right, which was designed for me to go off-tackle to the right. The blocking was perfect and I popped through the hole and ended up going 14 yards for the score with about a minute left to win the game.

I lived about a block away from the Rose Bowl Stadium, so after all the post-game interviews and team stuff

I walked home that night. It was like a dream. It was strange to realize I had just played in a game in that stadium. During the game, when you're on the field, all you see is eleven guys in front of you. You just don't notice 100,000 fans surrounding you.

The reality of that game and our victory hit me the next morning when I woke up sore and read about the game in the paper. Playing in the Rose Bowl is something that stays with you forever.

1991

Legendary actor/comedian/ TV show host Bob Hope was a good friend to Iowa coach Hayden Fry since his days coaching at SMU. Here, in a 1982 College Football All-American TV special he hosted, Bob uses his nose as the kicking tee with 1982 Rose Queen Kathryn Potthast holding for the kicker.

Hayden Fry, Head Coach, Iowa

One of my cherished Rose Bowl memories was working with the ABC Sports staff of Keith Jackson, Lynn Swann and Bobby Goodrich. Bobby played tight end for me at SMU.

Bob Hope flew non-stop from the Persian Gulf conflict where he had been entertaining our troops to entertain our team and our fans before the Rose Bowl Game. He told me how they had to refuel his aircraft in mid-air during the flight back to California so he could arrive in time. He did benefit shows for me to help turn the football programs around at SMU and North Texas and he never charged a penny for his performances. He had a heart of gold.

Donald Jones, LB, Washington

I come from a town with a population less than 1000 people, and it's not listed on most maps. After I sacked Iowa's quarterback Matt Rodgers in the 1991 Rose Bowl, ABC Sports commentator Keith Jackson said, "I have been all over the country but I have never heard of Gladys, Virginia." The following year we made it back to the Rose Bowl and as one of the team captains I had a chance to meet Mr. Jackson at a Rose Bowl media luncheon. I told him exactly where Gladys, Virginia was located. During the 1992 Rose Bowl game after I sacked Michigan QB Elvis Grbac, Keith Jackson said, "Donald told me where Gladys, Virginia is. "It's right by Lynchburg. I know where that is." I guess you can say I put Gladys, Virginia on the Map.

Don James, Head Coach, Washington

My most memorable post-game memory was when we waited all night to see if we were national champs [after the 1992 Rose Bowl Game]. About six in the morning, the call came that we were indeed voted #1 in the country. It had been a long restless night and the longer we waited, the more convinced we became that we had not been voted #1. The cheering, the laughing and the tears all mingled together as we celebrated our success. WHAT A NIGHT!

ABC Sports television end zone cameraman at the 1992 Rose Bowl game featuring Washington vs. Michigan.

1992

1993

Gary Moeller, Head Coach, Michigan

One of the most memorable Rose Bowl moments for me was the winning drive in the 1993 game vs. Washington. You have to appreciate where the players had been the year before, especially Elvis Grbac. Washington had a great team, an awesome defensive line and we had to play without our starting center, Steve Everett. In order to protect Elvis better, we installed the shotgun and switched to a two-count snap. The first couple plays of the game the ball was mistakenly snapped on the first count and Elvis just got killed by the Huskies' defensive end. He was playing with his head down the rest of the game. We just didn't protect him well and because of that, we were not able to get the ball to Desmond [Howard]. Our whole offense was disrupted from that ripple effect.

Right: Michigan tight end Tony McGee scores the winning touchdown against Washington in the 1993 Rose Bowl Game.

In the 1993 game, you could see such a huge difference in the confidence Elvis was displaying on the field. It was really evident in the game-winning drive that ended with his touchdown pass to Tony McGee. That's a favorite memory of mine from all the Rose Bowl games that I've been associated with because if you compare it to the year before, the growth and maturity Elvis achieved was incredible. The adversity our team faced and endured in the 1992 game definitely helped them the following year. After that victory over Washington, the whole team went over to where our fans were congregated in the stadium and sang "The Victors" with them.

1994

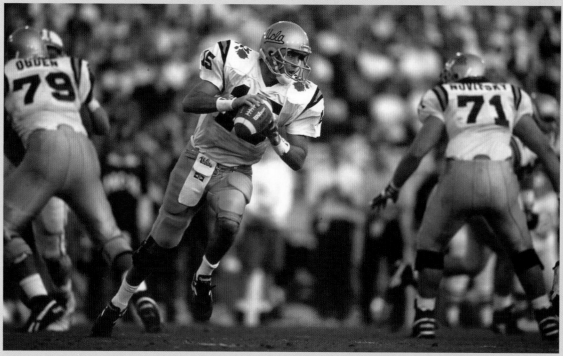

UCLA Bruin QB Wayne Cook rolls out to pass in the 1994 Rose Bowl Game vs. Wisconsin. Above: Richard N. Frank and son Richard R. Frank with the 1994 Royal Court before the UCLA half of the Lawry's Beef Bowl. Below right: Bruin receiver J.J. Stokes adjusts to catch a ball tipped by a Wisconsin defensive back.

Wayne Cook, QB, UCLA

I was sick the whole week before the 1994 Rose Bowl Game with Wisconsin. I had a very bad sore throat and I could barely talk all the way up to a day before the game. I missed all the Rose Bowl festivities except the Lawry's Beef Bowl. The entire night was spent doing interviews and taking pictures. All of my teammates were eating and I was still taking pictures with the Rose Princess. The Princess and I were sitting at a table with a giant cut of prime rib that was being used in our photos. When we finished the photos everyone was done eating. They told me they would make me a fresh plate but by that time I was really hungry and did not want to wait. I had been staring at the plate that we had been using in the pictures so I asked if I could have that one. They gave it to me and I ended up with the biggest and best cut of the night.

One of the great things about playing in the Rose Bowl is that for UCLA it has the feel of a home game. Not the 1994 Rose Bowl. I remember pulling into the Rose Bowl

parking lot and it looked like Wisconsin had taken over Pasadena. There was red as far as the eye could see. Once we got into the stadium it was not any different. The entire stadium seemed to be red.

The Rose Bowl should have been the Highlight of my career. UCLA had a great season and came out of nowhere to win a very strong Pac-10. We came into the game against Wisconsin very confident and expected to win the game. That season we had led the nation in

turnover margin. We turned it over six times that day. We had over 500 yards of offense and scored only 16 points. It should have been my best memory in college but instead it was my worst. I am still very proud to have played in the greatest Bowl game on earth.

J.J. Stokes, WR, UCLA

The Rose Bowl was the sole athletic reason I decided to go to UCLA. It was the best bowl that we could achieve as a team in college football. That's why they call it "The Granddaddy of Them All." The moment that I remember the most is walking down the tunnel headed to the looker room after getting off the bus. There were so many things running through my head that gave me an adrenaline rush like you could not believe. I remember thinking, "this is it, it doesn't get any better in the game of college football. I also recall thinking that the whole world would be watching, so I wanted to shine. I was so amped to play the game that when entering the looker room and preparing to get dressed I must have started to daydream. Typically, we have an hour and a half to get dressed to go out for warm ups. I must have been sitting in front of my locker for what turned out to be more like an hour and fifteen minutes. I do not remember who it was but they kind of tapped me on the shoulder asking me if everything was okay. Right then, it dawned on me that I only had a couple of minutes to get ready for the biggest game of my life, Da Rose Bowl. On the same note, I remember walking down the tunnel to the field still excited to showcase UCLA football because I felt that Pac-10 football got a bad rap. To the biggest surprise and shock of my life we entered the field to the amazing colors of red and white. Well, for those that don't know UCLA is blue and gold. In a stadium that holds about 105,000 people, about 80,000 thousand were Badger fans. We were on our home field playing the biggest game of our lives and we had less people in the stands than a team from Wisconsin. I believe that took some of the excitement away from our team to see more visitors at our home stadium than our own fans. We played for each other but we also played for the University of California at Los Angeles. We were disappointed as a team to see that lack of support. Nevertheless, we were proud Bruins.

Darrell Bevell, QB, Wisconsin

One of the first things I remember about the game was the lack of respect that we received about our chances to win the game. We were the higher ranked team yet were the underdog. The lack of respect even came up at the coin toss when the Referee John Laurie of the Big 8 (now the Big 12) said looking at the coin, UCLA and the block "W" of Washington and then proceeded to say that Washington will receive.

I try to stay focused during pre-game and don't usually notice the fans or what is going on around the stadium. When I stepped onto the field at the Rose Bowl for the first time, though, I was overcome with the feeling that after a 31-year wait, nobody from the state of Wisconsin wanted to miss this game. The stadium was filled to capacity with people wearing their Badger Red.

I wasn't known as a running QB and it was even joked with about how slow I was. I dropped back to pass in the 4th quarter and the left side of our great offensive line caved in the UCLA defensive front and opened a hole to the left. I proceeded to scramble in that direction to try and find an open receiver. Since we had called all deep routes, no one was to be found and I turned up the field looking to get at least a 1st down. Out of the corner of my eye I spotted wide receiver JC Dawkins coming back to get a block. I juked to the left and made a UCLA defender fall to the ground before ending up in the endzone for a 21-yard touchdown that proved to be the winning points. To this day, many Wisconsin fans joke that they went out to get a hot dog and came back in to see me crossing the goal line. I'm just glad I saved the longest run of my career for the right time.

Top: Wisconsin Badgers QB Darrell Bevell is lifted up by his teammates in celebration of his touchdown run in the fourth quarter of the 1994 Rose Bowl Game. Bottom: Badger QB Darrell Bevell and teammate Mike Roan are jubilant after Bevell's fourth quarter TD run puts Wisconsin up 21-10 over UCLA.

1995

Joe Schaffeld, Assistant Coach, Oregon

I played in the 1958 Rose Bowl Game against Ohio State, and it was as exciting then as it is now. I came from a small high school of about 300 kids in Vale, Oregon, and then I played at Boise Junior College before coming to Oregon. We went to the Rose Bowl my first year with the Ducks, but NOBODY gave us a chance to win. We came awfully close, missing a field goal that could have tied the game. Being able to come back to the Rose Bowl as the defensive line coach vs. Penn State was truly special and brought back many memories. The Rose Bowl is the greatest bowl game of them all.

1996

Darnell Autry, RB, Northwestern

I have never been so happy and so proud to be a part of a team like the 1995 Wildcats. We played not only for ourselves but also for all of the guys who played at Northwestern before us who never made it to the Rose Bowl.

Northwestern running back Darnell Autry scampers toward his second touchdown of the 1996 Rose Bowl Game vs. USC.

1997

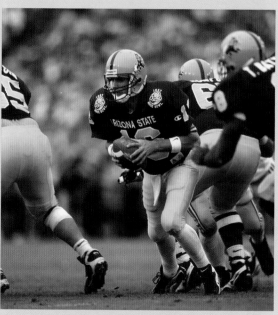

Left: Aerial view of the 1997 Rose Bowl Game. Right: Arizona State's offensive leader, QB Jake "The Snake" Plummer in 1997 Rose Bowl Game action.

Shawn Swayda, DT, Arizona State

You have touched a sore subject. We lost in the last minute to Ohio State, relinquishing our national title hopes. I was fortunate enough to be elected a captain for the team, and for that I am grateful. However, the only thing that came out of the game was a bunch of heartache and grief that is still very much with me to this day. The experience was awful because of the way we lost. Now, if we would have won like we were supposed to, then I could probably sit here and tell you how great an experience it was and all that garb. But all I can say is that to not win and lose how we lost was just totally gut wrenching and unacceptable.

Bruce Snyder, Head Coach, Arizona State,

Standing in the tunnel waiting for the TV and game officials to give the okay to run on the field for the kick off, I still remember the players and coaches behind me surging forward somewhat like a wave of energy. We were all very anxious to get going. I could not feel the concrete floor beneath my feet because they had gone numb from the emotion of the moment.

Late in the fourth quarter, we were behind in a real defensive struggle. Jake Plummer started a drive that included a fourth-and-two pass that was completed inside the 15-yard line. On the next set of downs, Jake went back to pass and an unblocked Buckeye linebacker rushed him. He made a spectacular run, making defenders miss him as he dove into the end zone. It would have clearly been the play of the game (maybe the year) had we been able to hold on to the lead. I missed the excitement of that play because I was so upset with the missed assignment that allowed the linebacker to rush unblocked. I was running toward the player "coaching" him as the team was celebrating our go-ahead score.

Bob Griese, Father of 1998 Rose Bowl MVP Brian Griese

Among my many Rose Bowl memories, the most vivid in my mind is broadcasting the 1998 Rose Bowl Game with Keith Jackson when my son Brian was playing for Michigan. I wanted to get down on the field before the game to see him for a moment and when I made it down there from the broadcast booth, it brought back a lot of memories of playing there 31 years previously.

Michigan was highly ranked and undefeated in 1997, so we covered several of their games during the course of the season. Keith Jackson would just sit back and laugh at me as I fielded questions about whether I could be objective and fair in my announcing with my son on the field. In reality, I was even more critical of his play than I was for the other athletes. If he did something great, it was just good in my book. If he did something bad, it was horrible from my perspective. I was harder on him because I wanted to make sure I came across as being fair. Well, when we got to the 1998 Rose Bowl Game, I enjoyed seeing Keith get peppered with questions about whether he would be able to announce an unbiased game since Washington State was his alma mater.

1998

Aerial view of the 1998 Rose Bowl Game.

I recall toward the end of the 1998 Rose Bowl game when it was apparent Michigan was going to win the game, Keith Jackson said, "Whoa daddy, you want to know who the MVP is? I'm standing next to his proud daddy right here!" It was a proud and emotional moment for me because as a parent you love to see your kids do well. Brian had thrown three touchdown passes and played extremely well. Once the game was over and we had completed our post game and signed off, we stayed in the booth for 45 minutes or so before I headed down to the locker room. Somewhere in the process you mentally and emotionally take off your broadcaster's cap and put on your father's cap. When I saw Brian for the first time after the game we didn't have to say anything—we just hugged each other. I'll never forget that.

Lloyd Carr at the Lawry's Beef Bowl opening ceremony with Richard N. Frank.

Lloyd Carr, Head Coach, Michigan

Outside of the Rose Bowl Game, the most enjoyable event of the Rose Bowl experience is the trip to Lawry's. It's such a great restaurant and the tradition that the Frank family has created surrounding the annual Beef Bowl is unparalleled. I had read about Lawry's and the Rose Bowl since I was a kid. What a thrill to finally go there in 1980 as a member of the 1980 Michigan staff. Since then I've been back eight times and it is always a great evening.

1999

DeShaun Foster, RB, UCLA

My freshman year at UCLA we played in the Rose Bowl. I originally thought it was going to be like any other game because we played there during the season. I remember driving to the stadium on game day and there was just so much excitement. I got off the bus and energy filled the parking lot. I could tell that this game was like nothing I had experienced. We lost the game to Wisconsin but I'll never lose the memory of the mystique from that game. I wanted to get back there so badly but unfortunately, we couldn't make it happen.

1999 – 2000

Aerial view of the 2000 Rose Bowl Game.

Jamar Fletcher, DB, Wisconsin

Going from Wisconsin to the Rose Bowl in Southern California, it was great to be able to experience an entirely different lifestyle. I was impressed by what a big deal the Rose Bowl is, and how well everyone treated us. Most importantly, our fans were incredible. It was fantastic to get out to California and see so much red out here. Having so many fans in red at the game supporting us—it felt like a home game! Coming into the 1999 game we felt disrespected. All the talk was about UCLA. We respected them, but we were anxious to show everybody what Wisconsin football was all about.

DeRonnie Pitts, WR, Stanford

The Rose Bowl week was the best team bonding experience ever. My favorite memory was when we chartered a bus to take us down Sunset Boulevard. The entire ride on the bus players took turns yelling out freestyle rap lines poking fun at everything from player's gear, girlfriends, play on the field, and hometowns. No one took it personal. It was just some good, clean and creative fun before a great night out on the strip.

We were out at Dublin's on Sunset one night and there happened to be a pretty exclusive party with stars like the Wayan's Brothers and Jamie Foxx. Ronnie Devoe from Bel Biv Devoe was there asking players on our team how to pick up girls. We all thought, "You are Ronnie from BBD and New Edition—that should work."

Our last night out at Dublin's we were in the upstairs lounge area packed with all kinds of people standing around and having drinks. Russell Stewart and Steve Coughlin (our tight ends) managed to clear some space and begin dancing (if it can be legally defined as such). What started as a good laugh, erupted into one of the best dance parties ever.

Badger defensive back #36 Mike Echols brings down Stanford receiver #81 Dave Davis while #26 Bobby Myers arrives on the scene.

2001

Drew Brees, QB, Purdue

When I arrived at Purdue my freshman year, the Boilermakers had been 3-8 the year before. In fact, they hadn't experienced a winning season in more than ten years. They had a new coach (Joe Tiller) and my recruiting class was ranked last in the Big Ten. There were only seventeen of us in that class, and when all was said and done, it was less than that. But, but we all made a commitment to each other that we were going to turn the program around, win the Big Ten, and go to the Rose bowl.

I recall seeing Michigan's Charles Woodson on TV my freshman year—he had a rose in his mouth after they beat Ohio State to win the Big Ten and a trip to the Rose Bowl, and I said to myself, "That's gonna be me someday."

Well, we fought and fought each year to get better and by my senior year we had worked so hard and only needed one more win to capture the Big Ten title. We were beating Indiana in the Old Oaken Bucket rivalry game and as the last seconds ticked off the clock, I thought about the roses that were on the sidelines ready to be distributed. It was a wild scene after the game. They had tee-shirts and baseball caps to hand out, and fans were hanging from the goal posts, but I made sure I got one of those roses to put in my mouth. I recalled that image I had seen of Woodson on TV and thought to myself, "So this is what it feels like."

Drew Brees, QB, Purdue

Marcus Tuiososopo, myself, and a few other college QBs (Carson Palmer, Kurt Kittner, A.J. Feeley) worked at a football camp the summer before our senior year and became fast friends. As we were leaving the camp, I said to Marcus, "See you in the Rose Bowl." When I found out we were going to be playing Washington in Pasadena, I gave Tui a call and said, "Hey, just like we said, we're gonna be playing each other in the Rose Bowl!" What a great feeling!

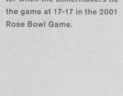

Top right: Purdue Boilermakers QB Drew Brees sets to pass in the 2001 Rose Bowl Game. Lower right: Purdue fans go wild in the third quarter when the Boilermakers tie the game at 17-17 in the 2001 Rose Bowl Game.

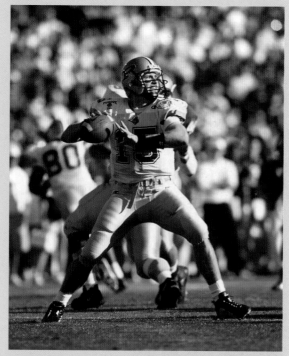

Joe Tiller, Head Coach, Purdue

During his opening monologue, Jay Leno welcomed the Purdue Boilermakers and mentioned that I had come in a few days before the rest of the team to shoot a Rogaine commercial. The crowd thought it was hilarious, but my wife, Arnette, sensing I wasn't particularly amused, leaned over to me and said, "At least he didn't say you were here shooting a Viagra commercial."

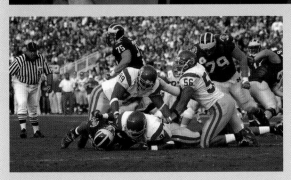

together any better for us. On game day, the Rose Bowl was full of cardinal and gold. Our players had prepared magnificently for the game and executed almost flawlessly. Michigan had a ton of talent, but we were able to overwhelm them on both sides of the ball. Winning the national championship in the Rose Bowl with all of our fans there. It doesn't get any better than that.

Kevin Painton, Event Staff, Lawry's Beef Bowl

I love being a part of the famous Beef Bowl tradition. It is a pleasure to see the joy on the faces of the players and coaches as they realize they are playing in "The Granddaddy of all Bowl games."

Top: USC head coach Peter Carroll joyfully accepts the 2004 Rose Bowl Game trophy from Tournament of Roses President Mike Riffey. Left center: 2004 Rose Bowl Game action. Right: Lawry's Beef Bowl event staffers at the USC Lawry's Beef Bowl event prior to the 2004 Rose Bowl Game.

Pete Carroll, Head Coach, USC

At USC, our goal every year is to win the Rose Bowl. We feel as if the Rose Bowl is our home away from home. In 2003, we felt like we did everything we had to do to play in the BCS championship game in the Sugar Bowl. But the computers didn't see if that way, so we were headed to the Rose Bowl to face an outstanding Michigan squad. Instead of being disappointed, our players saw this as a tremendous opportunity. We knew we would be playing a national championship game in what would be like a home game for us. It couldn't have come

BO SCHEMBECHLER, HEAD COACH, MICHIGAN (1969-1989)

Top left: Coach Bo Schembechler double-checks his game plan prior to the opening kick-off at the 1990 Rose Bowl Game. Top right: Bo presents Richard N. Frank with an autographed Michigan Wolverine team ball at the Lawry's Beef Bowl prior to the 1977 Rose Bowl Game.

Regarding the Lawry's Beef Bowl:

The kids all loved to go there and eat, especially when the server asked them, "How big of a cut do you want?"

On Ed Muransky and Bubba Paris and their chase for the record of prime rib consumed at the 1978 Lawry's Beef Bowl, prior to the 1979 Rose Bowl Game:

I let 'em eat because they were freshmen. They weren't gonna play anyway.

On being hired at Michigan:

When I was hired at Michigan, I was way down the totem pole on their list. Don Canham tried Ara Parseghian, Joe Paterno, and several others before he got to me. I'm sure Bump Elliott's recommendation helped me get the job. I never had a contract at Michigan. Every-thing was on a handshake. I told Bear Bryant that once and he said, "Bo, you're the dumbest !%$&# coach in football."

On Woody Hayes:

I played my last two years of college ball for Woody and then followed him as a graduate assistant on to Ohio State. When I was offered the job at Miami of Ohio, he told me I shouldn't take it because I was going to be the next head coach at Ohio State. I asked him how long he was planning on coaching and he said, "Oh, maybe four or five years at the most." He ended up coaching for nearly 17 years after that!

I was excited about coaching against Woody because I knew how he thought and how he acted. I told my staff in our very first meeting, "We're not here to beat Indiana, Illinois, or Northwestern because this is the Big Two and Little Eight. We're here to beat Ohio State and we're going to do something about it every day to make that happen. Woody's favorite play was off-tackle. We ran that all year long in scrimmage so our defense would recognize it easily when Ohio State ran it.

You didn't want to let Woody take a lead into the locker room at halftime. He knew how to control the ball and chew up the clock better than anyone.

On being voted out of the 1974 Rose Bowl Game:

We had a great team in 1973. We were undefeated and tied Ohio State 10-10. The Big Ten was paranoid about losing the Rose Bowl so they had a vote and because quarterback Dennis Franklin had broken his shoulder the Buckeyes were given the nod. That's why I campaigned to let Big Ten teams compete in other bowl games. Dennis Franklin was 30-1-1 as a starting quarterback and he never played in a bowl game. There's something wrong with that.

On the importance of the Rose Bowl Game:

I never set a goal for us to be the national champions. The way I figured it was you win the Big Ten and then you go to the Rose Bowl and win that game and let the voters figure it out afterward. Our season was a complete success if we won the Big Ten and the Rose Bowl Game.

On retiring:

I was coaching in the East-West Shrine Game with Bear Bryant and we were talking about retirement. He wanted to retire but he said, "If I do that do you know what'll happen to the 47 people that work for me?" That got me thinking. I took the A.D. job so I could name my own successor. I told Gary Moeller, "If you fire one single guy on this staff, I don't care if it's the equipment manager or the training room manager, I'll come back and kill you."

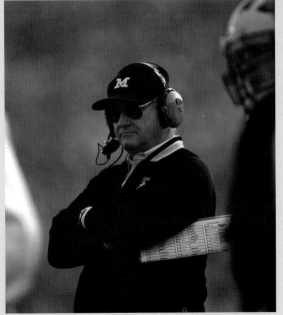

Top right: Coach Schembechler surrounded by his players on the sidelines during the 1990 Rose Bowl Game. Right: USC head coach Larry Smith, and his mentor, Michigan head coach Bo Schembechler at a press conference before the 1990 Rose Bowl Game. Bottom: Bo observes the action at the 1990 Rose Bowl Game, his last as a head coach for the University of Michigan.

ROSE BOWL GAME APPEARANCES

Teams with the most Rose Bowl Game appearances since the Lawry's Beef Bowl began in 1957	
USC Trojans	17
Michigan Wolverines	16
Washington Huskies	10
Ohio State Buckeyes	10
UCLA Bruins	8
Wisconsin Badgers	5
Iowa Hawkeyes	5
Stanford Cardinal	3

Teams with the most Rose Bowl Game appearances since the Big Ten / Pac-10 Conference pact began with the 1947 Rose Bowl Game	
USC Trojans	20
Michigan Wolverines	18
Ohio State Buckeyes	12
UCLA Bruins	11
Washington Huskies	10
Wisconsin Badgers	6
Iowa Hawkeyes	5
Stanford Cardinal	4
Michigan State Spartans	4
Illinois Fighting Illini	4
California Golden Bears	4

ROSE BOWL HALL OF FAME – INDUCTEE HISTORY

The Rose Bowl Hall of Fame was established in 1989 to honor members of the Rose Bowl family who have contributed to the history and excitement of the Rose Bowl Game, and those who embody the best of the passion, honor, strength and tradition associated with The Granddaddy of Them All.

1989
C.W. "Bump" Elliott - Michigan
W.W. "Woody" Hayes - Ohio State
Howard Jones - USC
Jim Plunkett - Stanford

1990
Archie Griffin - Ohio State
Bob Reynolds - Stanford
Neil Snow - Michigan
Wallace Wade - Brown, Alabama & Duke
Charles White - USC

1991
Rex Kern - Ohio State
John McKay - USC
Ernie Nevers - Stanford
Roy Riegels - California
Bob Schloredt - Washington
John Sciarra - UCLA
Russell Stein - Washington & Jefferson
Charley Trippi - Georgia
Ron VanderKelen - Wisconsin
George Wilson - Washington

1992
Franke Albert - Stanford
Bob Chappuis - Michigan
Sam Cunningham - USC
Bill Daddio - Pittsburgh
Bob Griese - Purdue
Hollis Huntington - Oregon & Mare
Island Marines
Shy Huntington - Oregon
Elmer Layden - Notre Dame
Jim Owens - Washington

1993
Frank Aschenbrenner - Northwestern
Dixie Howell - Alabama
Don Hutson - Alabama
Curly Morrison - Ohio State
Brick Muller - California

Julius Rykovich - Illinois
Bo Schembechler - Michigan
O.J. Simpson - USC
Bob Stiles - UCLA
Buddy Young - Illinois

1994
Vic Bottari - California
Jim Hardy - USC
Don James - Washington
Bob Jeter - Iowa
Lay Leishman - Tournament of Roses
Pat Richter - Wisconsin
Russell Sanders - USC

1995
Gary Beban - UCLA
Dick Butkus - Illinois
Harry Gilmer - Alabama
Pat Haden - USC
Al Krueger - USC
Doyle Nave - USC
Ted Shipkey - Stanford

1996
Eric Ball - UCLA
Pete Beathard - USC
John Ferraro - USC
Stan Hahn - Tournament of Roses
John Ralston - Stanford
Bill Tate - Illinois

1997
Terry Donahue - UCLA
Jim Grabowski - Illinois
Warren Moon - Washington
Erny Pinckert - USC
Ken Ploen - Iowa
Sandy Stephens - Minnesota

1998
Jack Crabtree - University of Oregon
Don Durdan - Oregon State

John (J.K.) McKay - USC
Rick Neuheisel - UCLA
Bill Nicholas - Tournament of Roses
Butch Woolfolk - University of Michigan

1999
Al Hoisch - UCLA
Keith Jackson - ABC Sports
Dave Kaiser - Michigan State University

2000
Johnny Mack Brown - Alabama
Marv Goux - USC

2001
BCS National Championship Game -
No inductees

2002
Ambrose "Amblin' Amby" Schindler - USC
Mel Anthony - Michigan

2003
Harriman Cronk - Tournament of Roses
Danny O'Neil - Oregon
John Robinson - USC

2004
Alan Ameche - Wisconsin
Rudy Bukich - USC
Wayne Duke - Big Ten
Jim Stivers - Tournament of Roses

LAWRY'S BEEF BOWL PROGRAMS

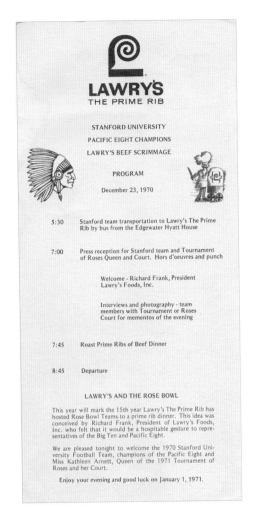

I was unable to locate any printed programs from the earliest years of the Lawry's Beef Bowl events in the Lawry's archives. I am reasonably certain a simple one-page program did exist as early as 1963. By the late 1960s, a one-page, 11-1/2" x 5-1/2" program was printed on heavy cardstock for each team's private event. Shown here is the 1970 program for Stanford (prior to the 1971 Rose Bowl).

By the early 1990s, a four-page, 8-1/2" x 5-1/2" booklet-type program was produced and used for both teams. The information was expanded to include both teams' season schedules as well as the Rose Bowl results since 1957.

In 2000, the program expanded to eight pages, adding a title page, two pages of brief history on the Tournament of Roses and the Lawry's Beef Bowl, and a Beef Bowl Highlights page. Shown here is the cover of the 2000 program for the 2001 Rose Bowl Game pitting the Purdue University Boilermakers vs. the University of Washington Huskies.

The 2002 Rose Bowl Game hosted the Bowl Championship Series National Championship between the University of Nebraska Cornhuskers and the University of Miami Hurricanes. It was the first time since 1946 that the Rose Bowl Game pitted teams outside of the Big Ten and Pac-10 conferences. It was also the first time ever the game was not held on New Year's Day (other than the infrequent

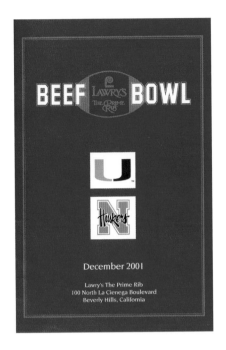

January 2nd games that are held when January 1st falls on a Sunday). The Lawry's Beef Bowl program expanded to 12 pages in full color, including four pages of color and black-and-white photos depicting the history of the event. It was felt that both teams might appreciate the tradition of the event more with the photographic history. Shown here is the cover of the 2001 program for the 2002 Rose Bowl Game.

The program remained in 12-page color for one more year when another team outside the traditional Big Ten / Pac-10 match-up, the University of Oklahoma Sooners, made an appearance in the Rose Bowl Game. The 2003 program for the traditional Big Ten – Pac-10 contest between Michigan and USC was six pages and two-color presentation. The same design was used for the 2004 contest between Michigan and Texas since the Longhorns were already familiar with the Beef Bowl tradition from their Cotton Bowl appearances.

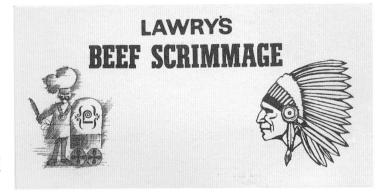

I found these small table signs in the Lawry's archives. They measure 3-1/2 x 2 inches. The pennant signage would have to be pre-1970 when the name change to "Beef Scrimmage" commenced.

BEEF BOWL AND BEEF SCRIMMAGE SIGNAGE

The earliest Lawry's Beef Bowl collectibles I could identify were mugs the players and coaches were given back in the mid-1980s. Shown here are Ohio State players displaying their 1984 Lawry's Beef Bowl/1985 Rose Bowl Game mugs. Mugs were also produced for a couple years in the early 1990s for the Rose Bowl Games featuring Michigan and Washington.

If you have ever been to the Pasadena Tournament of Roses Parade, you might recall there is an official pin for the Parade and one for the Rose Bowl Game. Every float and every sponsor have their own pins, too. The first Lawry's Beef Bowl pins were issued at the 1986 Beef Bowl events for the 1987 Rose Bowl Game between Arizona State and Michigan. There has been a pin for every year since 1987 and the design has remained consistent with some slight variations in the typeface. Shown here is the Lawry's Beef Bowl pin for the 2002 Rose Bowl Game with the words "National Championship" added at the bottom. The 2006 Rose Bowl Game pin will have the same words added at the bottom of the pin because the game is a contractual national championship with the Bowl Championship Series (BCS).

Lawry's has also issued pins for the Cotton Bowl version of the Beef Bowl in Dallas since 1987. Shown here is the Lawry's Beef Bowl pin for the 1997 Cotton Bowl between Brigham Young University and Kansas State.

Mini-footballs like the ones shown in this photo were first introduced at the 2002 Lawry's Beef Bowl for the 2003 Rose Bowl Game match-up between Washington State and Oklahoma and have been popular ever since. They feature the Rose Bowl Game logo and both team helmets on one side and the Lawry's Beef Bowl logo on the other side. They also come with their own miniature kicking tee.

As far as my research indicates, Lawry's issued the first ever Rose Bowl trading card at their 2004 events for the 2005 Rose Bowl Game pitting Michigan vs. Texas. Each team had their own card, and the players received both team cards. These cards were produced by CustomSportsCards.com on a promotional use only basis and they were limited to an issue of 1,000 cards per team. Shown here are the front and back of both the Michigan and the Texas cards.

Just before this book went to print, a 50th anniversary promotional card was produced in a quantity of 250 by CustomSportsCard.com and distributed to attendees at two separate events in Beverly Hills and Chicago. The Beverly Hills event celebrated Lawry's 50-year partnership with the Tournament of Roses and the Pac-10 Conference and the Chicago event did so with the Tournament of Roses and the Big Ten Conference. The action photo on the front of the card is from the 1960 Rose Bowl Game between Wisconsin and Washington (also seen in the 50 Years of Champions section of this book). The back of the card utilized text from The Power of Tradition section of this book.

LAWRY'S BEEF BOWL RECIPES FOR THE HOME

I haven't tried out these recipes for the home yet, but I can vouch for the real thing. Chef Walter Eckstein assures me they will be quite tasty if you follow the directions faithfully. Complement the main course menu with mashed potatoes or a baked potato.

Lawry's Prime Rib Roast
 1 (4 rib) standing rib roast
 Lawry's Seasoned Salt
 1 bag (5 lb.) rock salt

Sprinkle fatty cap of roast with Lawry's Seasoned Salt. Spread rock salt evenly over bottom of heavy roasting pan; place wire roasting rack on top of salt. Place the roast on the rack, fatty side up. Make sure no salt actually touches the beef. Insert meat thermometer in thickest part of meat, making sure it does not touch a bone. Roast in preheated 350 degree F oven until thermometer registers 130 degrees F for rare, 140 degrees F for medium, or approximately 20 to 25 minutes per pound. Remove from oven and let stand 20 minutes before carving. Using a sharp carving knife, slice meat across the grain for serving. Discard rock salt.

Makes 6 to 8 servings.

Note: If desired, use an instant read thermometer and insert to test internal temperature periodically; do not leave this type of thermometer in roast.

Lawry's Whipped Cream Horseradish
 1 cup whipping cream
 1/4 teaspoon Lawry's Seasoned Salt
 2 tablespoons prepared horseradish, well drained,
 or 4 tablespoons finely grated fresh horseradish root
 Dash Tabasco sauce

Whip cream until stiff peaks form. Fold in Lawry's Seasoned Salt, horseradish and Tabasco until well mixed.

Makes 6 servings.

Creamed Spinach a la Lawry's
 2 pkgs. (10 oz. each) frozen chopped spinach, thawed
 4 slices bacon
 1 small onion, minced
 2 cloves garlic, minced
 2 tablespoons flour
 1 teaspoon Lawry's Seasoned Salt
 1/2 teaspoon freshly ground black pepper, or to taste
 2 cups milk

Drain spinach well and squeeze out excess moisture with hands; chop finely and set aside. Fry bacon in heavy skillet until crisp; remove, drain and chop. Sauté onion and garlic in bacon drippings; add flour, Lawry's Seasoned Salt and pepper and blend thoroughly. Slowly add milk, stirring constantly until thickened. Add spinach and bacon; heat.

Makes 4 to 6 servings.

Creamed Corn
 1 1/2 tablespoons butter
 1 1/2 tablespoons flour
 1/2 teaspoon salt
 1 1/2 cups whipping cream
 2 tablespoons sugar
 3 cups fresh, frozen or canned whole kernel corn

Melt butter in heavy saucepan; add flour and salt, stirring to blend. Slowly add whipping cream, stirring constantly until thickened. Add sugar and corn, heat. For Au Gratin, place corn in a 9 or 10-inch shallow casserole dish; sprinkle with 1/4 cup freshly grated Parmesan cheese and brown under broiler.

Makes 4 to 6 servings.

INDEX

V

W

Y

I'm convinced that any book, regardless of genre, requires a supporting cast of dozens who provide research materials, creative collaboration, and encouragement along the way. Here's my supporting cast:

Howard Cohl and Peter Dombrowski at Silverback Books for understanding my vision for this book, as well as your expert advice and support. Lisa Tooker for expert project management. Christopher Hittinger and Stephen Turner at Turner & Associates for exceptional creative design & collaboration. Patty Holden for layout and production. Charlee Irene Ganny for indexing. Mitch Dorger and everyone at the Pasadena Tournament of Roses, especially Caryn Eaves, Adria DeBaca, Nicole O'Neil and Carrie Graves for archive research and support of this effort with a cheerful, professional attitude second to none. Richard N. Frank for your time invested in the Q&A process, and for opening up the Lawry's archives to help ensure this book was informative and accurate. Gayle Chick, Nancy Choe, Eileen Choe, Carolina Acosta, Colleen Donatucci, Bryan Monfort, Todd Johnson, Ellen Fremaux, and Linda Cirigliano at Lawry's. Tim Long and staff at Long Photography for outstanding photo work & rapid turnarounds on image scans. Squeege at Shark Bait Films for special scanning and photo restoration.

Special thanks to the incomparable Keith Jackson for your eloquent Foreword. May you be the Voice and Raconteur of the Rose Bowl for the next 50 years...

To all the players and coaches who shared their Rose Bowl recollections and personal photos: You are the heart and soul of this book. Thank you.

Special thanks to Jim Muldoon and his staff at the Pac-10 Conference, especially Wendy Heredia. Scott Chipman and Linda Arnold at the Big Ten Conference. Bruce Madej and Dave Ablauf (Michigan) Steve Snapp (Ohio State) Mike Lockrem (Minnesota) Justin Doherty (Wisconsin) Phil Haddy (Iowa) John Lewandowski (Michigan State) Jeff Nelson (Penn State) Mike Wolf (Northwestern) Tom Schott (Purdue) Kent Brown (Illinois) Pete Rhoda (Indiana) Tim Tessalone (USC) Marc Dellins (UCLA) Steve Fenk (Oregon State) Mark Brand (Arizona State) Gary Migdol (Stanford) Herb Benenson (Cal) Jim Daves (Washington) Rod Commons (Washington State) Geoff Turner and Jeff Eberhardt (Oregon) Tom Duddleston (Arizona) Keith Mann (Nebraska) Rick Korch (Miami) Kenny Mossman (Oklahoma) and John Bianco (Texas). Scott Yoffee (Chargers) Paul Kirk (Broncos) Brad Kuhbander (Chiefs) and Mark Loomis (ABC Sports).

Extra special thanks to Mark Bragg and Kevin Painton (Bruin Power!) for always being there and making each year better than the last.

"Coach" Jerry Stalcup: What a thrill to find out about your past life while researching this book. You never once mentioned playing in the Rose Bowl and the NFL when you coached at Rockford East HS. I'm fortunate to have had great men like you and your brother Craig as my coaches.

Thanks to my Danville connection: Glenn MacDonald, Greg Smyth and Denis Squeri. And across the miles to: Jim D'Arc, Mark Johnson, Bryan Boyd, Roger Cook, Bill Habeeb, Thann Illum, Chris Haynes, and Marc & Lisa Marriott.

Jeff, Kent, Van, Lance and Jon: Football and brothers! Now that's something that will always resonate in my heart. Mom and Dad (my first football coach) your words of encouragement will always inspire me. Special love and thanks to Andrew, Whitney and Zack, Noelle, Ariel, Miles and Sammy. And finally, to Susie: This book simply would not be possible without you. 3-O-3.

For Susan Jean.

Project Editor: Lisa M. Tooker
Writer/Photo Editor: Todd Erickson
Design & Typography: Christopher Hittinger,
Turner & Associates, www.turnersf.com
Indexer: Charlee Trantino

Primary Photo Resources:
Tournament of Roses Archives,
Long Photography, Inc.

Printed in China

ISBN: 1-59637-034-3